THE COLLECTED WORKS OF
LT.-COLONEL SIR REGINALD RANKIN BT.

THE INNER HISTORY OF
THE BALKAN WAR

The Collected Works of
Lt.-Colonel Sir Reginald Rankin Bt.

The Inner History of the Balkan War

By
Lt.-Colonel Sir Reginald Rankin Bt.

War Correspondent for *The Times*

'*Unoque die Romana reprendit
Quotquot ter denis acies amisimus armis*'
CLAUDIAN *De Bello Getico*

VOLUME ONE

LONDON
JOHN LANE THE BODLEY HEAD LTD

First published in 1914
Collected Edition . . 1930

Printed in Great Britain by
RICHARD CLAY & SONS, LIMITED
BUNGAY
SUFFOLK

TO

JAMES .BOURCHIER

THIS BOOK IS DEDICATED

WITH ADMIRATION RESPECT AND AFFECTION

CONTENTS

THE INNER HISTORY OF THE
BALKAN WAR

CHAPTER I

JAMES DAVID BOURCHIER

THE unattached diplomatist who has broken up the Turkish Empire in Europe is thus described in *Who's Who*:

Bourchier, James David, M.A., F.R.G.S., fourth son of late John Bourchier, J.P., of Bagotstown, Co. Limerick, and Maidenhall, Co. Cork.* Educated Cambridge (Scholar of King's College, and 1st Class Classical Tripos); previously Scholar and Classical Gold Medallist of Trinity College, Dublin. Was for some years Assistant Master at Eton; in 1888 acted as Special Correspondent of *The Times* in Roumania and Bulgaria, and has subsequently represented that journal in South-Eastern Europe; in 1895 investigated the atrocities at Dospat, Macedonia, and prepared a report for the British Government; in 1896 received the thanks of the Cretan Assembly for his services in promoting the arrangement with Turkey in that year; in 1898 accompanied the Emperor William's pilgrimage to Jerusalem; is Grand Officer of the Order of Prince Danilo of Montenegro, Commander of the Orders of the Saviour of Greece and of the Crown of Roumania, and Officer of the Order of St. Alexander of Bulgaria. Publications: numerous contributions to the *Fortnightly*

---

* Mr. Bourchier was a well-known authority on racing matters, and owned some good thoroughbreds, amongst them the famous Salamander, who, after changing owners, won the Grand National in 1865.

and other Reviews; and the articles, Athens, Albania, Bulgaria, Crete, Greece, Macedonia, Montenegro, etc., in the last edition of the *Encyclopædia Britannica.* Recreations: hunting, shooting, bicycling, golf, lawn-tennis, music, chess. Clubs: Athenæum, St. James's, New University; Athenian, Athens; Union, Sofia.

I first knew Bourchier in the year 1885, twenty-eight years ago now in this year of grace, 1913, when he was a young assistant master at Eton, and I was a small boy who was what we used to call " up to " him—*Anglice*, in his division or form for the time being. Although we were up to Bourchier, Bourchier was never up to us; he had already become very deaf, and, as boys are wont to do, we did not fail to take advantage of his infirmity. In the circumstances his deafness was perhaps a blessing in disguise, as it led to his abandoning a career for which nature had not intended him. A brilliant scholar, a man in the best sense of the word, kindly and gentle, treating little boys with more forbearance than they often deserved, ever mindful of *maxima debetur pueris reverentia*, he was not the stuff out of which your pedagogue is made. The masters at Eton, as a race, were a right good lot of men; but there has to be a touch of hectoring officialism about a successful schoolmaster; and this, and all other smallnesses, are conspicuously lacking in Bourchier's character. He was cut out for great things, and he has done them.

At the end of December 1887 Bourchier left Eton, to the sorrow of the boys and the masters alike. I next saw him in October 1912 at Sofia, and though twenty-five years had passed over his head he looked identically the same Bourchier as in the happy old Eton days: still slightly bald, without a grey hair in his close-cropped, reddish-auburn hair; the same ruddy, hard-bitten face, with its drooping fair moustache; the same humorous twinkle in the kindly grey eyes; the same boyish, hearty laugh.

During our conversations at Sofia Bourchier gave me some account of his early adventures in the Balkans. He was provided with a letter of introduction to Sir Augustus Paget, the British Ambassador at Vienna. He went to dinner at the Embassy, and happened to sit next the Vienna correspondent of *The Times*, an old Etonian, by name Brinsley Richards. The latter was interested to hear that Bourchier had come from Eton, and invited him to come and see him.

One day when Bourchier was at Richards' house, the latter asked him what he proposed to do in case he finally left Eton. Bourchier replied that he had a taste for writing, and that he proposed to write for the Reviews, and also possibly books, since his deafness would prevent his going to the Bar, as he had originally intended doing, having already " eaten his dinners." To a question of Richards', Bourchier replied that he had no political experience, and that he thought it doubtful whether *The Times* would care for his services.

Bourchier thought no more of this conversation, and shortly afterwards, by the advice of Professor Politzer, he went down to the Adriatic coast for change of air, and installed himself in the little island of Lussin-Piccolo, off the coast of Dalmatia.

Several weeks later, in April 1888, he received a telegram from Richards stating that *The Times* proposed to send him to Rumania, where a peasant rising had just taken place, and then to Bulgaria, which was still in a very disturbed condition, notwithstanding the recent arrival of Prince Ferdinand. Bourchier accepted this proposal, and then looked about for a steamer to convey him to Fiume, but found there was none for several days. He accordingly chartered a sailing-boat to the mainland, where he found a steamer, and eventually reached Vienna in about a week. When he reached Richards, the latter informed Bourchier that he had come too late, since the

peasants had been so disobliging as to allow their rising
to be suppressed.

However, with the assistance of Mrs. Richards, an
extremely charming and gifted woman, Bourchier finally
induced Richards to relent, and to allow him to proceed
to Rumania the next morning.

He arrived at Bukarest twenty-four hours later, and
found that the insurrection had broken out again, more
violently than ever ; Bukarest itself was at one time
threatened. He was consequently enabled to send some
interesting messages, which appeared equally to satisfy
Mr. Richards and *The Times* office. So when the insurrection was suppressed for the second time, Bourchier was
instructed to go to Bulgaria. He left Bukarest for
Rustchuk, with the intention of proceeding across country
to Sofia. But at Rustchuk he learned that Prince
Ferdinand was making his first tour through his new
domains, and would arrive at Tirnovo in a few days.
Bourchier therefore determined to visit the old Bulgarian
capital, where the Prince was about to spend Easter.
He thus describes his adventures there : *

Nothing can exceed the beauty of the rocky ravine
through which the northern road winds as it approaches
Tirnovo. Here and there the slopes are exquisitely green,
dotted with forest trees and fragrant hawthorn ; in other
places tall perpendicular crags obtain the mastery, and
frown down upon the traveller to the right and left, while
at his feet the foaming waters of the Jantra dash swiftly
along, half hidden by the luxuriant foliage, as they carry
the melted snows of the Balkans to the broad bosom of
the Danube. A sudden turn of the road brings him to the
entrance of the town, and it is not without a pang of
disgust that he finds himself in a dirty, ill-paved, mal-

* *Fortnightly Review*, July 1888. By the courtesy of Mr. W. L.
Courtney.

odorous street, the closely built houses of which shut out all view of the lovely valley through which the river winds as it almost encircles the ancient city of kings and priests. The town lies on a rocky peninsula, and it is necessary to descend to the banks of the river, or, if possible, to scale the dizzy heights on the opposite side, in order to appreciate the extreme beauty of its situation. The houses cluster on the precipice like sea-birds on some ocean crag, the red-tiled roofs rising one above the other in picturesque confusion, here and there relieved with trees and tiny vineyards, which seem literally to hang over the rapid torrent beneath. On the other side of the river one of those serrated ridges of rock so commonly found in this part of Bulgaria rises in the form of an amphi-theatre, almost completely surrounding the town, and crowning a verdant slope which, on the western side, is clothed with a forest of lofty trees.

Tirnovo is indeed a whited sepulchre, without most fair, but within so offensive that it is hard to say which of one's senses is most cruelly outraged. Butchers' shops and tanners' stalls abound; drains are unnecessary, for are not the streets themselves a sufficient receptacle for all super-fluities? " Sanitas sanitatum, omnia sanitas," said Lord Beaconsfield; but few of the worthy people of Tirnovo have heard of Lord Beaconsfield, and none of them put his precept into practice. The day after my arrival one of the most terrific thunderstorms I have ever witnessed broke over the town, and the process of purification which followed was an interesting and, indeed, a reassuring spectacle. The streets were converted into roaring tor-rents, in which huge paving-stones and piles of refuse contended with the surging flood. The inhabitants, taking advantage of the opportunity, bestirred themselves to rid their households of long-hoarded treasures, and by the evening of that day Tirnovo was tolerably clean. But with all its faults there is something charming and interesting in this quaint old city, in which there is nothing modern, and which still seems to slumber in a trance of centuries, unawakened by the restless din of latter-day civilization.

As we drove up to the entrance of the principal hotel, the streets were gaily decked with flags and evergreens in honour of Prince Ferdinand's visit. A couple of gen-darmes were standing by the doorway, and appeared to manifest great interest in our arrival. A little crowd collected round the carriage and eyed us with much curiosity. Strangers do not come every day to Tirnovo; but, as it afterwards turned out, we were regarded as no ordinary wayfarers. Winged rumour had gone before us, and our appearance was awaited with more than the usual interest. The entrance to the hotel consisted of a narrow dirty passage leading into a kind of coach-house, in which at night I have more than once stumbled over the recum-bent figures of sleepers reposing on the pavement, and into which a ladder descended by means of which the principal apartments were reached.

At the door we were met by the landlord, who expostu-lated with us for having telegraphed for rooms, saying that he had received previous information of our expected arrival. Here was a mystery, which at the time we did not connect with the appearance of gendarmes outside the house. Some difficulty arose with our host, who demanded a sum such as would be charged at a first-class Parisian hotel for our apartments. This was hardly arranged when a message demanding my presence at the Prefecture arrived. Believing this to be a mere formality, I sent my dragoman, Petro, with my card and my passport. A second message, however, was sent insisting on my appearance, to which I replied that it was not convenient to me to repair to the Prefecture at that moment, as the rain was falling heavily. At the same time, however, I instructed my dragoman to state fully my business at Tirnovo, and to show some letters of introduction which I brought with me to several members of the Prince's suite. In ten minutes' time Petro returned almost speechless with terror saying that the Prefect and the *chef de police* were in full conclave, and that I must come at once, hinting that otherwise my stay in Tirnovo would be a brief one. Not wishing to have my sojourn in such an interesting place curtailed, I proceeded to trudge through the mud and rain to the Prefecture, where I found the Prefect and the *chef de police*, an individual with a fierce expression, a red face, and a fiery moustache—in a state of suppressed excitement. The latter could only speak Bulgarian, but he made up for the deficiency of his linguistic powers by the fury of his glances. A long cross-examination followed, during which my persecutors occasionally turned on Petro, with the object of making him contradict me, or of confronting him with some previous statement of his own. Petro, who looked as if he were about to be led straightway into the torture-chamber, put on a ludicrous expression of mingled subserviency and fear. He had seen what I had not, the prison at Tirnovo, one of the most horrible dungeons in which suffering humanity has ever been confined. He was well acquainted with the police official, and his alarm, as I afterwards learned, was not unwarranted. This individual, as it turned out, had been the *fidus Achates*, or rather the Tristan l'Hermite, of M. Mantoff, the energetic Prefect of Rustchuk, and had ably seconded his chief in the vigorous measures, such as the flogging of respectable citizens without trial at the doors of their houses, by which he purged that town of the revolutionary element which was supposed to have infected it before his administration. When M. Mantoff, at the instance of the British Consul, was deposed by the Government, it was thought advisable to remove his faithful apparitor to some district where he had no enemies, and where awkward questions were not likely to be asked. And so Tirnovo obtained its Rufus. After a detention of about half an hour we were at length dismissed, but we soon became aware that we were followed closely by gendarmes, and from that moment until we left Tirnovo we were watched night and day by these vigilant guardians of the peace.

The interest which the good folk of Tirnovo took in our movements was much increased by the attentions paid to us by the authorities. The tales which Petro either overheard or was told by his friends with regard to our supposed object in visiting Tirnovo do credit to the inventive powers of the human imagination. Petro himself was thoroughly frightened, and counselled an immediate retreat from the dangers which surrounded us, saying that when he got to Rustchuk he would tell me all he knew, but that he dared not do so now. He could not understand my not taking matters *au sérieux*, though I told him that no doubt some mistake had occurred which would place the authorities in a ridiculous light, and that meantime I had no objection to the company of our gendarme, a good-natured young fellow, who sometimes gave us a light for our cigars, and provided us with any information we required. As a matter of fact, however, I had both written and telegraphed to the British Consul at Rustchuk ; but as I received no reply, I concluded, as indeed was the case, that the authorities had interrupted our communications, and that external assistance was unavailable for the present.

The spectacle which the town presented on Easter-eve was a most interesting one. All day the streets swarmed with peasants bearing on their shoulders the lambs which were to be slaughtered for the Paschal feast, many of the women carrying bags or pouches strapped to the waist, from which the lamb's head projected in kangaroo fashion. From morning till evening Tirnovo resounded with plaintive bleatings. Late at night crowds of worshippers made their way to the various churches, carrying lighted candles in their hands, and the streets were not empty till the break of day. It was after two o'clock when the clatter of the escort and the rattling of numerous wheels announced the return of Prince Ferdinand and his suite from their nocturnal devotions, and about the hour of three my faithful gendarme, who was always posted beneath my window at night, noticed that my light was extinguished—a circumstance which he communicated in confidence to my dragoman on the following morning, observing that I kept very late hours. The cause of my vigils will be readily explained by those who have had personal experience of Bulgarian hostelries and their denizens. The morning of the Orthodox Easter, which this year very nearly corresponded with the Western Whitsuntide, found Tirnovo wrapped in slumber, and it was well-nigh noon before any stir was noticeable in the streets. At half-past eleven Prince Ferdinand, in full-dress cavalry uniform, attended a grand service in the cathedral. All the congregation including the Prince, who stood alone on a high daïs, held lighted tapers in their hands. It was here that my red-faced persecutor ventured on a course of conduct which might have led to awkward consequences both for himself and me. Posting himself on my left hand—he had already stationed a gendarme on my right—he proceeded to inflict upon me at intervals a series of nudges, by way of reminder that he had not forgotten me. Respect for the sacredness of the time and place fortunately saved me from giving way to my natural resentment at this personal indignity; but I mentioned the matter to a Cabinet Minister on whom I called that afternoon, my gendarme remaining outside the house during the interview. The Minister made inquiries, as he afterwards told me, but was assured by the officer that he had only " taken the usual precautions." The incongruous nature of my position will be understood when I state that at this time I had already received official permission to accompany his Royal Highness on his tour, and had had more than one confidential interview on political subjects with the Minister I have mentioned, who had always received me with much kindness and urbanity.

At length the departure of the Prince for Rustchuk was announced, and Petro, by my orders, informed the authorities that they must send back my passport by special messenger. It arrived in the manner indicated, and in another hour, greatly to the relief of my faithful attendant, who afterwards asserted that he had saved my life, we were seated in our carriage *en route* for Rustchuk. As we left the door of the hotel our gendarme, with whom we had by this time established the most cordial relations, approached us, and with a winning smile intimated that he would regard a trifling *backsheesh* as an interesting souvenir of our stay at Tirnovo. This looked as if his attentions had come to an end, but such was not the case. As our carriage proceeded at a walking pace he still followed us, and it was not till we reached the confines of the town and started off at a brisk trot that we left him behind. I watched him as he stood beneath a triumphal arch at the entrance of the town, gazing wistfully after us, until our carriage rounded a distant eminence and he was lost to view. He was instructed, no doubt, to see that we made a *bona fide* departure.

It was not until we arrived at Rustchuk that the mystery was solved. A few days before leaving that town for Tirnovo I had sent a telegram to Bukarest concerning a revolver which I had left there. In Bulgaria every telegram is read by the authorities, and nearly every letter is opened. The intelligent officials at Rustchuk concluded that I was an assassin, and that I had arrived in Bulgaria with the express object of murdering the Prince. They communicated their suspicions to their equally intelligent *confrères* in Tirnovo, and warned them of my coming; and I am not quite sure that they did not inspire the Prime Minister himself with a certain amount of alarm. Prince Ferdinand, however, when informed of the circumstances, expressed his regret to me in the most courteous manner, stating that he had ordered the police at Tirnovo to send explanations, and adding the hope that I would consider myself a member of his suite during the remainder of his tour. I need not say that I accepted the hospitality so graciously offered, and my journey as his Royal Highness's guest through Eastern Bulgaria and up the Danube will remain one of the most agreeable reminiscences of my life.

Soon afterwards Bourchier started with the Prince for Shumla, where they witnessed a grand review of the Bulgarian troops. They then went on to Varna and Silistria, and thence, in the Prince's yacht, up the Danube, passing Rustchuk, Sistova, Nikopol, and Widin.

The enthusiastic receptions which the Prince met with throughout the journey convinced Bourchier that the people were far from sympathising with the designs of Russia for his expulsion from the country.

They then returned to Sofia.

During the journey Bourchier had many opportunities for conversations with the Prince, on whom at that time the eyes of Europe were fixed. Opinion in England was unfavourable to him, but Bourchier believed in his success. The great and ill-fated Stambuloff was with them, and from him, too, Bourchier gathered the essential factors in the problem of the Balkans—a problem he afterwards set himself to solve, and solved.

The Prince's affection for Bourchier resulted in many more excursions together—to Rilo Monastery and the frontier of Macedonia; to Kustendil; to Euxinograd on the Black Sea, and to many other places besides.

The Balkan Alliance.

The behaviour of the Young Turks in Macedonia in 1910 convinced Bourchier that only a resort to arms could free the subject Christians from an intolerable persecution. In that year ten thousand peasants were beaten on the feet so mercilessly that many of them were crippled for life; and yet no newspapers told the tale of the horrors; not a Government issued a Blue-book stating the facts; there was a conspiracy of silence.

This silence was due largely to the influence of the financiers and Jews who control the European Press and whose interests are wrapt up in the preservation of Turkey.

The Young Turk movement started in Salonika, a Jewish town, and, from the first, Jews were at the back of it. That movement may be said to have been a combination of two or three factors. A group of exiles in Paris, driven out by Abdul Hamid, had imbibed French revolutionary ideas. Long away from their own country, they had ceased to understand it; and they believed, or professed to believe, that Turkey might be regenerated by the revival of the constitutional régime instituted in 1877 during the Russo-Turkish crisis. They preached Liberté, Egalité, Fraternité, and imagined that the principles of the French Revolution could be applied to Turkey. Some undoubtedly were sincere and honest men, but they had forgotten the conditions obtaining in their native land.

Another factor was the military element in Macedonia. The young Chauvinist officers were indignant at the presence of an international gendarmerie in their own provinces, and at the prospect of the institution of foreign control for Turkish rule. The meeting at Reval between Edward VII. and the Tsar, and the discussions between England and Russia in 1908 as to the gendarmerie and other things, frightened them. The movement was thus in the nature of a revolt against foreign interference.

Thirdly, a great many of the population, including the Turks themselves, were ready to rise, hoping for better days, disgusted with the misrule of Abdul Hamid, and at the possession of all privileges by a small palace clique.

Salonika and Monastir became the rallying-points of the movement—Salonika, as has been said, being the home both of many rich and influential European Jews, and also of many Mohammedan or Crypto-Jews, who formed a link between the Jewish community and the *soi-disant* Reformers. The movement spread with great rapidity in the army, chiefly among the junior officers. The Sultan became alarmed, and having formally denounced the accursed thing at the palace, issued orders for the arrest or thirty or forty of the chief officers in the conspiracy, amongst whom was Enver Bey.

This precipitated a revolt. Enver Bey and Niazi Bey at Resna went to the mountains. The thing spread rapidly. The Young Turks captured Monastir and Salonika, and the Constitution was proclaimed. The Sultan, finding that he could no longer depend on the army, decided to temporise, and agreed to proclaim the Constitution.

Accordingly in November elections were held for the new Parliament, at which the Young Turks showed the cloven hoof. They secured the election of their own nominees—all Mohammedans except a few Bulgarians and Armenians and a slightly larger number of Greeks, many of whom were representatives of the islands and Asia Minor.

Parliament met in the winter, and a few months afterwards a reactionary movement took place at Constantinople, and the Old Turks gained over the greater portion of the garrison at Constantinople. Then Mahmud Shevket Pasha, the general of the Young Turks, established his forces in Macedonia, was joined by Bulgarian and Greek *Komitadji* bands, and advanced to Tchataldja.

Finding his throne tottering, Abdul Hamid tried negotiation, for the Young Turks believed that he had arranged the counter-movement. The latter, in fact, were masters of the situation, and a party of them entered the palace and made the Sultan sign his abdication. He was hurried into a train and taken to Salonika, and imprisoned in the Villa Allatini. There he remained till November 1912, when the victories of the Allies forced the Turks to take him back to Constantinople. The new Sultan was over sixty years old, and had been imprisoned all his life; he was a mere puppet in the hands of the Young Turks.

Having already got the whole army behind them, the Young Turks were now secure, and began to show the real character of their government. They began to put into practice their principles of Ottomanism—the doctrine that all Turkish subjects, without distinction of race or religion, were to be made simply " good Ottomans "; to abandon their native habits and inherited traditions, and to give up all the privileges that had been accorded to the subject races by former Sultans. Thus, under the outward form of a liberal constitution, they aimed at the obliteration of the various nationalities, and at the extinction of their national ambitions.

After April 1909 these doctrines were applied in European Turkey, and at once provoked violent opposition among the Albanians, who began a succession of revolts.

The curtailment of the old privileges of the Christian races was based on the pretext that as all were equal under the Constitution these special privileges need no longer be maintained. The churches were of course involved; the rights accorded to them were interfered with; religious animosity was excited : it was a process of levelling down to the Ottoman depth which struck at the most sacred ideas of an intellectual and progressive Christianity.

The schools were brought directly under the Ministry of Education, in order to prevent the racial propaganda being carried on. Thus, by a great variety of measures all pointing in the same direction, discontent was bred among the Christians, who had been promised equality, and now had to digest reforms aimed at their racial extinction, and passed by a packed parliament of Mohammedans.

At the same time the Young Turks tried to Ottomanise the half-Ottomanised Albanians. They insisted on their paying taxes they had never paid before; and while allowing Albanian schools to be instituted in Albania, they imposed the Turkish language as the sole medium of instruction, and insisted on the use of the Arabic characters in writing Albanian.

Then a series of revolts followed, and after the suppression, with ferocious cruelty, of one in the north of the country in the spring of 1910, the Turks decided on a general scheme of disarmament.

At first it was to apply to Albania only, but it subsequently was extended to the whole of Macedonia. Disarmament was carried on by the proclamation of martial law, at first among many Albanians, and then among still more Macedonians, who had never revolted.

Disarmament continued throughout the spring and summer of 1910, accompanied with hideous cruelty to the people. At least ten thousand peasants were bastinadoed, or beaten on the feet, many of them with such incredible barbarity that their feet were smashed into pulp. A Frenchman, a priest at Yenidje-Vardar, said that men came to him on their knees for treatment. The settlement of French Jesuits at Yenidje was not molested by the Turks, and those men saw all that happened. The

Bulgarian priest at Yenidje was beaten to death. One of the Turkish devices for compelling the villagers to give up their arms was to keep all the men standing night and day. When they fell down, exhausted, they were prodded with bayonets until they got up again. In Sofia, in 1913, there was a woman who at this time was outraged and then burned, so that she lost both her eyes.

For the sake of appearances the disarmament was carried out in the Turkish villages, but no one there was beaten or molested. At the same time the Young Turks encouraged the immigration into Macedonia of a large number of Bosnian refugees; these they planted in the Christian districts, often ousting the Christian proprietors, and gave them arms with which to terrorise their neighbours.

All these outrages went on without any effective protest from the Great Powers; the Press of the world was gagged; the conspiracy of silence, under Jewish auspices, meant the silence of extermination for the subject races in Turkey in Europe. For money had been laid on the Young Turks, and what do financiers of the Hebrew or any other brand care about torture and outrage and suffering and death so long as they get their prescribed rate of interest? From Shylock to Putumayo the fearful story is ever the same.

But not only the financiers were callously indifferent to everything but their financial interests; there was an odious competition between the Embassies at Constantinople to get concessions, from which our own Government did not stand aloof.

Bourchier, with a knowledge of the conditions prevailing in Turkey and in the Balkans, on the one hand, and at the councils of the Great Powers on the other, superior to that of any other man living, saw that things must go from bad to worse. The end would be the extinction of the subject nationalities. All hope of the intervention of the

Powers had gone shipwreck. Bourchier realised that the only remedy was a combination of the free nations, kinsmen of the oppressed peoples, either to bring such pressure to bear on the Young Turks as to induce them to mitigate their rule, or, if they resisted, to put them out by force.

He came to this conclusion at the end, I believe, of 1910. He did not want an immediate war; the first thing to be done was to apply pressure.

But there was little probability that this would succeed. The Young Turks were elated by success and by the praise which their admirers in Western Europe had lavished on them. They had spent all the money which they could obtain from their financial friends or by taxation in creating a powerful army, and could snap their fingers at the little States; so the programme of pacific remonstrance seemed to end in a *cul-de-sac*.

So Bourchier turned his attention to the other possible solution of the problem. What forces could the four States of the Balkans—Bulgaria, Serbia, Greece, and Montenegro—command for the purposes of bringing pressure, of one kind or another, to bear upon the oppressors of their co-religionists and kinsmen? The Bulgars were ready; their army was excellent, reorganised by Savoff, who had seen the evil effects on other armies of politics in cafés, and had inspired in his junior officers an enthusiasm for hard work which has borne its due fruit. The Bulgars could put 250,000 men in the field on the day of mobilisation. The Serbian army had improved since the Bulgars hammered it; it could provide at least another 150,000. The Greek army had had latterly the advantage of the instruction of French officers. English officers had been reorganising the fleet, and their *Averof* was a bigger and better man-of-war than any the Turks possessed. Little Montenegro could certainly put up a gallant fight.

Here was the germ of the Balkan League—the first cause of the war whch drove the Turks out of Europe after nearly five hundred years of misrule—a calculation simmering in the brain of an unofficial Irishman who, for love of them, had given half his life to the service of the Balkan peoples.

So it came about that during the winter of 1910–11 Bourchier had long talks with M. Venezelos, the Greek Prime Minister, and the two men discussed the scheme of a defensive and eventually offensive alliance between the Balkan States against the Turk.

Events marched rapidly in favour of the project. The difficulty of achieving secret unity and co-operation between nations whose sole common ground was their hatred of the oppressor gave way before the blundering rancour of the Jew-inspired Young Turks.

Everybody knows that Greeks and Jews are the wiliest traders in the Levant. There is a story the moral of which is that a Greek can give a Jew seven pounds and a beating over any commercial course. However that may be, the trade of the Near East is in the hands of Jews and Greeks, and rival traders never love one another very much. Possibly that is why the Jews have found it impossible to accept the New Testament.

It has been pointed out that the Young Turk movement was backed by Jewish funds and influence. The apparent success of their movement gave the Jews a temporary *cachet* at Constantinople; and in the councils of the State their not unjustified demand for some pecuniary compensation for their disinterested services was listened to with an attention usually foreign to the Turkish temperament on similar occasions. Turks never make money themselves; they watch others make it, and then take it. In an access of generosity they informed the Jews that, as an *ad hoc* and temporary measure only, they would relax their salutary rule that no plundering was to be done by

anybody but themselves. The Jews were delighted.
They saw the Greeks ruined, and all the gold they made
in their own pockets. An anti-Greek boycott was established, and the stream of Pactolus was diverted into
Jordan. At the same time anarchy was deliberately
encouraged in Asia, and when the Greeks of the kingdom
showed any interest in Cretan affairs the Young Turks
threatened war.

These things—the disastrous boycott of Greek pro-
ducts, and the condition of their kinsmen in Crete—
roused the Greeks to fury and disposed their Prime
Minister and King to embark on the great enterprise
counselled by the unofficial Irishman.

The pressure put on Bulgars and Greeks alike caused a
rapprochement between the peasants of the two races.
Warfare between them, almost chronic in the past,
entirely ceased; and the stupid Turks went on bullying
both with the utmost impartiality without in the least
comprehending the danger of a combination. This
evidence of the possibility of a real fusion of the masses
of the different races naturally strengthened the hands of
Venezelos and Bourchier. At this time the latter was
striving to bring about a Greco-Bulgarian alliance, which
the other States might subsequently join, and to this end
he directed all his influence to the sedulous fostering of the
nascent friendliness between the two races.

M. Venezelos is a very old friend of Bourchier's, and
their talks, those talks that were to change the face of
Europe for all time, were not held in the official atmosphere of council chambers; they met in various places,
and made a pilgrimage to the tomb of Byron at Meso-
longhi, and rode on muleback over the slopes of Pelion.

At last, one day in May 1911, the decisive step was
taken. The two men had climbed the steep flank of
Mount Pelion—surely an omen from the wisdom of the
prophetic past! For with a vengeance that had been long

deferred they were about to pile Ossa on the mountain where they stood! It was here that Venezelos told Bourchier that he had finally approved the draft treaty of an alliance with Bulgaria against Turkey.

Thus did Bourchier achieve a purpose that will make his name for ever famous. But it must not be supposed that this was his first essay in international politics. During the insurrection of 1896 in Crete he had helped the insurgents in their negotiations with the commanders of the Turkish fleet for reconciliation with the Porte, and his diplomatic skill, profound knowledge, and recognised integrity obtained for the Cretans terms which they knew very well they could never have got for themselves.

Some time ago St. Paul wrote a letter to his friend, Titus, who was in Crete for his sins and the Cretans', and humorously alluded to the national incapacity to make the most of a situation.

Poor Cretans! With their own prophet and St. Paul alike profoundly convinced of their mendacity, to say nothing of their other qualities, what chance have they ever had successfully to conduct negotiations with unbelievers like the Turks? But they and the Turks alike felt confidence in British straightness. Indeed, they were so grateful for all Bourchier had done for them that the Cretan Assembly passed a vote of thanks to him, and every member signed the resolution—a document of which he is naturally very proud. The Turks failed to keep the agreement, and in 1897 the insurrection broke out again. Life in Crete without an insurrection or two proceeding is said by old residents to be very dull.

Bourchier is an Irishman, and has no objection to fighting when the occasion presents itself. In 1896 he joined the insurgents for a while in the bleak red Cretan mountains. The insurrection of the following year was under Sphakienakis and Venezelos. These two born leaders, one of whom was afterwards to take the first step which broke the power of the Turk, made Bourchier one of themselves, and frequently consulted him. Later on, Prince George came to Crete, and Bourchier was with him every day for some hours. The Prince and Venezelos fell out, but this did not prevent Bourchier from visiting his comrade. Venezelos was dismissed from office, and though Bourchier did his utmost to effect a reconciliation between him and the Prince, he was unsuccessful, and Venezelos went to the mountains with an armed following. The strong man carried the day; Venezelos was master of the field; eventually the Prince had to go. In 1908, when Austria annexed Bosnia and Herzegovina, Crete declared for union with Greece. On the 23rd of July in that year the Young Turks rose, and their unwise policy towards Greece has brought about their own and their country's downfall. The chagrin of the Greeks at their failure to obtain union with Crete, after Prince George's departure, led to the formation of the Military League, and a revolution at Athens, followed by the rise to power of a military Junta.

But all soldiers are not Napoleons; a good many of them are but indifferent legislators. The Greek officers could not control the political machine; all the former party leaders were discredited; the harassed generals cast about for a statesman, and found one in Venezelos in Crete. So Bourchier and Venezelos renewed their ancient friendship, and Bourchier stood with the new leader on the balcony in Athens when he made his first speech to the people.

For some time Venezelos had his hands full. One of his chief difficulties was the delicate character of his relations with the King, who had by no means forgotten the quarrel between Venezelos and Prince George, and the recalcitrant attitude subsequently taken up by the Cretan leader.

And here it may be mentioned that, though Venezelos

was born in Greece, he comes of an old Venetian family.

The strained situation was prejudicial both to the interests of Greece and to the prospects of the alliance Bourchier already had in view. As an intimate friend both of the King and of the Premier, he was admirably equipped for the task of bringing about a reconciliation between them. The *rapprochement* was effected, and since that time King George's relations with his great Premier have been of the most cordial nature.

As before narrated, the Greek proposals were sent to Bulgaria in May 1911. Some months later, Bourchier went to Sofia and put his arguments in favour of the alliance before King Ferdinand and M. Gueshoff. Just as, nearly a year before, he had persuaded Venezelos and King George to take the first step towards the formation of the Balkan League, so again in Sofia he persuaded the Bulgarian Government to fall into line with Greece. In February 1912 he himself brought back to Athens from Sofia a reply favourable to Venezelos' proposal of a defensive alliance.

Up to that moment only five people had an inkling of what was going on, namely, King George of Greece and M. Venezelos, King Ferdinand of Bulgaria and M. Gueshoff, and Bourchier.

After Bourchier's return to Athens negotiations were put on a diplomatic basis, and the Greek Minister at Sofia was informed of the alliance and instructed to conduct the negotiations at the Bulgarian capital. That made six people in the plot.

February and March passed ; the negotiations went on in absolute secrecy ; in April a definitive treaty was signed between Greece and Bulgaria.

Bourchier had not left Serbia out of the hunt. At the end of December 1911 he went to Belgrade, and broached his plan to M. Milovanovitch, the Foreign Minister.

He urged on him the idea of a combination between the Balkan States—a defensive combination to protect and maintain the rights of the Christian nationalities in Turkey. Milovanovitch was favourable in principle, but he pointed out the great risks that Serbia would run—in the first place from Austria, if that Power got wind of the project, and in the second from Turkey herself, who could kill Serbian commerce by closing the Salonika route.

But M. Milovanovitch, who had already had a secret interview with M. Gueshoff, was sound on the question, and Bourchier left him, not doubting the ultimate issue, and went back to Bulgaria to inform his friends there how matters stood in Belgrade. In due course the Serbo-Bulgar Treaty was signed a week or two before the Bulgar-Greek Treaty.

Montenegro had no treaty with either Bulgaria or Greece, but there was a definitive treaty between her and Serbia.

Bourchier went back to England in July 1912, and at that time the Balkan League was practically formed, although further details and military conventions were agreed on a little later. He had done his part in the great task, and none too soon, for the futures of the peoples his statesmanship was to liberate.

In the early autumn things got rapidly worse between the Turks and Bulgarians on the one hand, and the Turks and the Serbians and Montenegrins on the other. There was a frontier dispute, followed by a series of massacres which did nothing to alleviate the situation.

But matters did not come to a head till September, when the assembling of a large Turkish force at Adrianople caused the fear of an invasion to spread throughout Bulgaria.

At last, on September 30, the four States mobilised simultaneously. The rest of the story is sketched elsewhere.

As for Bourchier, in the middle of September he went

to Sinaia, in the hope of contributing to an agreement between Rumania and Bulgaria, so as to secure the friendly neutrality of Rumania during the impending war. He received no encouragement at the time from the Rumanian Government; but who knows how far the subsequent neutrality of Rumania during 1912 was the outcome of his journey ?

Of course a factor contributing to the Balkan War was the war between Italy and Turkey. When the former became inevitable the Turks and Italians made haste to make peace. If her war with Turkey had gone on Italy would have been practically the ally of the Balkan States, and as such might have been involved in war with Austria. Naturally, therefore, the conclusion of peace between their foe and the Italians was a serious blow to the Balkan League, particularly in regard to the operations of the Italian fleet, which had usefully confined the Turks to land. Now the whole brunt of the blockade must fall on the Greek fleet, whose efficiency had yet to be proved.

The Allies asked Turkey, very politely, for reforms in Macedonia, and guarantees for their execution. The Turks sent no reply. War followed immediately, begun by King Nicholas of Montenegro. King Nicholas did this entirely off his own bat, and was remonstrated with from both Sofia and Athens. But the intrepid Nicholas was determined to have war. When the Powers intervened he thought a settlement might be arrived at, and a settlement by aught save the arbitrament of arms was the last thing he desired.

I happened to get sight of the following telegrams, sent by King Nicholas and M. Venezelos to Bourchier on the outbreak of war :

Profondément touché je remercie de tout cœur le noble ami du Monténégro et de l'indépendance balcanique.—NIKOLAS.

Je vous remercie et je vous serre la main comme à un des principaux artisans de cette œuvre magnifique qui est l'union étroite des peuples chrétiens de la péninsula balcanique.—Venisélos.

So far as I know, only one Englishman hitherto has had the information to ascribe to Bourchier his approximate rôle in the Balkan drama. That man is the special correspondent in the Balkan War of the *Westminster Gazette*—a truly admirable paper, which all wise Tories read when they believe that no Radicals are looking. A message from that correspondent, published in the *Westminster Gazette* of November 11, 1912, contains the following, dated Sofia, November 2, 1912:

A ROMANCE OF THE BALKANS

It has been assumed, perhaps everywhere, and it is generally believed in Bulgaria, that some definite agreement has been drawn up by which the allied kingdoms have arranged among themselves the details of any departure from the *status quo* that victory may bring with it. M. Dimitroff * is himself, of course, a diplomatist; and it was too much, perhaps, to expect him to-day, while there was still a possibility of a last Turkish stand at Tchataldja, and while Salonika, Monastir, and Janina remained in Turkish hands, to admit that the settlement had been cut and dried in this way. He would not even admit that any one statesman had been responsible for the alliance, though he said enough to lead me to attach more import-ance than I had done before to a current belief that is almost a romance of the Balkans.

Some days ago, in writing of the rejoicings at the fall of Kirk Kilisse, I mentioned an English resident who, for no ostensible reason, was made the hero of the moment.

* The Secretary-General of the Bulgarian Foreign Office.—Author.

To be strictly accurate, I should have called him Irish,
and described him as an absentee landlord who has spent
about half of a long life (*sic*) among these Balkan peoples.
More than a generation ago he was a master at Eton.
Now he spends a vagrant, bachelor life in a corner of
Europe to which he has become profoundly attached, and
in which he pulls an incredible number of strings.   He
makes Sofia his headquarters, winters in Athens, spends
the heat of the summer in Sinaia, and pays frequent visits
to Bukarest and Belgrade.   He was expelled * from
Bulgaria once, during a political crisis, but was soon
recalled, and the Greek Press made bitter attacks upon
him when, a few years ago, he began to point out the
necessity of this Balkan alliance.   He has the full confidence of every Court in the Peninsula, though ; and his
advice is more eagerly sought by responsible ministers,
and more frequently adopted, than that of professional
diplomatists.   He is known here to every man in the
street as " Bourchier " ; he is believed to have the British
Press in his pocket ; and when he takes his daily ride on
a handsome little grey Arab pony almost every hat is
raised as he passes.   M. Dimitroff is not prepared to
contradict anybody who suggests that " Bourchier's "
personal influence has done more than anything else to
bring about the Balkan alliance.

It only remains to attempt to determine James
Bourchier's place in history.   The task is a difficult one,
because a basis for comparison is, so far as I know, wholly
lacking.

Let us first of all briefly sum up the achievement, and
then try to find an historical analogy ; if that is wanting
let us formulate our own opinion, for what it is worth.

A man of genius travels to far-distant countries—not
to one country and to one people, but to four or five widely
differing countries and peoples, whose sole points of

* " Withdrew " would be more accurate.—AUTHOR.

contact are, firstly, that all of them profess the Christian religion, and, secondly, that all of them have kinsmen and co-religionists who are groaning under the brutal tyranny of a Mohammedan Power. In the course of his work he learns the languages of these peoples; he gets to know their varying habits of thought, national characteristics, and political ideals; he learns to understand and sympathise with all of them, and all of them love him in return. To the problems which have been vexing the hearts of these peoples for hundreds of years he for five-and-twenty years devotes his unremitting attention. Sciolism and genius do not co-exist. During those hundreds of years two distinct forces have been at work to mitigate the lot of those Christians oppressed by the Turk: the Christian populations have on countless occasions rebelled, and as often have been mercilessly punished for their rebellion; and the Great Powers of Europe have on countless occasions represented diplomatically to the Porte the enormity of its methods, and as often have failed to effect any reforms whatsoever. The man of genius ponders these things; he sees that there is one solution of the problem that has been talked of in the past but has not yet been tried; he knows that all other possible solutions have been tried and have failed.

The idea was nothing less than the uniting of the four Christian States in arms against the Mohammedan Power; to fight for the religious and political liberties of their kinsmen subjects of that Power. This he deliberately set himself to do, and this he succeeded in doing. The four States, temporarily united by the force of his genius, by common respect for his abilities, and by common knowledge of his devotion to their cause, sank their ancient differences; allied themselves; simultaneously made war; conquered the Turk, and drove him out of Europe.

That is Bourchier's achievement. The liberty that

hundreds of thousands of flayed and tortured Christians could not win for themselves; the justice that four nations of their own blood could not exact for them; the very civilisation that the Great Powers of Europe tried and failed to enforce on a barbaric State; that liberty, that justice, that civilisation James Bourchier has bestowed upon the Christian populations, and the millions of their descendants, of what before his day was Turkey.

The magnitude of this achievement on the part of an Irishman with nothing but ability and single-hearted sympathy for the oppressed may be looked at from two different points of view—the fact itself and its results.

When it is remembered that so short a time ago as 1885 Bulgarians and Serbians were at one another's throats, and that Bulgars and Greeks hated one another like poison, and fought whenever they met, as they did invariably before the war, and have done immediately after it, it will be admitted that the feat of inducing Serbians, Bulgars, and Greeks to combine for so gigantic a task, and one so particularly dependent for its success on complete unanimity and instant co-operation, was a great one, and one only to be accomplished by a great man. More men were engaged at Lule Burgas than at Mukden, Sedan, or any previous battle in the history of the world. If Bourchier had not gone to the Balkans and made the aspirations of its peoples his own, Lule Burgas would never have been fought. The issues of that epoch-making battle are sufficiently momentous.

Vast tracts of territory have changed hands; millions of people have changed their rulers; a Power and a creed which at one time threatened to dominate Europe have been practically evicted. Christianity has triumphed over Islam, civilisation over barbarity; the European has proved himself a better man than the Asiatic; the apple of discord has been lifted out of reach of the Great Powers; Europe will not allow Constantinople to any one at present but the Turk. Fifty years hence, or much less, the Crescent will not float over Constantinople ; but that is by the way—a prophecy, and therefore not an issue of Lule Burgas.

Few of the conquerors of the world have permanently effected more than this. The great founders of religious movements gained their triumphs because they worked, not for themselves, but for mankind ; Bourchier has succeeded for the same reason. For ever will the soul triumph over the material. No earthly forces can withstand the onslaught of a great idea.

The Tsar Liberator set free his oppressed neighbours, the Bulgars ; but they spoke the same tongue as himself, and he was the Tsar of All the Russias. No single instance occurs to me of any foreigner ever having done as much for alien races. Patriots, as their name implies, work for the good of their own country. Patriots from Ireland generally go into the House of Commons, and pretend there that their country is going to the dogs for the want of Home Rule. Other persons, equally patriotic, say that it will go to the dogs if it gets Home Rule The only conclusion an unbiased third party can come to is that the *status quo* is not doing much harm, and that Home Rule wouldn't either. But all these excellent and worthy politicians have, if they could only see it, such a defective sense of proportion. Living in the best-governed country in the world they frequently talk as though the world would come to an end if they cannot pass some grandmotherly Bill or other ; living in the richest and most contented country in the world they frequently talk as if an extra halfpenny on the income-tax spelt national bankruptcy. This old country could govern herself, even if the back benches were used for firewood to-morrow. We are like a lot of overfed and lazy schoolboys disputing, after a huge dinner, who shall have the biggest slice of pineapple. The governmental momentum which this old country has acquired in the course of the past six hundred years is sufficient to keep her on her majestic path, venerated and unresting, as Bacon said of princes and the stars, were all our legislative apparatus abolished to-morrow.

We want no more than an executive and a defence committee ; and Mr. Asquith has shown his genius in admitting the folly of party politics by his invitation to Mr. Balfour to sit in conclave, cheek by jowl, with his bitterest (?) opponents. Thus is the tongue in the cheek turned vocal. Mr. Asquith has abolished the House of Lords ; the logical *sequelæ* of his purpose is to abolish the House of Commons, and to establish an executive composed of the best men of all shades of opinion. He has gone so far in this direction that bored readers of " guillotine " and " kangaroo " proceedings would be relieved to find that he had the courage of his convictions, and that to-morrow there was to be no more legislation for ever, and that Ministries of All the Talents alone, and for all time, were to direct our goings in the way.

At a critical time like the present the Cromwellian-Asquith dictatorial plan has abundant advantages.

No, politics here are not a serious business ; everybody has his tongue in his cheek. But in the Balkan Peninsula politics are too often a matter of life and death. Turkish politics meant death and rape and the bastinado for thousands of Christians annually. Nobody could defend these practices as Mr. Asquith defends Home Rule or Sir Edward Carson defends the Union.

Poverty, comparative, workhouse-relieved poverty, is the only thing in British politics. In the Near East you have gnawing, desperate, totally unrelieved poverty, and murder and rape and burnings and the bastinado thrown in. Which is the more promising field for a statesman ? Ah, but it is so much more comfortable to stick M.P. after your name, and to have a good dinner

every evening, and to ask absurd questions which are
carefully wired down to the local paper, than to be an
exile in strange, wild, half-savage lands where sometimes
it is hard to get anything to eat, where very often you run
a very good chance of getting a knife between your ribs,
and where your efforts for the amelioration of the lot of
the poor and the persecuted will most assuredly not
obtain for you even the reversion of an under-secretary-
ship !

Our present rulers lack imagination. Which of them
has ever lifted up his voice in defence of the oppressed of
other races ? Mr. Noel Buxton and the Balkan Committee
are not our rulers, but they are honourable exceptions to
our sordid insularity.

Ah ! Would that we had the *saeva indignatio* of a
Gladstone, denouncing atrocities committed against
Bulgarians, instead of the stony silence which has passed
over unrebuked atrocities more atrocious, committed by
the same unspeakable Turk within the last five years !
The names of Byron, of Gladstone, and of Bourchier will
be remembered and treasured in the hearts of millions
when tolerably well-educated men, a hundred years
hence, will have to get a book of reference to see who was
Prime Minister of Great Britain in 1913. Stein occurs as
a prototype of Bourchier, but then he was a German firing
the imaginations of Germans.

Frankly, I give it up, and it doesn't matter. *Securus
judicat orbis terrarum.* The statues which will rise in the
Macedonian towns will be time-bound witnesses to the
love and admiration which the unofficial Irishman, the
defender of the weak and the oppressed, excited in the
hearts of the people he liberated ; and when those stones
are dust his name and fame will be assured. *Exegit
monumentum aere perennius.*

CHAPTER II

SCENES IN THE BALKANS

HE following extracts from articles by Bourchier, which, apart from their interest, serve to show his admirable literary style, are reproduced by the courteous permission of the editor of the *Fortnightly Review*. Of Rilo he writes:

We advanced to the great gate of the monastery, which is sheltered by a portico adorned, like those at Mount Athos, with frescoes of saints and angels, and flanked by loop-holed projections in the wall on either side. Here the Abbot or Hegúmen, a portly, genial ecclesiastic, received us, arrayed in robes of purple and silver brocade, and accompanied by some sixty or seventy monks—all that remain of the once numerous brotherhood. A procession was formed; and, with incense and lighted tapers going before, we passed into the great quadrangle and directed our steps to the church which stands in its midst. The quadrangle is, properly speaking, an irregular pentagon; a number of galleries run round it, which lead to the cells of the monks; these long corridors are supported on stone arches, rising in tiers, and forming a series of picturesque arcades. Everywhere the colouring is rich and effective; the masonry is picked out in white and red, and the walls are bright with medallions and quaintly traced devices. The topmost gallery forms a kind of verandah beneath a projecting roof, which rests

34

on dark oaken beams. The court is overgrown with grass, and shaded by a few fruit-trees; around are numerous fountains, and the air is alive with the murmur of running water. The church is even more brilliant than the surrounding buildings with its variegated stonework, gay mosaics, and alcoves filled with frescoes. In contrast is the stern sombre aspect of the venerable keep, the oldest part of the monastery, looking down in the dignity of its eight centuries on the silvered domes and red-tiled roofs and cloistered shades below.

.   .   .   .   .

Leaving Rilo Selo, we began to ascend the superb mountain gorge in the heart of which the monastery lies. The slopes around us were clothed with thickets of dense brushwood; but after some hours' progress we entered upon the grand primeval forest which forms the distinctive feature of the Rilo scenery. At our feet a foaming torrent dashed swiftly along, half hidden by luxuriant foliage; from its margin to the confines of the rocky tracts above—a distance of some five thousand feet—the steep acclivity on either hand was covered with noble trees, the delicate green of the beech contrasting with the darker shades of the oak and ilex and the still more sombre colouring of the firs and pines. For hours we made our way through these leafy glades till at length an open vista in the woods revealed to us a prospect through the valley; and we saw before us the monastery of Rilo, with its domes and cupolas and battlemented tower, standing like some enchanted castle in the royal solitude of its vast domains. Close beneath it ran the sparkling stream; around were undulating lawns interspersed with tufted groves; beyond was the boundless forest, climbing upwards to where, in the heaven above, stupendous rocky summits stood ranged like a regiment of giants, surrounding and protecting the national sanctuary.

The monastery of Rilo has ever been the central-point

and focus not only of the national religion but of the national sentiment. Its history is interwoven with that of Christianity in the Balkans; it is to Bulgaria, as Jireczek says, what Mont Saint-Michel is to Normandy, or the Grand Chartreuse to Dauphiné; for ages it has kept alive the light of the faith in the heart of the Peninsula, though so many of the mountaineers close by—the Pomaks of Rhodope—have embraced the creed of Islam; and to-day it forms a link, both political and religious, between the free Bulgarians and their not-forgotten brethren in Macedonia. Its founder, St. Ivan Rilski, the St. Bruno of Bulgaria, was born in 876; he was the contemporary of the great Czar Simeon, and, as may be supposed, innumerable legends have gathered round his memory. For years the holy man wandered over the mountains of Bulgaria, seeking a spot where he might found a pious retreat; at one time he lived in a hollow tree, at another in a cave among the rocks. At length he fixed his dwelling in the mountain, above the present site of the monastery: his fame for exorcising demons and healing incurable maladies brought disciples to his side, and the little band constructed a chapel and some rude dwellings: the chapel still exists, and there is a grotto hard by, into which pilgrims descend through a chimney-like passage cut in the rock. Sinners, it is said, cannot pass this way; and the fat, who, it may be presumed, have had too much of the good things of this life, are fain to enter by a door from below. The saint was buried here, but his bones were afterwards removed to Sofia, where they remained for five hundred years. The Bulgarian Czars loaded the sanctuary with gifts and privileges; and their memory served to keep alive, through centuries of Turkish domination, the national idea and the record of a glorious past. Since the Ottoman invasion the monastery has had a chequered history. At first it fell into decay; then it was restored by three

brothers from Küstendil, who brought back the bones of
the founder; in later times it won the favour of successive sultans, who bestowed upon it by firman most of the
privileges it now enjoys. Twice it has been almost
destroyed by fire; it has stood innumerable sieges, and
more than once it has been stormed and captured by
brigands, who exacted a heavy ransom from the monks.
It has had enemies spiritual as well as temporal; but
notwithstanding all the efforts of the Greek hierarchy, it
has clung to the Slavonic language and ritual. In times
of political and religious persecution it was a refuge to the
oppressed, and at the beginning of the present century it
counted some six or seven hundred inmates, clerical and
lay. The Berlin Treaty gave the monastery to the new
principality, but its trials did not end here. The revival
of brigandage which followed the revolt of Eastern
Roumelia again exposed the brethren to danger; the
shepherds on the estate were compelled to supply the
robber-gangs with provisions; the monks found themselves obliged to carry arms, and many of them were wont
to sleep with a loaded rifle by their pillow. But the
energy of the Bulgarian Government has successfully
dealt with the evil; some fifty of the brigands have been
shot, hanged, or otherwise disposed of, and the remainder
have adopted less picturesque methods of earning their
bread. The trackless forest has now been cleared of its
human, or rather inhuman denizens; the bear, the wolf,
and the wild boar roam unchallenged in its weird soli-
tudes, while the chamois and the eagle divide the empire
of the rocky heights above.

　　　　.　　　.　　　.　　　.

Next morning when I left my cell and looked down
from the gallery upon the grass-grown court, I was
struck by a novel and interesting spectacle. The quadrangle was thronged with hundreds of peasants in their
charming holiday attire, their brightly-coloured costumes

contrasting with the sombre robes of the monks and the white summer uniforms of the soldiers. Some were sitting grouped on the greensward, enjoying their morning meal; others were asleep beneath the fruit-trees, fatigued by their long pilgrimage; others were standing in the alcoves of the church, gazing with wonder and admiration and awe at the pictured revelations of the wrath to come. A little crowd was assembled at a stall beneath the belfry, eagerly purchasing crosses and beads and pictures of saints. It was interesting to observe the tendency of the sexes to keep apart: the unmarried girls sat in rows on the steps beneath the arches, with gay ribbons and strings of coins in their hair, while the young men cast shy glances at them from a respectful distance. Fresh bands of pilgrims continued to arrive throughout the day, and before evening there were at least three thousand peasants at the monastery. After sunset a terrific thunderstorm broke over the valley; the lightning seemed to leap from crag to crag above our heads, and the thunder echoed grandly among the mountains on either hand. The peasants had crowded into the galleries, where they lay packed like sardines, most of them asleep and unconscious of the storm. It was after midnight when I was aroused by the sound of beating upon a *semantron*, or wooden board, followed by the loud tolling of bells, and I went down into the court. The rain had ceased; the peasants were all astir, and many of them were already on their way to the church, at the door of which a monk sat at a table lighted by a dim candle. As the worshippers approached he inscribed in a book the names of such of them as gave offerings, it being understood that the names should be mentioned in the church services for a time proportionate to the magnitude of the gift. A little group was gathered around, as the peasants fumbled for their purses in the folds of their garments, or stood debating within themselves how much

they should give—it was a conflict of interests spiritual
and temporal—or bent their swarthy sunburnt faces over
the table as they eagerly watched for the inscription of
their names. They had given of their penury, and they
meant to have their reward.

The services continued through the small hours of the
morning, and at nine o'clock Prince Ferdinand attended
one of them, the peasants crowding densely to see their
sovereign. Already many of the pilgrims had departed,
making their way down the valley in a long picturesque
train with their waggons and their oxen. The women were
seated in the waggons, the men for the most part going
on foot. I chanced to speak to one of the former, a
sturdy countrywoman and a mother in Bulgaria, who had
come hither with her two stout sons, aged twenty-one and
eighteen respectively. It was her second visit to the
monastery, she said ; the first was before the birth of her
firstborn, when she came to make her vows ; and now that
he was grown to man's estate she had come again. She
had brought an offering of twenty-five francs, and received
in return a paper with some pictures of saints and a
promise that her name should be mentioned in the prayers.
Not much for her money, some may say ; nevertheless the
investment was a good one because it made her happy.
So too with the others who left their hard-won savings
here ; they returned to their homes happier, and perhaps
better, than before. " Vain superstitions," says the Spirit
of the nineteenth century. Yes, but what would life be
without its superstitions ? What would passion be
without its romance, or faith without its mysteries, or
hope without its illusions ? And why quarrel with a
superstition which calls these children of toil from the
furrow and the pasture to spend a holiday in this delightful
spot, and gives them at least a landmark in the monotony
of their lives ? The time may come when men will
believe only that which has been proved, the darkness of

credulity may yield to the daybreak of reason; but the
moonlight and the stars and the enchantment of the night
will vanish as well in the cold dreary mist of the dawning.

. . . . .

It was a magnificent summer evening—for there is
little or no spring in the Balkan peninsula—and the
wooded hills on the Bulgarian shore were glowing red
in the gorgeous light of sunset as we sped rapidly down
the swollen tide, which seemed to spread as far as eye
could reach over the lowlands of Roumania as it reflected
the splendid colouring of the sky above, and into which
the sun appeared to sink as into the waters of a boundless
ocean. A short pause was made at Turtukai, where the
enthusiasm of the people surpassed anything I had yet
seen, and the twilight was already falling as we came in
view of the famous fortress of Silistria. The pale crescent
of the new moon, which heralded the commencement of
the Ramazan, had already risen above the towers of the
impregnable city, and the coloured lights were twinkling
on the minarets, from which the call to prayer and the
proclamation of the great festival had but a moment
before been delivered. We found Silistria *en fête*; and
late as was the hour, the Prince managed to hold an official
reception and to inspect the garrison before sitting down
to the banquet given in his honour by the town. Silistria
proved its loyalty by providing us with an excellent *ménu*.
Both the cook and the viands had been brought all the way
from Bucharest. It was near midnight when the *Orient*
turned her head against the stream, and starting amid a
blaze of fireworks, steamed out into the dark silent river.
We spent a portion of this night, and the greater part of
the following one, at anchor in the stream. Before with-
drawing to my cabin I went on deck, where, to my
surprise, not a single officer or member of the crew was
to be seen. All had apparently retired to rest, and there
was not even a look-out man at the prow. The stars

were glittering overhead with that wild, wonderful
brilliancy which they only display in the southern heavens,
and the rays of light were reflected on the countless
eddies of the gigantic river. All was stillness but for the
ripples of the water against the vessel's side and the flute-
notes of the nightingales in the dense thickets of the
Roumanian shore, from which we lay but a hundred
yards distant. A dozen boats might have put out from
the bank with torpedoes or dynamite bombs without any
fear of an alarm being raised. But we had little to fear,
for nobody knew where we were, the order to drop
anchor being always given unexpectedly and carried out
immediately.

EXTRACTS FROM "THE GREAT SERVIAN FESTIVAL"

By James D. Bourchier

("*Fortnightly Review,*" *August* 1889.)

"Happy the people who have no history." In one
sense of the word the Servians have no history, or at least
no written record of events worthy of that name; and yet
it can hardly be said that the retrospect of the past is a
happy one. A few chronicles preserved in the monasteries, some biographies of kings who were regarded as
saints, and an essay on general history by Raïch are almost
the only Servian sources of history extant. Even these
were written in the liturgical language, unintelligible and
practically unknown to the people. But the popular
imagination and the popular love of song has made up for
the deficiency of authentic records. The Servian *pesmas*,
or heroic songs, are the real annals of the nation. They
form a national epic of the highest interest and value,
thoroughly indigenous, untouched by external influence,
and containing at least the outlines of historical facts,
while affording a vivid picture of the life, the manners,

the ideas, and the aspirations of former generations of the Servian race. Composed soon after the events they narrate, and in a style suited to please the audiences of the day, they have much of the fresh, spontaneous charm of the *Iliad* and the *Odyssey*; and though no Servian Homer has arisen to weld them, like the old Greek rhapsodies, into a harmonious whole, they continue to furnish the simple, half-educated peasantry with a life-like and fairly connected idea of the heroes of olden time and their achievements. There are few peasants who cannot recite half a dozen or more of these primitive lays to the accompaniment of the *gouslé*, a kind of one-stringed violin made of sycamore wood and played with an arched bow. Every event in Servian life which brings the people together— the village festival, the wedding, the *slava*, or patron saint's day—furnishes an occasion for the recitation of the *pesma*, as well as for the dancing of the *kolo*, or national dance; wandering minstrels go from village to village, and the *haïdouks*, or brigands, in their winter lairs pass the night in singing the exploits of mighty men of old, many of whom were adepts in their own particular trade. And so it is that every Servian peasant is familiar with the names and deeds of those who fought and fell at Kossovo —the good Czar Lazar, his wife's father, the brave Young Bogdan, his brothers-in-law the nine Yougovich, and his two sons-in-law, the nobly-descended traitor Vouk Brankovich, and the low-born but valiant and handsome Milosh Obilich, the Scaevola of Servia and the darling of the popular legend. Perhaps there is no people in Europe more familiar with its ancient folk-lore. " Littérairement," says Émile Montegut, " il n'y a pas en Europe de peuple plus intéressant. Par lui nous pouvons pénétrer le mystère des poésies primitives."

. . . . .

At Lubostin there was a scene which, more than anything I have ever witnessed, recalled visions of the golden

age. It was a magnificent summer day, and the rays of the
noontide sun were streaming brightly through the foliage
of the noble walnut trees which surround the monastery.
Some thousand peasants in holiday costume were scattered in groups beneath the shade, the brilliant hues of
their garments forming a pleasant contrast with the rich
verdure of the greensward. They had come with their
waggons and their oxen ; and the handsome sleepy-eyed
animals were reposing hard by, chewing the cud of
peace, and apparently as happy and contended as their
masters. Horses, too, bearing on their backs gorgeously
coloured rugs, on which their riders sleep at night when
they undertake long journeys, were standing beneath the
trees ; lambs and sucking pigs were turning on wooden
spits over pine-wood fires ; rudely made picturesque
country carts were being utilised as pantries and wine
cellars, and I saw an ecclesiastical dignitary in his robes
pushing one of them under a shed. We approached some
of the picnic parties and found they were enjoying excellent fare—roast lamb, brown and white bread, both of
good quality, very palatable cheese, good wine and
komovitza, a liqueur brewed from barley. The people were
most hospitable, offering us a share of their repast with a
courtesy and frankness which was very winning, for they
are unaccustomed to the existence of social superiors, and
feel none of the *mauvaise honte* created by artificial distinctions of rank. The costumes of the men were in
many cases very handsome, their homespun jackets being
embroidered with silver, their waistcoats tastefully worked
in flowered patterns of silk, and their worsted stockings
shewing wonderful varieties of design in brilliant colouring. The dress of the women was scarcely as picturesque,
but very effective in the distance, owing to the brightness
of its hues ; many of them wore yellow silk handkerchiefs
round their heads and strings of coins in their hair. It
would seem as though the Servian women exhausted their

æsthetic faculties in the adornment of their lords. They
are prettier than their Bulgarian sisters, but nature, in
the case of both nations, seems to have lavished most of
her favours on the men. It was impossible to look upon
these sturdy countrymen, with their well-nourished
frames and contented faces, without reflecting that
something at least may be said for a system of peasant
proprietary. They have each of them a small estate of
at least nine acres, which they are forbidden to sell or
pledge ; and if they want more land they can easily obtain
a grant from the Government if they can give satisfactory
proofs of industry. Sometimes they work together in
associations of families, or *zadrugas* ; and this system of
practical socialism has been found so advantageous
owing to the pressure exerted upon the idle, that the
Government encourages it by remissions of taxation and
military service. But there is a difficulty, I regret to say,
in inducing the women to live together in peace. The land
is fertile, and supplies the modest wants of the Servian
peasant without exacting any great amount of labour ;
he has time for a holiday such as this—in the middle of
the harvest, and for many more besides. It seems deplor-
able to our commercial instinct that the most should not
be made out of the soil ; but there is really no reason why
the Servian peasant should be richer than he cares to be.
He is happy, and that is enough. And it would be rash
to assert that the average of happiness is lower in this
sunny land of ease and plenty than in a certain island in
the far north-west, where, amid fogs and smoke, millions
toil unceasingly for wealth they have no time to enjoy,
and Mammon and Respectability are as gods, with Mrs.
Grundy for their archpriestess. There is a kindly reason-
ableness—shall I say a Christian charity ?—in the habits
and even in the laws of these unsophisticated people ;
they have not yet been hardened by the greed of gain
and the daily sight of poverty and rags amid enormous

wealth. The village inn, for instance, is open free at night to the poor wayfarer; he is neither driven to the nearest haystack for shelter and then prosecuted for trespass, nor is he arrested for the crime of having " no visible means of subsistence." There are no beggars in Servia, for the blind and the maimed earn their living as village minstrels, and the healthy and strong find abundant occupation, and can become landowners if they will. Mrs. Grundy would not approve of the Servian peasants; but they are nearer to the kingdom of heaven than she is. It is interesting as we stand on the threshold of the twentieth century to follow the life and manners of these last survivors of a patriarchal age:

> . . . . extrema per illos
> Iustitia excedens terris vestigia fecit.

EXTRACTS FROM "THE STRONGHOLD OF THE SPHAKIOTES"

By James D. Bourchier

("*Fortnightly Review*," August 1890.)

The shadow of night was falling as we entered the mountain village of Lakkos, passing on our way a small encampment of Albanian gendarmes—surly, ill-favoured-looking fellows, who, as we afterwards learned, lead a cat-and-dog life with the villagers. The latter, most of whom were veritable sons of Anak, apparently regarded us with some distrust as we entered the little khan, but as soon as we produced our credentials they received us with all cordiality. We were conducted to one of the largest houses in the village—a two-storeyed mansion, the lower part serving as a stable, and the dwelling-rooms on the floor above being reached by a terribly steep flight of steps. Here we were hospitably entertained by the man of the house, a fine-looking mountaineer, who attended to our wants in person, while the women of the family, grouped together in a dark corner, seemed contented to watch us with a shy curiosity. Presently the villagers dropped in one by one, till soon we were a goodly company; and the flickering light of our tiny lamps, falling dimly on their swarthy, handsome, black-bearded faces, their herculean frames and picturesque costumes—at the same time faintly shadowing the outlines of female forms in the background—revealed to us a scene worthy of a Jordäens or a Teniers. There were few of these wild warriors who had not taken human life in this land of the vendetta and religious feud; most of them had carried a rifle in the two last insurrections; and yet now they told their tale of outrage and wrong with an almost touching *naïveté*, resembling the frank simplicity of children. Many of their narratives scarcely stood the test of inquiry, but there was no conscious attempt to deceive, nothing but an overwhelming conviction that all their evils must be traced to the hereditary foe.

. . . . .

We proceeded to a point at the southern end of the plain, where the rocky barrier before us seemed to afford no possible means of egress, when we unexpectedly came upon the Xylóscala, or " Wooden Ladder," the end of the southern entrance to the Sphakian stronghold, and without doubt one of the most extraordinary mountain passes in the world. We stood upon the brink of a steep declivity, descending at least three thousand feet into a narrow gorge, where, amid the dense foliage of overhanging trees, we seemed to catch the sparkle of a running stream; to our right an enormous pile of dark-blue rock, frowning grimly at us from out of the sky above, broke off into a terrific precipice, and sank sheer into the abyss beneath our feet; to our left stupendous mountain forms, massed and contorted by some fierce convulsion of nature, appeared to leap and rage and battle together in the wildest confusion, while above them all Mount Holy Ghost, like a monarch among giants, rose glistening in a royal mantle of the purest white. It was one of those sights which, when once seen, can never be forgotten.

The Xylóscala has been given a bad name by the travellers and the guide-books; * but our mules, like the Tommy Atkins of after-dinner speeches, were fit to go anywhere and to do anything, and our human companions were equally reliable. We accomplished the descent without mishap, and rested for a while beneath the shade of beautiful plane-trees, near by the running stream, which, springing suddenly from a cleft in the rock and vanishing again into some mysterious aperture, disappears and reappears again several times in its progress down the valley. We followed the course of the stream as it wound its way among the immense boulders which had fallen from the beetling cliffs around us ; sometimes the bed was dry, and afforded a kind of path ; at other times it was necessary to scramble up the mountain-side to a considerable height, where the way, leading up and down among pinnacled rocks or sharply turning by the verge of some unexpected precipice, was even more trying to the nerves than the Xylóscala itself. The absolute indifference of my mule, which would sometimes stop to browse on some choice fern or mountain shrub, at a point where a single false step would have hurled us both to destruction, would

---

* Pashley, who did not descend the Xylóscala because he distrusted his horse, relates how " not long since a Sphakiote went with his mule for the first time ; the poor beast started back on seeing the precipice and, losing its footing, was precipitated to the bottom " (see *Travels in Crete*, vol. i. pp. 148 and 157). " Les mulets eux-mêmes," says Perrot, who also took another route (*L'Ile de Crète*, p. 75), " y sont exposés à être pris de vertige, et on en a vu souvent rouler avec leur charge au fond de l'abîme." Murray is equally discouraging. But under favourable conditions there is no real danger. The name Ξυλόσκαλα is derived from the wooden beams which are here and there fastened into the rock in order to make a path.

certainly have been a little irritating were it not a consoling sign that the animal had no tendency to vertigo. Every moment the scenery changed, as one gigantic mountain succeeded another on either hand, but no sign of human life broke upon the deep solitude till we approached a little ruined monastery half hidden among beautiful cypresses. The form of these graceful trees has ever been connected in the Cretan mind with the ideal of feminine beauty, and one may hear the muleteers singing some such love ditty as this :

> My slender little cypress-tree,
>   With purple cap so neat,
> What happy youth shall fondle thee
>   And linger at thy feet ?

.   .   .   .   .

Proceeding on our way, we soon came in sight of the fine bay of Suda, where seven vessels of the Turkish navy were riding at anchor, and then approached the foundations of the ancient Aptera, the " wingless town," where the Sirens, vanquished in a contest of singing by the Muses, lost their feathers, and, casting themselves into the sea, were changed into the rocky islets which lie in a group at the mouth of the harbour. Descending a rugged path by the edge of the sea, we came, for the first time, to a track which almost deserved the name of a road ; here we met with a body of Turkish troops on the march, light-hearted youths, who were singing at the top of their voices, and beating time by clapping their hands. It was a sultry day, and none of them had partaken of food since the night before, for it was the time of the Ramazan ; and yet these cheery souls were as happy as kings. Some of them rebuked our Mussulman gendarme, who was smoking a cigarette, for indulging in this luxury during the time of the fast, for the true son of Islam, as I have often heard, is vexed in his righteous soul by the laxity of the Cretan believer. Here was a real Salvation

Army, hungry, thirsty, ill clad, and toiling beneath a burning sun ; yet jubilant and joyous in the hope of a world to come.

EXTRACTS FROM "THE POMAKS OF RHODOPE"*

By James D. Bourchier

("*Fortnightly Review,*" October 1893.)

We began to ascend the romantic valley of the Yadenitza, which sparkled at our feet, half hidden by luxuriant gardens of maize and beans and hops ; no vines are to be found at this altitude, but along the water's edge immense green gourds lay cooling themselves and turning a yellow-tinted side to the sun. The lofty slopes on either hand are now, alas, clothed only with brushwood, for the noble forests which once covered all this region have disappeared, " exploited " by Baron Hirsch when making his celebrated railway. In half an hour's time we came to the spot where, exactly three years ago, two railway officials, MM. Ländler and Binder, were captured by brigands, who, I think, must have been woodland spirits in human form, determined to avenge the destruction of their ancient home. These denizens of the forest, however, styled themselves " political agents," and told their prisoners that before long they would " remove " Prince Ferdinand, inasmuch as all true Bulgarians wished to be governed by their brother Slavs, the Russians.

We soon reached the charming little town of Belovo, half Pomak, half Bulgarian, with its deep-eaved wood-built houses clustering round the stream, its balconies adorned with creeping plants and flowers, its quaint Turkish bridge, its glittering minaret, and its " decent church " topping the neighbouring hill. Here we left the valley

* Pomaks are Moslemised Bulgars.—Author.

and began to ascend the mountain path on our left.
Before long we had left the ravages of Baron Hirsch
behind us, and we entered upon the grand primeval
forest which stretches away to beyond the monastery of
Rilo, some fifty miles to the west. Yet soon it was evident
that here, too, the work of destruction was going on
apace. Every now and then we met peasants coming
down the mountain-side with oxen laboriously dragging
timber, the lower and heavier portion of the felled tree
being supported on a single pair of wheels, while the rest
trailed behind, acting as a drag in places where the
descent became precipitous. The sun was now declining,
and the golden rays fell gently on the forest-clad slopes
around us, revealing here and there some patch of
exquisite verdure amid the gloom of the pine trees and
the spring-like freshness of the beechwood. Far beneath
us the little town lay sleeping amid the shadows, a charming spectacle but for the ruthless desecration of the
woodland on either side ; above us the rocky peaks stood
robed in flaming carmine or towered in deepest purple
against the western sky ; away to the north the spreading
plain of Philippopolis lay steeped in a soft blue mist.
But the splendour of the sunset vanished rapidly ; and the
stars had long been twinkling overhead when at last we
reached the summit, famished and fatigued. Our
" sumpter-horse " had lagged behind, so we were fain to
support life with a crust of black bread, borrowed from
one of our gendarmes, and a draught of ice-cold water
tempered with a few drops of *raki*.

The descent was steep and we were often obliged to
dismount and lead our horses. Again we entered the
dense forest, now so dark that we could scarcely see a yard
ahead ; but my gallant grey, still keeping the van, went
merrily forward till my hat was suddenly swept from my
head by a stray telegraph wire—unexpected trace of
civilisation—which somehow managed to cross the path

at this point. Had that fateful line been a few inches
lower this veracious narrative would never have been
written. We continued to ride through the wood for some
hours, till at length the sound of men's voices was heard
in the darkness. Had a fresh band of brigands come over
the frontier ?—that was the question. No, it was only
some half-dozen " notables " of a neighbouring village
who had ridden out to welcome us. There were hand-
shakings, greetings, and presentations, instead of pistol
shots and the flashing of yataghans ; our friends had
provided a primitive vehicle for our use, lest we should
have been wearied of the long ride on horseback, and in
this we bumped and splashed and jolted for another hour,
till at length, long after midnight, we arrived at the
Pomak town of Lijené-Banya, to which we were bound,
catching a glimpse of its ruined walls in the starlight, and
entering the main street through an arched gateway,
which much resembled the late lamented Temple Bar.

The place of our domicile at Lijené-Banya was a large,
clean, new mansion, well furnished in the Turkish style.
Over the principal entrance was the inscription—" This
is the house of Ali Effendi, the son of Hussein Aga."
Ali Effendi, our host, is a man of mark in his native town.
He is a mufti of high reputation, and conducts the
services in the mosque which adjoins his dwelling. Tall
in stature, with hair and beard slightly grey, his bronzed
oval countenance, with its high arched nose and flashing
eyes, surmounted by the turban which denotes his rank,
he looks the type of a Mussulman ecclesiastic of high
degree, and there is nothing either in his appearance or
manner to suggest a trace of his Bulgarian origin. I was
startled to hear him greet us in Bulgarian ; and, indeed,
for the next few days I could hardly get over my surprise
at hearing Bulgarian spoken everywhere, so little do the
Pomaks resemble their Christian cousins. Ali Effendi
had built his goodly house as a speculation, for a comfort-

able hostelry is needed by the well-to-do citizens of Tatar-Pazarjik, who come hither in the summer-time to enjoy the pure mountain air, and to bathe in the warm ferruginous spring from which the village takes its name.

The cleanliness of Ali Effendi's mansion was in pleasant contrast with the usual squalor of a Bulgarian village khan. Cleanliness is enjoined in the Bible as well as the Koran, but somehow or other the Eastern Christian falls sadly behind his Mahometan neighbour in this respect. Sound and undisturbed was our slumber beneath Ali Effendi's speckless coverlets, and in the morning we rose refreshed, and eager to welcome the novel impressions supplied by a Pomak village. Lijené-Banya looked, indeed, a charming little spot in the bright morning sunshine, with its tile-roofed houses nestling among fruit-trees, its little mosque adorned with a graceful minaret, and its limpid streams of running water coursing at random through the streets. In front of Ali Effendi's abode was a patch of greensward shaded by lofty trees, beneath which the turbaned fathers of the village were seated on gorgeous carpets, sipping their morning coffee, and smoking with calm, austere dignity the long-stemmed pipe of peace. If appearances count for anything, there is no perfect tranquillity of mind beyond the pale of Islam. Before the door ran a clear, swift rivulet, tickling the roots of two magnificent willows ; beneath their shade a bridge-like platform was constructed over the stream, fitted with seats all round like a family pew, and furnished with a kind of removable trap door in the midst, which enabled the company to gaze upon the running water—always a delight to the Pomak as it is to the Turk.

Right opposite was a smithy, where at the present moment an ox was being shod by a bronzed, handsome son of Vulcan, while some dozen peasants, who seemed not to be in a hurry about anything in particular, were standing or sitting around. The animal lay on his back, his four legs being drawn together, and attached to a horizontal beam, which rested on a stout tripod. It was not the spectacle, however, but the spectators that attracted my attention. Tall, athletic, clean-limbed figures, aristocratic features stamped with the mastery of centuries, eyes that looked at you straight in the face without defiance indeed, but without fear, and with just a suspicion of supercilious indifference, reminding you that you are but a Giaour . . . what dignity of pose and gesture, what superb bearing, what splendid nonchalance of mien and manner! Peasants indeed, but gentlemen every one of them, who would treat you to their best with a courtly hospitality, and run a yataghan to your heart if you insulted their womankind or slighted the creed of the Prophet. I have seen many a handsome type of humanity among the Bulgarian peasants, but nothing so picturesque, so *distingué* as this. It was only among the younger Pomak men, whose beards were not yet grown, that I detected a trace of relationship to the Bulgarian race; the Bulgarian peasants, with the exception of the popes and the elder men, do not wear the beard, whereas the Pomaks invariably allow it to grow. Young Pomak men who have lately been married wear a flower, either attached to the turban or inserted behind the left ear; the Bulgarians of the Tirnovo district do likewise. And what of the Pomak women? Assuredly they are beautiful; they must be beautiful. But I have never seen a Pomak woman's face; for the Pomaks are in all things more zealous for the law than their teachers, the Turks; and not only do the women screen their faces with the *ferejé*, but they turn aside, and sometimes even take to flight, at the approach of an unbeliever.

Want of space compels me to record as briefly as possible my impressions of this interesting people. A casual observer might imagine them to be Turks; but there were certain differences in the type which would hardly escape the notice of any one familiar with the East. The only parallel instance I know of the change which a comparatively recent conversion to another faith can effect in the characteristics of an Oriental race is that of the Greek Mussulmans in Crete. No one could possibly mistake the Greek Mussulman for a Christian Greek, though some might mistake him for a Turk. The apparent similarity between the Pomaks and the Turks might perhaps be accounted for by a common Turanian ancestry, for it is hard to say to what extent the genuine Bulgarian is really a Slav. Adopting the language of the Slavs whom he conquered, he became a Slav; adopting the religion of his Ottoman conquerors, he almost becomes a Turk. It may be suggested that intermarriage with the Turks has brought this apparent fusion; but this is not so; the Pomaks are of purer Bulgarian blood than the Bulgarians themselves, because the adoption of Mahometanism preserved their women against the licence of the Ottoman conqueror. A few customs still existing among them bear witness to the fact that for eight centuries their forefathers were Christians. They still celebrate some Christian holidays; they will attend the consecration of a Christian sanctuary; they will sometimes, I am told, invite the prayers of a Christian priest in cases of illness. The women lament over the graves of their departed relatives, using the old Christian prayers *mutatis mutandis* to suit their present creed. At the feast of Bairam the maidens dance the Bulgarian *khoro*—unveiled this once, for it is then that the Pomak youths select their brides; the young men may not dance, but stand at a becoming distance and take stock of their future partners for life.

.   .   .   .   .

I must only sketch briefly one or two other scenes of my pilgrimage. It was a chilly evening when, fatigued by a long day's ride over the mountains, we descended into the valley of Batak, the scene of the famous massacre some fifteen years ago. The last gleam of sunset was lingering in the west; beneath us a damp cold mist hung over the ruins of the hapless village; around us the purple hills, those mute witnesses of an appalling crime, looked down in gloomy majesty upon the Valley of the Shadow of Death. Arriving at the village we passed along the main street, which seemed to form the bed of a mountain torrent; new houses had risen among the ruins, but here there was nothing picturesque, no trace of the old-world charm which characterises a Bulgarian village. We entered the mud-floored khan, where some twenty of the inhabitants were assembled. What a contrast was here to the lordly race of highlanders among whom we had been sojourning! Pale, dejected, dispirited, half stunned, it would seem, by the blow which had fallen upon them, the Christians of Batak bore the mark of ages of servitude; and they and their descendants will bear it for many a day, for the stamp impressed by centuries of subjection is not easily effaced. It is sometimes hard to realise in Bulgaria that the servant has become master and the master servant.

Next day we visited the church and the schoolhouse, the principal scenes of the tragedy, as well as the hospital built by Lady Strangford, and now used as a church. It was strange to see an English inscription, two Union Jacks, and a coronet painted on the plaster over the door of the hospital. But the church, which formed the last refuge of the unhappy villagers, was the principal object of interest. It was on the 7th May, 1876, that Achmet Aga and his warriors appeared before Batak. He summoned the inhabitants to give up their arms, but mistrusting him, they refused to do so, and defended themselves for two days, until it became evident that the Pomaks were getting the best of the fight. Then came a parley; Achmet Aga swore a solemn oath that if the villagers would deliver up their arms not a hair of their heads should be touched. They did so; and next came a demand for all the money in the place. This, of course, was given up. Then the Pomaks entered the village, and put all the inhabitants to the sword without distinction of age or sex. The houses were burned, and nothing was left of Batak save a pile of smouldering ashes and corpses. When all was still and the work was done, Achmet and his mountaineers returned to their villages.

We were accompanied to the church by the *kmet*, or mayor, a well-spoken, good-looking man of about thirty-five years of age. It is a low, strongly built structure, which might have been defended successfully by a few resolute, well-armed men posted at the narrow windows. But the occupants on that terrible day were mainly women, and the men who were there had given up their arms. We passed through a little churchyard surrounded by a high wall, and stooping low beneath the arch of the narrow doorway we entered the temple of Death. At first it was impossible to see anything in the darkness; then gradually the bare white walls became visible—whitewashed by the Turkish officials, in order to remove the bloodstains and the traces of burning. The same officials, with praiseworthy energy, took up the stone floor, in order to make things presentable for the European gentlemen who came to investigate the crime. Every trace of the woodwork had disappeared, for the Pomaks set fire to the interior before the wretched occupants had all been slaughtered. There was nothing in the way of furniture, except a kind of wooden stand, on which a number of skulls, some sixty or seventy in all, were ranged in rows, and some boxes containing charred bones. Many of the skulls had been perforated with bullets, others had evidently been slashed by yataghans, most of them from behind. On some of them lay small bouquets of faded flowers; on one, that of a young girl—almost cloven asunder by a sword-cut— lay a tress of dark brown hair. The *kmet*, at that time a lad of twenty, was one of the few who escaped from the church. I shall never forget the story which he told us, as he stood with us in this dark charnel-house, with a lighted candle in his hand.

" When we heard that the Pomaks were coming," he said, " my father, who was one of the two popes of the village, told me to take my wife and the other women of the family to the church, where the women were assembling. I never saw my father again—he was tortured by the Pomaks, and his eyes were torn out while he was alive. The other pope was treated in the same way. About a thousand of us were crowded in the church, and the door was made fast. When the Pomaks began firing through the windows my wife was struck in the shoulder by a bullet. As the bullets were entering the church from all sides, I endeavoured to make my way to the door, which had been forced by the Pomaks, and through which some of those in the church were endeavouring to escape, most of them being shot down by the Pomaks as soon as they came out. When near the door I fainted and fell among the corpses. When I regained consciousness I found myself lying under several dead bodies, which were so thickly piled above me that I could scarcely breathe. I freed myself with difficulty, and went out of the church. The Pomaks had gone, but I was immediately arrested by a Turkish official. One of my sisters, who was in the church, disappeared, and I believe she is now living as a slave somewhere over the frontier. Many of the younger women disappeared in this way. After the attack on the church had continued for some time, those who were inside were told that they might come out in safety, as they had been pardoned. Achmet Aga stood by the door, and as the men came out one by one he gave orders that they should be executed. They were taken down to the river-bank, where the Pomaks stood ready with drawn swords, and were beheaded there. The bodies were thrown into a pit close by."

We went out of the church into the pleasant sunshine, and descended to the margin of the clear, swift stream near at hand. Its banks were once covered by busy timber-mills, which were burnt with everything else in Batak. On the grassy slope we could discern the traces of the pit, since filled up, into which the bodies of the victims were thrown. Close by was the large new school-house, raised on the site of the former building, in which more than a hundred women and children were burned alive. Five thousand human beings perished on that fatal day. The bodies lay piled in the streets and in the church-yard, and choked the mill-dams in the stream. Many of them were eaten by dogs, for the few survivors were so crushed by the misfortune that they never attempted to bury the dead.

Tantum religio potuit suadere malorum.   Religion, religion alone, was the cause of all these horrors. For let it not be supposed that the massacre of Batak was the deed of alien conquerors, of strangers, of invaders, like the Israelites in Canaan, or like the Turks themselves in Europe five hundred years ago. No, the crime was committed by neighbours upon neighbours, by kinsmen upon kinsmen ; by men of the same blood and language as their victims, descended, like them, from ancestors who had resisted the Ottoman invader ; by Bulgarians upon Bulgarians. And in what respect did the murderers differ from the murdered ? In the tenure of a dogma, in divergence of opinion as to the mode of reaching Paradise. . . . The massacre of Batak was the crowning tragedy of 1876. The Turkish Government acquiesced in what had been done, and Achmet, defender of the faith, received the Order of the Méjidié. Well-meaning but ill-informed persons in England imagined, and imagine still, that the horrors of Batak were perpetrated by the Turks. They were perpetrated by Bulgarians upon Bulgarians.

EXTRACT FROM "PRINCE ALEXANDER OF BATTENBERG"

By James D. Bourchier

("*Fortnightly Review*," *January* 1894.)

Rarely in these prosaic days do we find a figure in which is centred all the interest and romance of the departed age of chivalry. The world, as heretofore, is not wanting in great men ; our age yields to none that have gone before it in magnificent achievement; but the romantic element is absent, and the poet or historical novelist of the future will pass over the latter end of the nineteenth century when in search of an attractive hero. An exception will perhaps be made for Prince Alexander of Bulgaria. Every attitude that can kindle the historic imagination or touch the chords of human sympathy will be found united in the person of the first Bulgarian sovereign. Youth, beauty, valour, distinction, and a rare personal amiability—all were his ; in his brief career were compressed as in a drama the vicissitudes of a long life-time—hope and disappointment, blighted love, the brilliant success of a moment, followed by a tragic downfall and retirement into comparative obscurity. Before he was thirty Prince Alexander had learned the lesson which most men only master when their hairs are grey. His premature death seems a fitting termination to an existence which had realised too soon the conditions of human destiny.

I do not propose to write a biographical sketch of Prince Alexander, or to enter minutely into the details of his private life in accordance with the growing tradition of our Americanised literature. It is rather as the first sovereign of the young Bulgarian nation that I wish to speak of him here. The services rendered by Prince Alexander to his adopted country were splendid and distinguished. The future historian, indeed, will hardly allow him the title of great; his faults were undoubtedly many, but his position was one of exceptional difficulty, and few men with his youth and inexperience would have committed so few errors or conquered so many obstacles. Prince Alexander was by no means a mere soldier, as some have imagined. He possessed no inconsiderable talent for diplomacy, a gift which laid him open more than once to the charge of insincerity. His intuitive insight and perception of character developed rapidly during the short period of his rule in Bulgaria, and displayed itself sometimes in a way that astonished those with whom he was daily brought into contact. In dealing with Orientals he could show upon occasion a subtlety and acuteness of which the open frankness of his manner betrayed no symptom; and those who believed they had outwitted him sometimes discovered that the tables had been turned upon themselves. His principal fault as a ruler was a want of resolution and tenacity of purpose, qualities essential to success in any career, and indispensable to the leader of a people in whose nature these characteristics form a striking ingredient.

It is difficult to estimate the exact amount of popularity which Prince Alexander enjoyed amongst the Bulgarians. Tall, handsome, well made, noble in aspect, and amiable in manner, he was the type and impersonation of that ἠνορέη ἐρατεινή with which Homer clothes his heroes, and which, as a rule, enthrals the affections of the multitude. But the Bulgarians are an unimpressionable people, and their hatred and suspicion of foreigners amount to a passion. They welcomed their young Prince with, for them, a wonderful display of enthusiasm, spontaneous and genuine, no doubt, but perhaps as much inspired by self-congratulation over their newly acquired liberty as by devotion to their future sovereign. They had learned before the Prince's arrival that his family had objected to the ultra-democratic character of the constitution bestowed on them by Russia, and during his first journey through the country the young ruler of Bulgaria passed beneath triumphal arches on which the ominous words " Constitution of Tirnovo " figured in large letters. The political honeymoon was already dimmed by a cloud : it was an omen of the trouble that was to come. During the first five years of his reign Prince Alexander can hardly be said to have possessed any real popularity. He was a foreigner—a *tchuzhdenetz*, a German, and a Protestant. The people, taciturn, suspicious, ignorant, and unresponsive, regarded him with indifference, if not with distrust ; it was hard for them to unlearn the lesson which they had been taught from childhood by their priests and by Russian emissaries—that the great orthodox Tzar was the real ruler of Bulgaria. Whatever advantages accrued to him from his personal charm, his sincerity of motive, and his honest efforts to promote the welfare of the country, were neutralised by the systematic detraction to which he was exposed on the part of the Russians and the rival Bulgarian politicians, who dragged his name into all their disputes, and bandied it to and fro with a total disregard of decency. It was not till September 1885, when he came forward as the champion of a united Bulgaria, that he began to feel himself in touch with the national sentiment. From this date also began his popularity with the army, for it was then that the Russian officers, who occupied all the superior posts, were withdrawn by order of the Tzar. It was not till Prince Alexander had bidden them a final farewell that the Bulgarians began to appreciate his real merit : *virtutem incolumem odimus, sublatam ex oculis quaerimus invidi.*

CHAPTER III

A CORRESPONDENT'S DIARY

I LEFT London for the Balkans on October 19, 1912. The great journal for which I was setting out to work that morning most opportunely published a leading article eminently calculated to cheer and encourage those about to take part in the imminent war. I think a severe frost-bite was the slightest injury that any one could hope to escape with ; for the vast majority there were reserved alternatively, mutilation, typhus, no quarter, typhoid, dum-dum bullets, cholera, and forty degrees below zero. When I had finished the article my spirits rose to such an extent that I found myself praying that either there might be a collision before we reached Dover, or else that the boat would sink before we reached Ostend. The game was up ; death was inevitable ; it were far better to get done with it at once.

At Ostend I had an opportunity of seeing how admirably the registered baggage system is worked. Two trains stood alongside a platform—one for Holland, the other for the Near East. My heavy baggage lay between them, and presently came officials and porters, who perhaps had strong views on the subject of international arbitration, and had privately decided that a nice new Wolseley valise would constitute a striking trophy for the decoration of the Temple of Peace, and therefore they would lose no time in despatching it to The Hague.

However that may be, it is certain that pugnacious-looking mule-trunks destined for Bulgaria were put into a van bound for some absurdly pacific spot, and I believe one of the conspirators in the cause of arbitration was making out fresh labels addressed to Mr. Carnegie. But fortunately for me, who was about to enter what would undoubtedly have been an ineffectual protest against this diversion of my property, there exists at Ostend one railway official who has not yet succumbed to The debilitating influences exerted by the proximity of the Hague. The hawk eye of this stern individual at once detected the plot of his subordinates, and in peremptory terms, some of which seemed to have the true Army-in-Flanders ring, he commanded the conspirators to place my luggage in the Orient Express.

I was going to Sofia, but it was impossible to get a ticket beyond Buda-Pesth, and, as was natural, fellow-passengers regaled one with lurid and wholly false accounts of the disorganisation of the railway system beyond Austria, and of the weary weeks that must elapse before one could hope to feel a dum-dum bullet or gaze on a cholera camp.

There was a Yorkshireman going to visit his oil-mines in Bulgaria—apparently a paying investment—and an Austrian, who lived most of his time in England, returning to his native land; why he was returning to his native land I wondered, for the whole tenor of his conversation was the depreciation of Austria and the exaltation of England. This person spat as he harangued, and beslavered Englishmen and English institutions with fulsome and indiscriminating praise. And yet there are foolish persons who maintain that as a nation we are not popular in Europe.

At length we came to the huge monastery of Melk, set on its rocky bluff above the glittering Danube, where the valley is wide and fertile, and the hills are covered with trees, and the whole countryside smiles at the memories of hundreds of years of loving cultivation at the hands of the excellent priests. And at night we ran into Buda-Pesth, where the luxuries of travel ended. The view from my bedroom window was entrancing. Myriads of lights twinkled on the rounded contours of the hills, contending with the stars; the broad river threw a mysterious belt of darkness through the coruscating city; a shadowy bridge loomed out of the purple distance; nothing was solid, nothing real in that fairyland.

Buda-Pesth is beautifully situated, but it smells like a composition of drains, coffee, and bad tobacco; and many other places in Eastern Europe appear to emulate its undoubted priority in this direction.

Of medieval Buda, Busbecq wrote in 1564: " On the following day we pursued our journey towards Buda, the doctor being as nimble as before, in spite of his terrible bruises. When we were just in sight of Buda, by order of the Pasha some of his household came to meet us, along with several cavasses; a crowd of young men on horse-back formed the most remarkable part of our escort, on account of the strangeness of their attire, which was as follows : They had cut a long line in the skin of their bare heads, which were for the most part shaved, and inserted in the wound an assortment of feathers; though dripping with blood they concealed the pain and assumed a gay and cheerful bearing, as though they felt it not. Close before me were some of them on foot, one of whom walked with his bare arms akimbo, both of which he had pierced above the elbow with a Prague knife. Another, who went naked to the waist, had stuck a bludgeon in two slits he had made in his skin above and below his loins, whence it hung as if from a girdle. A third had fixed a horse's hoof with several nails in the top of his head. But that was old, as the nails had so grown into the flesh that they were quite immovable." *

* Forster and Daniell, vol. i. p. 396.

Lady Mary Wortley Montagu wrote, in 1717, of "Buda, once the royal seat of the Hungarian kings, where their palace was reckoned one of the most beautiful buildings of the age, now wholly destroyed, no part of the town having been repaired since the last siege, but the fortifications and the castle, which is the present residence of the Governor-General Ragull, an officer of great merit. He came immediately to see us, and carried us in his coach to his house, where I was received by his lady with all possible civility, and magnificently entertained.

"The city is situated upon a little hill on the south side of the Danube, the castle being much higher than the town, from whence the prospect is very noble. Without the walls lie a vast number of little houses, or rather huts, that they call the Rascian town, being altogether inhabited by that people. The Governor assured me it would furnish twelve thousand fighting men. These towns look very odd; their houses stand in rows, many thousands of them so close together, they appear at a little distance like odd-fashioned thatched tents. They consist, every one of them, of one hovel above, and another under ground; these are their summer and winter apartments.

"Buda was first taken by Solyman the Magnificent, 1526, and lost the following year to Ferdinand I., King of Bohemia. Solyman regained it, 1529, by the treachery of the garrison, and voluntarily gave it into the hand of King John of Hungary; after whose death, his son being an infant, Ferdinand laid siege to it; and the Queen-mother was forced to call Solyman to her aid, who raised the siege, but left a Turkish garrison in the town, and commanded her to remove her Court from thence, which she was forced to submit to, 1541. It resisted afterwards the sieges laid to it by the Marquis of Brandenburg, 1542; the Count of Swartzenburg, 1598; General Rosworm, 1602; and the Duke of Lorraine, commander of the Emperor's forces, 1684 ; to whom it yielded, 1686, after an obstinate defence, Apti Bassa, the Governor, being killed, fighting in the breach with a Roman bravery. The loss of this town was so important, and so much resented by the Turks, it occasioned the deposing of their Emperor Mahomet the Fourth the following year."

Next morning (21st), I arose at 5.30, in order to take train to Belgrade. It is surprising how many of the best sort of trains start in the middle of the night. There must be some reason for this ; but the desire to attract a larger travelling population is probably not the true one.

The country hereabouts is very dull. A vast plain of rich soil, unencumbered with fences, grows a prodigious quantity of maize. The plough-horses look like thorough-breds, and stride down the illimitable furrows at a pace that would astonish an Essex farmer. Perhaps because of the excessive toil involved in following racehorses at farm-work the Hungarian rustic seems to do as little as he possibly can when otherwise employed.

The navvies on the line are chiefly engaged in relighting long pendent china pipes, which nearly break on the permanent way if their owners are so incautious as to use their shovels. The stations are crowded with sackcloth-clad peasants emigrating, and the inference is that wages are very low. In the afternoon we arrived at Semlin, where the broad yellow Save separates Hungary from Serbia, and saw across the river the city of Belgrade, set on the flat top and steep flanks of a long low hill. Kinglake, in *Eothen*, written in 1837, describes the abrupt and start-ling difference between Western Semlin and Oriental Belgrade, though only a river divides them ; but to-day all is changed ; the Turk has retired from Serbia ; Belgrade apes the methods of Brussels, and the Serbian is outwardly as civilised as his neighbour across the Save.

A ferry-boat took us from Semlin to Belgrade, and the moment we set foot on Serbian soil we realised that here the gates of Janus stood open. The landing-stage was crowded with armed men—reservists, probably, coming back to the colours—and the inevitable chorus of women and boys. Evidently some of our fellow-passengers were persons of distinction, for a great cheer went up as they struggled to the street. And what a street! Narrow, dirty, and paved with a cobbled irregularity that must be felt in a victoria to be properly appreciated. There can be no question that the coach-builders of Serbia are pre-eminent in their profession.

This indictment applies only to the flanks and lower part of the town. On the flat summit there is one very long, very wide, well-paved street, with some excellent houses and shops in it, as well as the hideous, yellow, square, rococo palace, in the purlieus of which the hideous murder of King Alexander and Queen Draga took place. As one looks at that street, so modern and civilised, and thinks of the crime committed in it, reminiscent of the bloodiest periods of medieval history, one cannot avoid the conclusion that the unspeakable Turk indeed arrested the spiritual development of the peoples he misruled by just the length of time he exercised his blighting influence, and that was more than four hundred years. I left Belgrade as soon as I could, by a train which started at the comparatively reasonable hour of seven in the morning.

All along the line, at short intervals, stood peasant-guards, with long thin bayonets fixed; there were no Turks within two hundred and fifty miles, but if there had been those unfortunate sentries would have been massacred in detail.

The scenery is small and unimpressive: low hills, narrow valleys and winding streams, with hardly a distant view. Maize and grass seemed to be the chief crops. At every station there was a great concourse of peasants, clad in dark-brown sleeveless Zouave jackets embroidered with

black cording, and trousers thrust into gaily coloured
socks encircled and protected by straps led from the heels
of the *tsavouli*—the raw-hide moccasins universally worn
by soldiers and labourers in these Slav countries.   A
better form of foot-gear than this does not exist.   Why are
we so many centuries behind Red Indians in the matter
of boots ?

These *tsavouli* are light, pliant, easily dried and easily
made.   I saw many a soldier, later on, busily skinning a
horse.   Indeed, it was almost necessary to be present at
the demise of a horse in order to see one dead and still
integumented.   With the horse-hide the soldier made
himself a new pair of boots.   Now our soldiers cannot
make their own boots so the kindly contractor supplies
them with an article that is either too long or too short,
too wide or not wide enough, that is very heavy and tiring,
impossible to dry easily, but when dried inflicts savage
injuries in the shape of corns, blisters, and sores.   Then
the kindly contractor charges the taxpayer for those boots
a sum that in Serbia would buy seven pairs of *tsavouli*.
Certain aspects of civilisation seem to denote a tendency
to dissociate the instrument and its function.   This is a
sign of decadence.   The army contractor would be
surprised and incredulous if you told him that the best
boot was the boot in which you could march longest
without pain ; he would almost certainly reply that the
best boot was necessarily the boot that cost the most
money.

We got to Nish, Mr. Jackson and I, at 8 p.m., and
having subsisted on some bread and grapes during the
past twenty-four hours, we were not sorry to see a refresh-
ment room again.   The place was crammed with hungry
men, and two tired-looking women, half asleep, shook
their heads like mandarins to a thousand requests for food.

Here I first had an opportunity of noting the perfect
manners of the commonalty of Serbia and Bulgaria.

There was no shouting, no pushing and shoving, no scowling at new-comers, no recriminations hurled at the women behind the buffet, as there would have been in countries nearer home. What we saw there—order, dignity, restraint—I saw invariably later on under conditions often very adverse to their exercise. However, Jackson had skilfully obtained a bottle of wine, and Signor Bevione, Correspondent for *La Stampa*, of Turin, most generously presented us with half a chicken, so we did not do so badly after all. A railway-carriage closely packed is a poor place to sleep in, particularly when you are woken up at every station by demands for passport and tickets; but it was not for us to grumble. Everywhere stood long trains of trucks full of huddled men, patched with white and red; they were the wounded from about Uskub going back to Nish.

I saw Sofia for the first time early in the morning (23rd), in a haze of rain. The vast plain ended mysteriously; beneath a long purple cloud there was a city; and high above the cloud the rising sun lit up snowy peaks.

Their capital summarises the qualities of the Bulgarians —an intense desire for progress, continuous industry, reticence. Fifteen years ago Sofia was a collection of adobe buildings on the usual Turkish plan; the streets narrow, tortuous, filthy, and uneven; the houses designed as though to stand a siege, with blank walls and massy bolted doors. Now it is a modern city, with spacious boulevards and well-planted squares, remarkable for the excellence of its paving of yellow tiles. The street that leads from the station to the centre of the town is so straight and so long that after a time you come to the conclusion there is no end to it; then you come upon an old Turkish mosque, reverently preserved in the heart of the Christian city, and suddenly dash past a palace bowered in trees, and brilliant with vermilion salvias. Here you might be in Paris or in Brussels, except that Sofia is ampler in her streets and open spaces. And there is another huge difference now. Sofia is not a city of the dead, but the city of those who have gone forth to die for her if need be ; and the wide streets are silent and empty, and no children's voices echo across the deserted squares. For the fathers are gone away to fight the foe, and their children are all helping their mothers to fight that other foe, Poverty.

I remember going into a tobacconist's, and finding the tiny shop under the sole control of two diminutive urchins, hardly out of the nursery. They skipped up ladders to dizzy heights in quest of choice cigars ; they gravely consulted one another as to the proper price to charge ; they counted out the change with the assurance of expert financiers. I am not sure that they thought taking my little present of a franc apiece was strictly professional, but I know I had tears in my eyes as I went into the street. Of course there are lacunæ and hiatuses in Sofia ; it must be so in every city only fifteen years old. But it is safe to say that in another ten years Sofia will be worthy of the great nation whose capital she is.

I went to the Hôtel de Bulgarie—as good an hotel as is to be found—and saw Bourchier, after a lapse of twenty-six years. He was the same Bourchier—ruddy, red-haired, with the merry laugh—that I last saw in mortar-board and gown, striding briskly to instruct naughty little Eton boys, who with their usual acumen had discovered that Bourchier is not of the stuff that most pedagogues are made, and, I am afraid, traded on the knowledge. At all events, Bourchier was tremendously popular ; to be " up to " (i.e., in the division taught by) Bourchier was a coveted distinction, which meant a great deal of fun and not too much work, and the absolute certainty that even if caught red-handed shying a lexicon at Brown minor's head you would not spend " after twelve " in durance vile. Little did those wicked boys imagine that their too-good-natured master would live to be acclaimed by hundreds of thousands of grateful Christians as the chief factor in their liberation from the bondage of the Turk.

At the excellent Union Club I was introduced to Mr. Graeme-Scott, Bourchier's private secretary, and to Mr. Heard, our Vice-Consul. Life is full of curious coincidences. A fortnight before I got to Sofia I was travelling in Kerry, and was told of the beautiful garden on the island of Rossdohan (the Point of the Two Birds) made and owned by Dr. Heard. I determined to see the garden, and with great audacity sent Dr. Heard a wire asking if I might come over. I got the kindest of replies, and a most hospitable welcome, and, best of all, a whole day of the society of one of the most talented gardeners in the United Kingdom. What a perfect gem, set in the blue waters of the Kenmare estuary, with the mountains all purple and gold with gorse and heather! and the trees and shrubs—the cordylines, Benthamias, Eugenias—all growing jungle-like on a spot where thirty years before there had been only one hawthorn bush! An English gardener must go to Ireland if he wants to garden.

Dr. Heard told me one of his sons was on his way back to his post at Sofia, the last place in the world I ever expected to go to; and yet, a fortnight later, the first man I met in the Union Club was Heard.

At the Club, too, I was presented to H.B.M.'s Minister, Sir Henry Bax-Ironside, and met Herr Kolmers, a distinguished young German doctor who had come to Bulgaria at the Queen's request to take charge of the hospitals organised by Her Majesty.

Late that evening I got a telephone message from the Prime Minister telling me he was sending me a permit to go to the front, and asking me to call on him next day at 10 A.M. M. Gueshoff is a man of about sixty; round-headed, square-jawed, with straight eyebrows and mouth. His eyes are kind in expression, and mitigate the sternness

of the rest of the face—a sternness increased by a loud
and commanding voice. His moustache and imperial are
white, and his hair so closely cropped as to look as though
his head had been shaved. Decision, action, and vigour
are the characteristics of the man.

The Prime Minister was most cordial, and he and
Bourchier (whom I had persuaded to accompany me) and
I had a very interesting talk. M. Gueshoff told us how
he acquired his perfect knowledge of English : he was
educated at Owens College, Manchester, where Mr.
Spencer Wilkinson was one of his friends. Bourchier
told him that he had been my master at Eton, and the
Prime Minister jokingly replied that he must have been
a very good master. I don't believe Bourchier had ever
been called a very good master before ; and he was so
pleased that he laughed consumedly. We then discussed
the function of the Greek fleet, and M. Gueshoff said
there was no written undertaking as to its rôle. Bourchier
urged that it should cut off sea-communication between
Asia Minor and Salonika, for the Greek battleship *Averof*
was more powerful than anything the Turks had got.
The Turks, on paper at all events, had the stronger fleet,
but the officers were a poor lot. The Premier and
Bourchier agreed that the taking of Thasos by the Greeks
was as a *point de départ* against the mainland. I took my
leave of one of the great men of the twentieth century with
the feeling that here was a statesman who not only was a
great man, but who looked and talked like a great man.
His study, in which he received us, is a comparatively
small room, with a fumed oak parquet floor, and a high
dado of the same wood. The writing-table and two big
wire-fronted bookcases match the floor and dado, and the
latter is surmounted by a paper of dull gold. There are
a few red leather arm-chairs ; portraits of the King and
Queen, and the inevitable telephone. On the pink
blotting-paper lay a newspaper—it was *The Times*.

Before we went away, M. Gueshoff wrote and gave to me the following open letter to M. Stancioff, lately Bulgarian Minister in Paris, and now Chief of the King's Bodyguard at Headquarters (Starazagora):

MON CHER MINISTRE—Je vous recommande tout particulièrement le porteur de cette lettre, M. le Colonel Rankin, correspondant du *Times*. Veuillez lui faciliter la tâche d'historiographe de notre guerre et croire, mon cher Ministre, à mes sentiments cordialement dévoués.— J. E. GUECHOFF.

The small boy who had eventually admitted us to the house then showed us out. His duty is to say " Not at home " to everybody, and he says it. The difficulty Bourchier had on our arrival to get him to understand that I had an appointment with the Prime Minister was prodigious. The diminutive and sceptical Cerberus had barred the door against us while he went to obtain confirmation of his inflexibility, and he finally let us in with a disappointed air.

My interview with the Prime Minister had ended by his saying that he had to go to the station to see the Queen off to Philippopolis, whither Her Majesty was proceeding in order to attend a Red Cross Society's meeting for the organisation of hospitals.

Bourchier had just received £100 from Mr. Noel Buxton, the Chairman of the Balkan Committee in England, and he wanted to know the Queen's wishes as to the disposal of it. This seemed a good opportunity to find out, so we presently took one of the neat little victorias, with their pair of fast ponies, that abound in Sofia, and dashed down the never-ending street towards the station. It was not difficult to gauge Bourchier's position in Bulgaria from the way he was treated by everybody, from Royalty downwards. Outside a door stood the Royal car. Bourchier walked straight in, and presently came out saying that the room was full of ladies-in-waiting, and that perhaps we had better wait until the Queen came out on to the platform. I fancied that was distinctly the better way, and so Bourchier elbowed his way through the throng of waiting people until he got to the fringe of bayoneted sentries guarding the carpeted space reserved for the Court. I thought that the sentries would at least challenge him, but no, when they felt his elbow in their backs they merely looked round, saw Bourchier, and stood on one side. I kept so close to Bourchier that I got through the line before I could be bayoneted. At length the Queen of Bulgaria appeared. Attended by the Prime Minister and uniformed dignitaries of her suite she walked towards her carriage, close to which Bourchier and I had stationed ourselves. Her Majesty is petite, dark, and pale, with an expression of goodness that is unmistakable. Bourchier went forward bowing, and preferred his request for Her Majesty's commands as to the destination of Buxton's £100. The Queen replied, in excellent English, " I will let you know when I return." Then I had the honour of being presented to Her Majesty, who spoke a few gracious words. And so the Royal lady started on her errand of pity and succour, turning to bow smilingly to the dense cheering crowd of her subjects.

That afternoon (24th) it was evident that the Sofians were expecting something. The almost deserted streets began to fill up ; the quiet groups gravitated towards the Press Agency ; and soon a large crowd had assembled, framed by the waving acacias and vermilion salvias of the great square. Suddenly a roar of cheering broke out, and as the news flew from mouth to mouth the whole city vibrated from end to end with a storm of hurrahs. Kirk Kilisse (Lozengrad) had fallen, and the keen wits of the soldierly Bulgarians realised that the key of Adrianople was theirs. Moreover, it was the first victory the Bulgars had ever gained over the Turks, and in the popular imagination it seemed a certain augury of the ultimate success of their country's arms.

That was a tremendous evening. There was no riotous mafficking, but every man, woman, and child in Sofia turned, laughing, cheering, and handshaking, into the streets, and the bells of the churches rang, and lights gleamed in every window. Opposite my hotel a group took up the National Anthem—a sweet and plaintive melody. A white-headed figure, hatless and bowing, comes in sight; it is M. de Sazieff, a hero of Slivnitza and the Serbian War. He is hoisted shoulder-high, and carried through the cheering throng. Then a huge wave of humanity surges down on the Hôtel de Bulgarie, and Bourchier, another Bulgarian national hero, ex-assistant-master at Eton, is discovered at length in the midst of the multitude, somewhat the worse for wear, but still able to laugh his jolly laugh. He is carried up to a room facing the street and deposited on a balcony, amid loud cries of the Slav equivalent for "Speech, speech!"

Bourchier made a speech; it was a model of brevity and conciseness; in Slav he said "Good night," and that was all. The crowd laughed and moved away, and Mr. Jackson and I took a stroll down the principal streets, for there is no spectacle in the whole world so exhilarating as that of a nation rejoicing. But you can never get away for long from the dark side of the war-picture. There were women in Sofia who wept that night.

As we strolled along I saw two men with long hair flowing over their shoulders marched rapidly through the street by guards with bayonets fixed, and I called Jackson's attention to them.

"Those fellows are followers of Tolstoi," he said, "and they go about preaching the wickedness of war. This town is under martial law, and those chaps will never see another sunrise. They will be tried by court-

martial in barracks to-night, and they haven't got a
cat-in-hell chance. Personally," finished up Jackson,
" I hate those fellows that try to set people against defend-
ing their country."

Then we went into the Market-hall—a huge brilliantly
lighted and spotlessly clean building 200 ft. long and
150 ft. wide, with meat and vegetables ranged orderly in
rectangular blocks—beef and mutton, potatoes, cauli-
flowers, paprikas, lettuce, egg-fruits, tomatoes, and dozens
of other things—all splendidly clean and healthy-looking.

The next day (25th) I bade farewell to my kind friends
Bourchier and Graeme-Scott and Jackson, and took train
for Starazagora. Hundreds of officers and thousands of
men were being sent off to the front, and every seat was
taken. I was fortunate in my companions, who were all
officers of the Bulgarian army, except the handsome young
man who sat opposite to me and talked about hunting in
England and big-game shooting in Uganda in faultless
English. We exchanged food, and I got some lovely rosy
stuff that looked like a rare and costly jam, but was really
a cheap but excellent caviare.

The country we passed through has a smooth, polished
look, due to the absence of trees and the scantiness of all
forms of vegetation—a drab and featureless land in which
the yellow and red of the dying leaves of the oak-scrub
planted on the hills burnt by the Turks in 1878 is a
welcome oasis of colour. We met truck-loads of wounded
Bulgars and truck-loads of captured Turks, and at all the
stations there were crowds of happy peasant-folk cheering
the never-ending procession of fighting-men.

The costumes of the peasant women of Bulgaria have
certain small local differences; but there is a family like-
ness about them all. The thing that strikes the Englishman is the use of colour. In his own country, women who
used colour in their dress profusely and contrastively
would be thought mad or vulgar. But the Bulgars live

in a clear-skyed land where sharp contrasts are the usual
effect of the atmosphere; and they know their reds of the
oak-scrub, and their greens of the young wheat, and their
brilliant whites of mid-day sunshine; and they paint them
in their dresses as God paints them in their fields. Over a
white short-sleeved chemisette they wear a black Zouave
bodice embroidered in filigree. The arms between the
shoulders and the elbows are bound with green and
yellow circlets, and a white coif comes low and straight
across the forehead, enclosing the hair, which falls beyond
the limits of the coif in a loose queue. Most of the
young girls wear a bright green pinafore. In Oriental
countries the use of black in dress is the recognised badge
of a subject race, and it seems likely that the almost
universal black Zouave jacket of the Bulgarian women is
a relic of the days when they quailed beneath the rule of
the Turk. But the bright hues of freedom are creeping
fast over the dark habiliments of woe; and nearly all the
Bulgarian women ornament their skirts with chequers of
brilliant colour contrasts—red and white, or green and
red, or these two and white—the national flag, of which
they are so justly proud.

At a station where an enterprising journalist was busy
photographing a squatting group of Turkish prisoners my
vis-à-vis in the railway carriage took me to the end of the
train, opened the side of a truck, and showed me three
magnificent horses, one of which was Irish, and the other
two Hungarian. He offered to lend me one if we were on
the same job, and I am sorry I never had the chance of a
gallop on one of those splendid animals—sixteen-hand
blood hunters up to fifteen stone, all of which had won
steeplechases. Behind the horses came a 60-h.p. motor
belonging also to my friend, so one realised that his
ability to traverse all sorts of country was reasonably
assured. Later we exchanged cards—Prince L. Windischgrätz, Chamberlain to His Imperial Majesty the

Emperor of Austria, and as delightful a person as ever existed.

Cantilever bridges, of the archaic and picturesque type that one sees in Baltistan, span the infant Maritza as it rushes through its narrow limestone gorges ; and near the city of Philippople (as it is hideously spelt on the railway station) the flat lands are cut up into paddy-fields and irrigated for rice. There, too, are large orchards of mulberries—the commonest fruit-tree to be seen both in Bulgaria and Turkey.

"Compulsory Greek " is a subject that has been exercising the minds of pseudo-educationists lately, and a visit to Serbia and Bulgaria furnishes the thousandth reason why that language should be taught to everybody. It was like going back to Eton to see the old familiar letters, and they threw the glamour of heroic antiquity over the newest and ugliest railway station. Bishop Cyril, the great missionary, brought them to these parts a long time ago ; and he would undoubtedly turn in his grave if he knew that the city of Philip now called itself Philippople in Roman characters.

At eight in the evening we arrived at Starazagora. It was dark, and I did not see the victoria which Head-quarters had most thoughtfully provided for Prince Windischgrätz and myself ; so I got hold of a porter and marched off through the rain, over miles of cobbled roads, to an hotel.

I have seen a good many inferior inns, but my guide at last ushered me into the bar of the meanest and filthiest one of its kind. There were eight or ten dirty fellows drinking at small tables ; there was no room for more. I could not make the host understand me in French or German, and I was meditating a bolt into the street when the most extraordinary little person insinuated himself under my notice. He was extremely small and thin, about four feet two, and his dilapidated black clothes hung

about him limply. His face was very pale and his nose
very red, his eyes very watery, and his long hair very
greasy, and from his unshaven chin protruded half a
dozen hairs an inch long. A more farcical parody of a
man never existed. But he spoke excellent French, which
was accounted for solely by the fact that he was a Frenchman, and he told me that every hotel in the town was full
to overflowing with correspondents, and that I should do
well to get a bed at the Tsar Osvoboditel Hotel, or Tsar
Liberator Hotel, which in truth was the magniloquent
name of the pothouse in which I found myself. In
Starazagora all the principal streets and all the smallest
inns appear to be called Tsar Osvoboditel ; and there is
certainly an attractive rotundity, a sesquipedalian roll,
about the words which almost condone the confusion
caused by their ubiquity.

After a while I was led through a dirty kitchen into a
dirtier backyard, and taken up a flight of creaking steps
into a passage so narrow that one could hardly walk
straight in it, and then a door was flung open, disclosing
a very small room into which three beds had, by some feat
of juggling, been crowded. " You can have one of those,"
said the host. I shuddered at the prospect of passing a
night in such a place with two companions from the bar
below, but if all the hotels were full what was to be done ?
So I left my bag in the room, got hold of the weary little
Frenchman, and induced him to take me round the town
on a tour of investigation. He was very difficult to
persuade ; the town was under martial law ; it was very
late ; we might be arrested or shot ; besides which, it was
ridiculous to imagine that there was a hole or corner left
vacant in all Starazagora except that one miraculous bed
in the hotel Tsar Osvoboditel. But when I had made it
clear that I would reward him for his services he became
amenable, and beguiled our tramp through the rain with
the melancholy tale of his misfortunes ; he had lost all his

money; he had left France in order to teach the Bulgars French; he had a wife and two daughters to support; his affairs were not prospering. It seemed incredible that so abject a little creature could ever have induced any woman to marry him. But the ways of Nature are inscrutable.

By the time my small guide had reduced himself to tears, composed two-thirds of bad cognac and one-third of want of the money to buy any more, we arrived at the hotel Zelantan Lieve, or Golden Lion, which is the Ritz of Starazagora. The whole front of the place seemed to be made of door, which was very hard to open, and equally hard to shut, and designed with a view to giving all concerned with it the maximum of noise, draught, and irritation. Within were a swarm of diners lingering over their coffee and cigars—military attachés in uniform at a long table on the right, war correspondents in the middle distance, and natives in the offing under the cinematograph sheet.

That restaurant had a fine sense of the inestimable value of caste distinctions; everybody got exactly the same food, but if you sat to the right of a certain pillar you paid eight francs for your dinner, and if to the left, only four. The right seemed usually more crowded than the left, which is a proof that newspapers like their correspondents to be comfortable.

I saw two Englishmen at a little table (dangerously near the social boundary; they might easily have been mistaken for four-frankers), and when I advanced unhesitatingly upon them through the maze of tables they got up and greeted me. They were Mr. Pryor, Director of *The Times*, and Mr. Maxwell, of the *Daily Mail*, who in the intervals of the merriment produced by the sight of my weird guide told me they had come down to meet me at the station the previous day, and had procured a room for me at the Zelantan Lieve. This was good news indeed, and my Lilliputian Frenchman was straightway allowed to indulge his evident partiality for brandy, before staggering back to the nauseous hotel of the Tsar Liberator.

Pryor and Maxwell, after having been cooped up in Starazagora for weeks doing nothing except abuse the censors, were in high feather at the prospect of an immediate advance, and they were very kind in putting me on to the right authorities for the procuring of the necessary passports, brassards, and permits. The steps taken by the Bulgars to identify and control correspondents were many and successful. One had to carry one's photograph about with one on a little red card, with one's signature on it; one had to wear a red brassard with B.K. and a number on it; and one had to have a document informing the various persons concerned who you were and what Headquarters would allow you to do. For instance, Nevinson of the *Daily Chronicle*, Maxwell of the *Daily Mail* (running in coulples with *The Times*), and I had permits to go anywhere we liked; but of course that did not mean that we were free to go whenever we pleased; the jealous vigilance of the local commanders saw to that; and not a few correspondents who violated the limits of their liberty by as little as a kilometre found themselves back in Sofia, with orders to repair to their native climes after such an interval as would render useless to the enemy any information they might have obtained. But the great bulk of the correspondents were tied down to definite areas; some were deported at once. Later on Mustafa Pasha swarmed with them, even as Starazagora; whereas at Tchataldja, the only battle at which correspondents were present, there were only ten out of the hundred and fifty or so who started.

The next morning (Oct. 26) Prince Windischgrätz came round and told me M. Stancioff wanted to see me. As I had a letter for him from the Prime Minister which would, I knew, expedite all necessary arrangements for getting away to the front, nothing could have been more opportune. The Prince told me about the victoria that had been sent for us the night before, and laughed when he heard of my adventures. He told me that M. Stancioff had been, before the war, Minister at Paris, but was now Chief of the King's Bodyguard, and quartered in the same house as His Majesty, where the Prince was living.

M. Dimitri Stancioff (which may be pronounced Stantchoff, but the former is the spelling on the ex-Minister's cards, just as M. Guechoff spells his name with a " c," whereas all foreigners spell it with an " s ") is one of King Ferdinand's favourites, which one can so easily understand. He is one of those people with fascinating manners and an attractive personality ; gifted too with great mental power—an able diplomat.

I can never be sufficiently grateful for all his kindness to me at a time when he must have been working twelve hours out of the twenty-four. He gave me notes to all the principal understrappers of authority, telling them to give me passes without delay, and refused to hear of my stopping at such a place as the Zelantan Lieve ; I should find Madame Dimtcheff's house far more comfortable. (I thought of the hotel Osvoboditel and smiled.)

" The Marquis de Segonzac and M. Puaux of the *Temps* are there," he said. " You will find them both quite clean," and then he laughed. He had seen too much of war correspondents not to know that certain of them import the habits of active service into ordinary life.

He wrote down on a slip of paper, with surely the largest blue pencil ever fabricated, the name and address of Madame Dimtcheff. It is not necessary to add that she lived in the Ulitza Tsar Osvoboditel.

I spent the whole day rushing from office to office, and when evening came I was in a position to leave Starazagora for the front next day.

Starazagora is a new town, built on the site of the one utterly destroyed by the Turks in 1878. It lies on the dark flank of the treeless mountains, and overflows into the flat fertile plain—a straggling, wide-spaced, rectangular city, dotted with mulberry trees yellowing under the autumn rains. Its position as the railway centre of the richest corn-producing area in the country has earned for it the name of the granary of Bulgaria, and no Bulgarians have better reason to hate the Turk than its inhabitants. But like Winnipeg in the old days, and other great cities in their infancy, Starazagora strikes the Western traveller as inchoate and unfinished. The streets are broad and planted with trees, but the houses are not on the same scale as the boulevards, and the breadth of these latter is only accentuated by the depth of the ruts which striate them. But the site is good, and the surrounding plain extraordinarily fertile, and there can be no question that in days to come Starazagora will be a great city.

Madame Dimtcheff's house was a revelation. There was a double flight of steps leading up into a spacious hall, which opened through folding-doors into a court filled with all sorts of flowers in tubs and pots, the delicious scent of which filled the whole house. My room opened out of the hall; and I do not think there was an upper story. Everything was palatial: the linen, gilded candelabra, silken easy-chairs, and pots of cyclamen. Alas, it was only for one night that I exchanged the awful discomfort at the Golden Lion for the soft luxury of Madame Dimtcheff's abode! I got up at six the next morning, and found Madame Dimtcheff already among her flowers in the court. She was in deep mourning and so were her children, and I realised the inhumanity of war in forcing strangers into her house in the hour of her sorrow. One of her children could talk a little French, and so I expressed my gratitude for her hospitality and took my leave. When I got back to my room to fetch my coat I found an exquisite little breakfast laid out on the large table in the centre of that delightful room. How good it all tasted after the relative privations of the last few days ! It was the last decent meal I was fated to have for six weeks.

That same morning (Oct. 27) Maxwell and I set out for Mustafa Pasha. Before leaving I called on Colonel Lyon, D.S.O., H.B.M.'s Military Attaché to the States of Bulgaria, Serbia, Rumania, and Greece, and got from him some valuable information and some less valuable maps ; for most people had bought maps with a view to a Turkish irruption into Bulgaria, and not with a view to a Bulgarian irruption into Turkey ; and consequently the maps were all north and no south, which is a defect in a map.

Our caravan consisted of a 10-h.p. Delage four-seated motor—one of the best little cars that ever ploughed through bogs—and its chauffeur Alexander Mamegonian ; a light four-wheeled hooded wagon drawn by two grey horses, or rather ponies, and their driver George ; and a cook called Alexis.

Alexander is an Armenian—a bullet-headed, black-haired, aquiline-nosed, brown-eyed, corpulent fellow of twenty-eight ; an admirable driver over ordinary roads, but certain to lose his head and get into the worst place when things get difficult. He is not of sanguine temperament, and viewed some of the difficulties he was called on to face with a horror that was comic. On such occasions he would spit on his hands and ejaculate, " O mon Dieu ! mon Dieu ! " and I fear we only ruffled his patriotism by genially insisting that as the track got worse the more it resembled the streets of Sofia, in which he had been wont to drive, and which he considered, and not unjustly, the acme of all that is perfect in roadways.

Alexander is not a fighting-man, but was liable, as a Turkish-born subject, to service in the Turkish Army.

To escape this he had fled to Sofia; but when the war broke out the Bulgarian authorities pounced upon him as a transport-driver. Now, Mr. Alexander Mamegonian had been getting two pounds a week as a chauffeur in Sofia, and he had a vivid, if not distorted, conception of the horrors and hardships incidental to the life of a transport-driver in war time; so when Maxwell managed to secure him by judicious use of consular authority, Alexander was full of gratitude and hope. But there was another side to the question. When Alexander, weary with much driving, and appalled by the terrors of the track, became restive or sulky, which not infrequently occurred, his benefactor reminded him of the life led by Bulgarian transport-drivers, and the extremely exiguous proportions of their pay; and then, if Alexander still persisted in remaining restive and sulky, a lurid picture was promptly sketched in graphic outline of the probable fate of a deserter handed over to the Turks. At that Alexander's beautiful olive complexion would grow ashen, and his plump cheeks visibly contract, while at the same time a marked desire to please would take the place of his former recalcitrancy.

Alexander looked like an Indian; he was an Oriental *au bout des ongles*. Vanity is a common trait in the Oriental character, and Alexander's favourite device for proving the excellence of his driving was to turn round and look at the departing scenery or at the hind wheels. He kept a motley collection of old rope and empty benzine tins affixed by means of rotting straps somewhere on the footboards, and if the scenery was too ugly for words, or the back wheels had just had new tires put on, he would lean round and gaze affectionately at this rubbish. He would have told us—in fact, when remonstrated with, he did tell us—that this retrospective mood was induced solely by the desire to look to the safety of our property. But I knew better; it was induced by the desire to show off. Now a little failing of that sort in one's chauffeur is venial in broad-wayed Sofia, but on the edge of a Turkish precipice it becomes a trifle irritating.

It is only fair to the Armenian to add that he had the eye and hand of an expert, and that however near he brought us to destruction we always actually escaped it. With regard to discipline Alexander was hopeless; though repeated lessons eventually improved him in this respect. He would not admit that it was possible that any one but himself could drive a motor; and it was only necessary to tell him to keep to the right in order to see him go to the left. From some of the directions Maxwell gave him I am inclined to think that my colleague had not only noticed this peculiarity but was acting on it.

On the thousand and one occasions when we had to get out and push behind, an invariable custom of Alexander's, directly the groaning and panting little car had gallantly vanquished the mud, was to crack into top speed and have a run by himself. No vocal efforts on our part ever arrested his wild career; his joy in freedom, the absence of four compelling eyes sternly fixed upon his sideways cap, constituted an irresistible call to his blood.

If I, however, with unreasonable intolerance of a fellow-mortal's free exercise of his volition, ever ventured to hint to Alexander that I resented such behaviour, as tending to loss of time, to cause me unnecessary fatigue, to load my boots with portentous quantities of mud, and, finally, as a breach of discipline, my colleague would remind me, with a judicial air, that as we were entirely dependent upon the benevolence of our chauffeur towards us, it were well to treat him with the utmost consideration, and not to allow such a trifle as a two-mile tramp through the worst mud in the world, shouting all the time, to mar the cordiality of our relations. Seeing myself in a minority of one on this and similar questions, I schooled myself to accept all the avoidable misfortunes that occurred with a laconic stoicism that, I am proud to say, won the warm-hearted Oriental's admiration, and towards the end of the journeyings he several times paid me the very high compliment of asking my advice on technical matters.

It only remains to add that Alexander was a convinced teetotaler; but it was astonishing how frequently a very severe pain in the pit of the stomach induced him to apply to us for brandy, for whisky, or for any other medical comfort containing a high percentage of alcohol. He considerately warned Maxwell and myself that his colleagues George and Alexis were immoderately addicted to the bottle; and I have several times noticed him putting temptation, in the shape of the contents of the large wine-flask, out of their way, when firmly convinced that no one was present to observe and commend his noble deed.

Géorg, or George, was a very different stamp of man. He was a tall, lean, hard-bitten fellow of about thirty-five, with huge brown moustaches sticking out on either side of his face, and intelligent grey eyes. One could guess, without being told, that he was a horse-master. As with horsy men all over the world, his trousers were rather close-fitting in a land of baggy trousers. If one gave George an order one knew that it would be carried out, even if the poor fellow had to pawn his coat to do it, as George, in straits for money, and having four horses to feed, actually did on one occasion.

His walking powers were wonderful; all day he would tramp through the deepest of all possible mire, wading through streams and bodily lifting wheels when they jammed against boulders, often on the scantiest ration of bread, and yet he never once grumbled. He was always willing, always up to time, and his first thought was always for his horses. What we should have done without George Heaven only knows!

Alexis, the cook, was a scoundrel. Maxwell declared that once in Philippopolis Alexis had prepared a dinner

such as he had never eaten farther east than Vienna.   If
so, I am disposed to believe that someone else cooked it.
Certainly the specimens (they were not many) that I saw
of Alexis' culinary achievements awoke no suspicion in
my breast that I was no longer in Turkey but snugly
ensconced in the Café Voisin.   I have a firm belief that
once Alexis was my cook in Tunis, and that after he had
threatened to stick a knife into me I had him removed to
prison by two gendarmes.   At all events the facial resem-
blance was remarkable.   Alexis never once talked to me
about the advantages of Tunis as a winter-resort, but he
finally decamped with my nearly new Wykeham saddle.

Of the horses it suffices to say that one was very much
better than the other—a dappled grey about fifteen hands,
a free-goer and stout-hearted, whereas his companion
was smaller, with a coat like an ox, and a disposition to
stop and kick if the work in his opinion were too prolonged
or too severe.

On October 27 Maxwell and I set out from Starazagora
in our little Delage, amid a crowd of persons, including our
friend Colonel Lyon, who were apparently animated by
a desire to know how all that luggage and three men could
possibly get on to or into so small a vehicle.   Our departure was kept a secret, known to everybody, in order not
to ruffle the susceptibilities of all the correspondents who
had no cars, and who had to travel later by a plebeian
train.

The motor itself had been kept in an obscure shed, in
the midst of a labyrinth of slums, in order that no jealous
person might make a hole in the radiator, or put spokes in
wheels which Alexander considered had their proper
complement already.

At last the ultimate bag was secured to the groaning
foot-boards ; Maxwell's head alone emerged from a sea of
baggage ; and in front Alexander, in horrible French,
represented to me the difficulty of pedipulating the clutch

with water-bottles, haversacks, and revolvers trying to find their own level on the floor. On the right of the screen fluttered the Union Jack, on the left the red, green, and white horizontal bars of the Bulgarian flag. The crowd cheered; we were off to the war.

It was Sunday, and the vine-trellised streets (what picturesque and delightfully useful things are those same pergolas of vines!) were full of women in gay attire, of which the Romanys were by no means the worst dressed or the least favoured. A church was discharging its early congregation, and the bells rang merrily as the black-robed, high-hatted, long-haired and bearded Papas, or Pope, smiled on his departing flock. In front of us the road flew away as straight as a dart for thirty kilometres over a dead flat black alluvial soil, in which the young corn was already emerald.

The villages we passed were small and half-deserted; the houses of adobe with red-tiled roofs, or with rough walls of wattle covered with mud and thatched. Only old women and boys and fowls were left; all the men and horses and oxen had gone to the war.

After a prosperous spin of fifty kilometres over a road which contained no holes over a foot deep we got to Tirnovo Semen, on the right bank of the Maritza. The only way across the broad river appeared to be by the fine railway-bridge, and that was completely blocked by stationary trains. However, a local worthy put us on a track which I fancied was a practical joke, and down the awful declivity we bumped and skidded until we struck a military bridge, over which Alexander dashed at a pace which would have killed the paternal engineer, had he been looking on.

But on the far side our wild career was abruptly brought up by a bog and a precipice, and had it not been for the kindly help of a dozen gunners (into whose camp we had plunged) we should have been there to this day.

As Bulgarian soldiers all look alike, I may as well describe their uniform here. Their tunic and trousers are of a rough brown cloth, very warm and durable, with black shoulder-straps and letterings. On their feet they wear the *tsavouli* already described, and round their legs they bind with many thongs thick white felt-like gaiters of woollen material. Their caps are like our Guards' caps, without the German exaggeration in height—dark blue with a red band round the edge. Many soldiers have told me that their caps made excellent targets for the Turks (who themselves wore green khaki, like their tunics), and there is no question that details of this sort make a lot of difference in war. Officers have an oval enamelled device on the front of their caps, and they replace *tsavouli* and gaiters with the leg gear of the West; but there is such a wealth of invention shown in their permutations and combinations that the brain boggles at the task of describing them all.

The fact which impressed an observer accustomed to our beardless battalions was that all the Bulgarian soldiers were men, not hobbledehoys—fine, broad, deep-chested, hairy men, reared on sour milk and brown bread, with clear pale skins and resolute brown eyes, and black locks flowing out behind their tattered and dirty headgear. Splendid fellows, splendidly trained and led, they furnish some of us with an example we should do well to follow. There is no need for a crusading Lord Roberts in Bulgaria ; every man there understands very well the first and primitive duty of citizenship. God help England if before long we don't produce a statesman capable of seeing, through and beyond the sordid haze of party politics, the eternal realities that make for a nation's peace !

Fifty quick-firing guns were limbering up as we left the camp ; for all the Bulgarian world the cry was, " Forward to the front ! " In the station close by I saw three very curious-looking objects, the like of which I had never seen before. They were huge metal skeps, or beehives, out of each of which protruded a vicious little gun. I suppose those armoured beehives could hold four or five men apiece ; and while they were sending out their droning swarms to gather honey from the flower of the Turkish army they would be completely protected from the waspish bullets of their foes.

These beehives were mounted on four wheels, and six oxen were dragging one down the road. I think our War Office might do worse than adopt this idea, which called up the exquisite lines of Dr. Watts :

> How doth the little busy bee
> Delight to bark and bite.

There were also four 5-inch (Creusot ?) guns on the line, bound for Mustafa Pasha and the besieging of Adrianople.

We motored from Tirnovo Semen to Hermanli, but we did not go by road, we went across country. In England, walls and hedges would make it difficult, though not impossible, to drive a motor across country ; in Bulgaria there are no walls and no hedges ; but the boulders are just as difficult to negotiate as walls, and the mud is much more retentive than any blackthorn fence.

If you can imagine eighteen consecutive miles of black ploughed field churned by guns and bullock-wagons into a congeries of ruts eighteen inches deep, you have some faint adumbration of the delights of motoring in Bulgaria. But the reality of it all will escape even the most vivid imagination. I had to jump out very quickly about three hundred times, and tore my breeches worse each time I did it ; then came a period of frenzied pushing behind, which left the arms in a state of agonising pain, and the heart thumping like a sledge-hammer ; and after that you had to jump into the car in motion before Alexander could get clear away. Then for five minutes you panted in your seat ; and when Alexander saw that you had got your wind he would purposely drive into the stickiest place, and make you go over the performance all over again, just like an encored dog, or one of those silly tunes with *Da Capo* at the end of it.

At one place we had to cross a stream, and the Bulgarian flag hit a tree and snapped short off, which some people would have regarded as a very dreadful and portentous omen. To us, however, the far bank was more ominous ; there the car stuck, and pushing, I am glad to say, became a work of supererogation. Luckily a bullock-wagon and six bullocks came up, and their driver very obligingly unhitched the leaders and brought them up the bank. Alexander then proceeded to attach a rotten rope to the axle ; but the rope resented the corpulent Alexander hanging on to one end of it ; it broke and threw Alexander backwards with great force on to the hock of an unsurprised bullock. An English beast would have displayed serious annoyance if a fifteen-stone man had suddenly alighted on its hock ; but these Bulgarian animals have lived so long under the Turks that when anything startling happens they just mutter *Kismet* under their breath and go on ruminating.

I wandered in the drenching rain up the little watercourse in which we had stuck, and was rewarded for my inattention to the hauling operations by finding *Crocus speciosus*—pale blue instead of lilac, but otherwise just like our meadow saffron (*Colchicum*)—peering shyly out of the grass. Close by grew a clump of dark blue columbine (*Aquilegia*), with flowers and seeds on the same plant. In all Bulgaria I do not believe there are so many flowers in one place as in that little watercourse.

We were now passing through a land of rolling hills, boulder-strewn and oak-scrub-covered, until at last with incredible efforts we got to Hermanli, and struck a road once more. From Hermanli to Mustafa Pasha the country flattens out ; a poor, sandy soil takes the place of the rich black humus round Starazagora, and trees are few and far between. Three miles from Mustafa we entered Turkish territory. The boundary between Bulgaria and Turkey is marked by the dwelling of the customs officer —a very ordinary-looking brown-tiled wooden house, but distinguished by the proximity of a most remarkable erection. This is a four-legged, spindly structure 20 feet high, on which rests a small rude platform of boughs, and above a still ruder roof of straw. It looks like an invitation to a pair of storks matrimonially inclined, or a *mechán*, as they call it in India, from whence to shoot tigers; but Maxwell gravely assured me that it was a bedroom, and that he had passed many nights most agreeably in similar places. For my own part, I would sooner sleep in the mud than in such a crazy-looking, ramshackle affair, where, if a neighbour borrows your ladder before you are awake, you are bound to stop till he is good enough to return it.

Close to the railway station, which is a good three miles from the town of Mustafa, we came on a large field-hospital, admirably placed for sending cases easily and without unnecessary hardship to the base.

It has become almost a fashion to decry the Bulgarian medical arrangements in this war; but I hold that, considering the enormous difficulties of transport, their medical organisation was as good as could be expected. A superfluity of surgeons in the firing-line there was not, nor yet stretcher-bearers in abundance; but the wounded got their wounds dressed, and were taken back to the rear in ox-wagons—an excruciating form of torture for many of them. This sounds like a condemnation of the system; but it is not. No other methods could have been employed.

No wounded were left for days untended on the battle-field; and, except in one respect, the field-hospitals were conducted on up-to-date lines. The exception is in regard to sanitation. No soldier, no general, no surgeon-general, paid the least attention to sanitation.

Men drank at any foul pool they came to, and no one cared. They did these things at home; why not let them do it now? So argued officers I have remonstrated with, forgetting the multiplication table.

Our good friends the Bulgars must send a mission of keen young surgeons to study Japanese methods—far and away the most thorough and successful in the world; for with men such as theirs a fighting-man lost through preventable disease is a crime committed against the nation.

Mustafa Pasha is a pretty place, when you're not in it. The broad yellow Maritza comes sweeping down out of the brown hills, and the willows and poplars along its banks are graceful lines of subdued colour in these autumn days. There are more trees round Mustafa than anywhere else in Turkey; it is really extraordinary that the consuming desire for firewood which seems to animate the Turk has allowed so much good fuel to remain standing.

A fine stone bridge of seven or eight spans connects the two banks of the Maritza, and nearly the whole of Mustafa is on the left bank. In the centre of the bridge there is a high stone alcove, graven with a long Turkish legend; and above this floats the Bulgarian flag. The Turks tried to blow up this bridge, but they only succeeded in breaking down two or three yards of parapet, without in the least affecting the strategical value of the bridge. Day after day, guns, men, and munitions poured across in an increasing stream, with the swollen Maritza, 200 yards broad, foaming and eddying below. If the bridge had been destroyed the investment of Adrianople would have been impossible.

When you are over the river you come almost at once upon a good-sized brick house, standing back from the roadway, guarded by high iron railings, and wearing the unmistakable air of the premier building of the district. This used to be the Spring Gardens of the Turks; and is now the headquarters of the Second Army, commanded by General Ivanoff. We boldly drove the motor into the courtyard, and sent up our cards to the great man. We were told to come in, and went up a reverberating wooden staircase into a bare hall, out of which many doors opened.

General Ivanoff is a big, heavy man, with a less distinctively Bulgarian appearance than most of his compatriots; he might be a German or a Russian. His manner is ponderous, and his expression somewhat dour. Before the war he was known as a man who allowed no considerations, earthly or otherwise, to interfere with his plans; and I believe the correspondents who followed us by the hundred found him a trifle intransigent. But we were the first on the scene; the very name correspondent had not yet had time to stink in the nostrils of the authorities they pestered; and we received a very dignified, if not excessively cordial, greeting from General Ivanoff, and were given tea in the Russian fashion—that is to say, with lemon juice instead of milk. But when we got to the subject of what we might do, and where we might go, a hard, cold look came over our host's impassive features; it was not permitted to go more than two kilometres on the road towards Adrianople, because the Bulgarian troops were getting into position, and did not want their time occupied by visitors.

This was out first intimation, from reliable authority, that the old business of war-correspondence was at an end. It was something of a shock; here were we, having travelled thousands of miles, and spent hundreds of pounds on our papers' account, within ten miles of an epoch-making siege, yet forbidden to travel those last essential kilometres! This plaint is now so stale that I shall say no more, except that the unqualified success of the Bulgarian *démarche* in preventing the leakage of information valuable to their enemy has undoubtedly established a precedent which will be followed in all future wars.

The war-correspondent as we have known him is no more; *fuit Carthago*. News will be got, of course; but probably it will be done by an elaborate system of smuggled despatches from educated privates in the trenches, whose patriotism is not impervious to cash.

We were billeted in the house of the Chief of Police; and as he keeps his men and their horses in the passage behind the front door, we felt reasonably secure from burglars.

In the evening we were invited to dine with the General and all the officers of the Staff at their club. There was any amount of food—soup, and beef, and *kusskuss* (which is a savoury mess of rice and raisins and odds and ends)—besides any amount of good, red, full-bodied wine, of which 300,000 litres had been found in the town. The officers took 100,000 litres, and gave the troops the rest; and in an incredibly short space of time there was no wine left in Mustafa.

" Those water-drinking Turks are topers on the sly," said some one at dinner.

The recent capture of Kirk Kilisse (which the Bulgars call Lozengrad) naturally formed a staple of talk, and the younger officers were uncommonly well pleased with themselves. " Von der Goltz said it would take Prussian troops three days to take Lozengrad, and we have taken it in three hours ! " was a phrase repeated more than once. One alone, out of all the crowd of officers and censors, spoke English. This was Vassileff, a little roundabout, spectacled, bald-headed gentleman, a professor somewhere, and a profound student of Macaulay, Spencer, and Mill. Maxwell remarked that Ivanoff resembled Stössel.

" Not in character at all," snapped the patriotic Vassileff.

The next day came the news of the beginning of the great battle known to history as Lule Burgas, and intense excitement was shown everywhere. Thousands of reservists marched cheering into the town, with chrysanthemums and zinnias in their caps, and sprigs of green in the muzzles of their rifles. No uniforms had these, but their ordinary brown clothes, with here and there a sheepskin coat with the wool inside, and on all legs were the white gaiters bound round with black ribands.

Perhaps this is the best place to give the substance of an admirable lecture delivered to a few of us a fortnight later by Captain Jostoff, of the Staff, brother of Colonel Jostoff, Chief of the Staff to General Dimitrieff, commander of the Third Army.

On October 21 the troops of the Bulgarian Third Army crossed the frontier near Kazi Kilisse and encamped in Turkey. Their objective was Kirk Kilisse. The force moved in four columns, the two strongest in the centre, the weaker on the flanks. Two columns marched down the right bank of the Teke Deresi, by way of Omar Abbas, Karamza, and Eski Polos; a third went down the left bank by way of Chesmekeui and Kermutli; while the fourth marched south-east to Tashtepe, Kicherlik, and Almajik.

Kirk Kilisse was to be taken either by a *coup de main* or by an investment; the two centre columns were first of all to attack the place while the outer columns outflanked it and worked round to the rear, cutting the line of communication with Baba Eski and Bunar Hissar. If a siege were necessary, the two inner columns would take the northern sectors of the investing line, and the two outer columns the southern.

At half-past two on the 22nd, Bulgarian patrols got contact with the enemy; the column marching on the left bank of the Teke Deresi found a Turkish cavalry regiment and a battery in bivouac near Frikler, and drove them south. At the same time another regiment and another battery came up from Kirk Kilisse in support of the retiring Turks, who then made a stand. The Bulgarian advance guard attacked these two regiments and drove them back, and many dead and a lot of ammunition were left on the field. At the same time the outer column on the right bank of the river was engaged at Eski Polos and Kermutli, and forced the Turks to retire on Petra, whence, seeing their retreat menaced, they fled to Kirk Kilisse.

On the 23rd the columns continued their southward march. This bit of country presented every difficulty that troops ever have to contend with. There are no roads ; narrow valleys alternate with boulder-strewn ridges ; there is no scope for manœuvre ; and the Turks brought a converging fire to bear on the Bulgarians, who were numerically inferior to their enemy. The engagement now became general over the whole front ; but the Bulgarian column on the left was delayed by bad ground, and its absence enabled the Turks to avoid a disaster.

As far west as Seliolo the battle raged that day ; and at night torrential rains fell. These conditions helped the Bulgarians ; protected by the swelter of the storm they made a night-attack ; with the bayonet they fell upon the Turkish trenches, and drove their foe helter-skelter back into Kirk Kilisse, which they abandoned to its fate.

In the soaking dawn of the 24th the whole garrison of Kirk Kilisse quietly retired, and left the key of Adrianople defenceless. The Bulgarians did not see the retreat of the Turks. On the 24th they advanced against the town, and were greatly surprised at encountering no opposition. They occupied the two forts to the north and east of the city ; in the former they found nine antiquated guns, and in the latter not a single piece.

Of the Bulgarian losses in the series of engagements which led up to the capture of Kirk Kilisse I am unable to give any idea.   Captain Jostoff certainly gave us no idea. It was part of the deliberate policy of the Bulgars, part of that reasoned and consistent theory of warfare which raised them at one blow to the position of a first-rate military power, to maintain absolute secrecy on all matters the publication of which might prejudice their fighting efficiency.   No lists of dead and wounded were ever issued ; mothers and wives only knew that their sons and husbands would never come back to them again because of a scrawl from a comrade who saw his comrade fall.

One of our English-speaking censors, towards the end of the war, was sad and depressed ; the horrible food nauseated him ; he ate nothing ; his cheeks grew paler and paler.   One day he came and asked me for medicine, I knew not why ; there were plenty of his own surgeons in the camp, and I had only Burroughs Wellcome's admirable tabloids, and not a whole pharmacopœia of those. The next day he came and thanked me, and said he felt better.   I ventured to ask him if it were not true that he had some grief which no medicine could cure.   The poor fellow's pale face twitched, and he said simply, " I believe my brother has been killed."

He did not know that his brother had been killed, a brother who was an officer, too ; he only believed it.   No official return ever put an end to his suspense ; if rumour was busy gnawing at his vitals that was something over which officialdom freely confessed it had no power.   One day, some time after, I met him again.   " He is dead," he said ; " they have seen his grave at Kirk Kilisse."

This narrative, or its too palpable paddings and lacunæ, affords a striking illustration of the way the Bulgars treated correspondents in the matter of information ; but to appreciate the situation properly it must be remembered that I had greater latitude given me than ninety-nine out of the hundred and ten correspondents who started from Starazagora.

My own feelings on the subject of what I was not allowed to see are so painful that I shudder to think of what the bulk of my confrères must have suffered, perhaps are still suffering. We cannot all aspire to the sublime imaginative heights of the journalist who, in the serene atmosphere of a Viennese Club, wrote brilliant accounts of battles which had yet to be fought.

But the military attachés were treated a great deal worse than the correspondents. They followed the operations at a distance that was hardly respectful. When all the interest had completely evaporated from any particular place the attachés were sent thither. They were herded about like sheep. Distinguished professors from the Staff College gave them elaborate lectures which contained few grains of truth.

One day, during the progress of an admirable disquisition on the site of a very old battlefield, one attaché was observed to quit the group of attentive listeners, and walk rapidly away. Scraps of his soliloquy floated back to the entranced audience sitting at the feet of Gamaliel : " Lies, lies, lies," it sounded like, " lies from beginning to end."

When the Rumanian attaché expressed his feelings with no uncertain voice he was promptly told that the Bulgars had not the slightest intention of letting him see how they made war. Shortly afterwards he went back to his native land. But all this is by the way, and we must return to the Third Army. At Petra, Captain Jostoff told us, the Turks held up the white flag, and then fired, at measured distances, at the oncoming Bulgarians, causing terrible losses.

From Kirk Kilisse the Turks retired to Baba Eski and Bunar Hissar ; but until the Bulgarian patrols got contact with them again they were in the dark as to their whereabouts. Some Turks made a stand at Kavakli, about seven miles south of Kirk Kilisse, on the Baba Eski road,

and were driven south again in great disorder. Questioned
as to the number of Turks who had fought at Kirk Kilisse,
Jostoff said, " Five divisions, and one division of Redifs "
(or Reservists). Putting a division at 10,000 men the
total amounts to 60,000 men.

On this day (24th) a Bulgarian cavalry division was
despatched to look for the enemy towards the south ;
for it was believed that if Turkish reinforcements came at
all they would come from the Rodosto direction.

On the 25th, 26th, and 27th, the Bulgarian infantry
marched slowly southwards, waiting for information from
the reconnoitring cavalry, who found nothing and nobody
towards the south and so the conclusion was arrived at
that the Turks must have gone to Bunar Hissar. So, with
their left flank refused, the Bulgars marched south-east ;
but they appear to have greatly under-estimated the
opposition that the Turks they found at Yenno and Bunar
Hissar were going to give them, for the bulk of the army
continued its march south-east, leaving the left wing to
dispose of the Bunar Hissar people. But it was very soon
discovered that the left wing had a very serious business
in front of it, and that unless direction was changed, and
the whole force swung round to the east, the Turks would
crumple up the left wing and enfilade the main body.
So on the 28th, at noon, the Bulgarian troops at Yenno
were made the pivot of manœuvre, and the great turning
movement began. All did not go well for the Bulgarians ;
the left got dangerously split up by difficulties of ground,
and a column engaged with the Bunar Hissar Turks had
to retire to Kara Agatch, over a difficult river which has
only two widely separated bridges.

All this time the Third Army was anxiously awaiting
the arrival of the First Army to support it on the right,
or south ; but again the fearful difficulties of the road came
into play, and the First Army arrived too late. The brunt
of the battle, from Bunar Hissar to as far south as Lule

Burgas, five-and-twenty miles away, fell upon the Third Army, under General Radko Dimitrieff, which had to take up a frontage out of all proportion to its numbers. The artillery, too, was delayed by the mud, and the Bulgarians had to endure a Turkish bombardment without the means to reply.

At Colever the Bulgarians rushed the Turks, and held the position with mountain guns; and a furious attempt to retake the place failed. Now the Bulgarian reserves were called up, and the Yenno or 5th division carried the heights to the east of Bunar Hissar. Here the colonel of the 5th Regiment was killed, and for a moment his troops wavered. But Radko Dimitrieff, as ever, was where the fight raged hottest, and knowing the immense danger confronting his whole force if the left were turned, he sent a message to the division to die where they lay rather than retire.

All through the night of the 29th to 30th October, the Turks and Bulgars lay opposite one another, and kept up a terrific and incessant fusillade.

On the 30th, the Bulgars holding the line Bunar Hissar-Turkbey advanced, entrenching themselves as they went, slowly but surely; they only gained little over a mile, but that mile, on the threatened left, was of the utmost consequence. Urgent messages were sent to the First Army to advance as quickly as possible against the Turks' left; and eventually the Third Army got the good news that the First Army were frontally attacking the enemy at Lule Burgas. A small force of Bulgarians managed to get south of Musclim, and enfiladed the Turks, while almost at the same time the Colever Bulgarians made a breach in their enemy's line near Kara Agatch.

On the 31st the Bulgars developed their success, and bringing up all their artillery made a desperate onslaught east of Lule Burgas. The Turks retired, not in utter disorder, as at Kirk Kilisse, but with the savage reluctance of troops that realise that they are finally and irrevocably beaten.

Lule Burgas was the decisive battle of the war, and its hero was Radko Dimitrieff. His great turning movement will live in history as a conspicuous example of military genius. But he could not have done as he did if the men he commanded had not been some of the best troops the world has ever seen. The awful carnage on that devoted left flank ! The grim resolve to die, but not to give an inch !

After this digression I must get back to October 28 at Mustafa. Maxwell and I agreed that it was no use being the first correspondents to reach the precincts of Adrianople, with a motor-car of our very own, unless we made use of it to see something. The worst of it was that motors are so aggressively and blatantly talkative, nothing will induce them to keep a secret. There in the court of Headquarters our motor stood, silent when we didn't mind what it said, and vociferous when we wanted it to keep quiet. However, it had to be, the handle was turned, and the talk began. I shall never forget the crowd of uniformed Jonahs assembled by that rhythmic voice.

" Where are you going ? " in French, German, English, and Bulgarian, and before we could reply, although we had not the smallest intention of replying, " You must not go there."

" Eet is varee dangerouse," piped our spectacled friend, the student of Macaulay and Mill, his round eyes dilating with affected terror : " de troops have orders to shoot all de civilians."

Observing with surprise that this trifling deviation from the truth did not blanch our cheeks, he tried another venue, and almost broke his spectacles by the intensity of his expression as he remarked : " Dere are tousands of Pomaks * lurking in de forest." But still the engine

* Pomaks are Moslemised Bulgars who out-Turk the Turk in fanatical savagery.

thrummed on, and Alexander, who, fortunately, understands not one word of English, was listening smilingly,
in the company of so many epauletted gentlemen, to
words which in Armenian would have drawn his features
into an agonised grimace.

But it was no good ; foredoomed to death, we appeared
utterly indifferent as to whether release came at the hands
of Pomaks or Bulgarians ; Lalage (I mean Delage) sang
on, and when we actually took our seats in the car the
ox-eyed absorber of Spencer saw that if he were going to
stop us he must act, and act quickly.   He disappeared,
while the excited throng of his compatriots kept up the
fusillade of threats and warnings, and in two minutes the
general himself—the iron Ivanoff—appeared.

Nec deus intersit, nisi dignus vindice nodus.   Suffice it to
say that in another two minutes Lalage had ceased to sing.
Maxwell and I were very angry, and the saddest part of
it all was that Alexander never knew what he had escaped
by the miraculous intervention of the great man in blue.
Deus ex machina was Ivanoff that day, and got us out of our
machine, too.

It is impossible to give an idea in words of a place like
Mustafa ; there is too much detail, too much variety, too
much dirt.   The High Street is very narrow, but very deep
in liquid mud, and the side-walks are so very exiguous that
if you meet anybody coming in the opposite dirtecion you
must instantly decide whether you will knock him into
the gruesome sea beneath or be knocked there yourself.
Most of the houses are tiny little things, all window by
day, and all shutter by night ; and there are actually some
acacias planted boulevard-wise in front of them.

When we came back the second time to Mustafa, there
were two foolish ponies in an ammunition wagon who
disliked the beautiful song of Lalage as she approached.
They ran away, and in a second the cart had cut down,
very neatly, one of the acacias.   I felt very sorry, but their

driver, when he had stopped his horses, seemed very pleased at their having unintentionally converted the boulevard into firewood.

What thousands and thousands of animals and vehicles ploughed and churned that historic mud-alley! I never saw it anything but crammed with a jostling mass of guns, ox-wagons, cavalry, infantry, correspondents, censors, and staff-officers.

Over the bridge from Bulgaria, and down the road to Adrianople, and far on towards Constantinople, poured the stream of deadly weapons and missiles, and food and men, and back along the same road came some empty wagons clamouring for cargoes, and some with limp and blood-stained figures stretched out in the straw. As the ox-wagon was practically the sole method of transport the Bulgarians used (they had a few pony-drawn carts, but very few), something must be said about that most important vehicle.

In the first place there was a really incredible number of them. In the dim haze across the long plain one fancied one saw a low line of hills; at length one saw that it was nothing more than a convoy of wagons three miles long. Everywhere they were in their hundreds, each with two meek, black-eyed, whity-grey bullocks, who were all so exactly alike that it is certain that even their drivers didn't know t'other from which, although no doubt they pretended they did.

Although these wagons carried the food and ammunition for great armies, it was the rarest possible thing to see anything in them but a little chopped straw for the bullocks to eat. Possibly the load was secreted under the straw; but in any case the wagons were very lightly loaded. The wagon frames are V-shaped, and very narrow, covered with a rounded hood of woven reeds, and set on axles of enormous breadth, to obtain the stability so sorely needed in negotiating what the Turks call roads.

The four lumbering wheels make very small pretence to being circular, their perimeter being formed of a great number of more or less curved timbers ; and so you can form some idea of what wounded men suffered in these cribs of torture.   The oxen are yoked in the usual way, without any restraining traces ; and consequently they were entirely free to twist their hinder parts out into the roadway at the precise moment that your motor was passing them—a liberty of which they frequently availed themselves.

Their drivers were generally Turks from Bulgaria, as you could tell by their rags of turbans ; skilful fellows in the practice of that art, which consisted in directing the oxen by prodding them in the required direction with a long stick with a nail in the end of it, or hauling them about with cords affixed to their horns.   It was really wonderful to watch the precision with which a tap here, and a thrust there, and a gruff " Haidee ! " to sum up with, kept the bullocks in the narrow way.   A great many of these drivers were boys ; and once I saw a little lady of about seven summers walking with a long pole beside her father's team, and abusing and beating the animals with a sting and venom that must have been a source of legitimate pride to the parental heart.

" Haidee " is the word on which you can travel all over Bulgaria and the other Slavonic countries.   It is not an oath, although it sounds so much like one ; and if it has any definite and assigned meaning, which I doubt, it may be roughly rendered by " Get on or get out." It is a remarkable word, and, like some Chinese words, I understand, a different inflection of the voice appears to give it a different meaning.   If you said it roughly to a bullock it got on ; if you said it gently it got out.

The performances of the ox-wagons were a triumph of organisation.   Hundreds of miles had food and ammunition and forage to be carried from railhead to the front ;

and each day the front got farther and farther from railhead. The method established a continuous chain of wagons from the bases to the front, each link of which, like a curb, had both an outward and a returning side.

From Mustafa, for instance, a certain number of wagons took their freight seven or eight miles, then handed it over to another set of wagons, and returned to Mustafa for more. This slow process was carried out with a completeness and regularity that enabled the Bulgarians to fire an immense quantity of ammunition and yet never run short of it, and to eat a prodigious quantity of bread and yet never lack flour. Soldiers will not need to be told that an efficient transport system conducted, by the necessities of the case, on these lines, presupposes an organising ability on the part of the responsible staff which is by no means common.

But Mustafa High Town was what we were talking about, and one of the features of the place when the Bulgars entered it was the extraordinary number of white crosses chalked up on doors and shutters. When the Turks fled to Adrianople they took with them all the able-bodied Bulgars in the place, but left the old and decrepit behind. These poor creatures, fearing lest the oncoming Bulgars should mistake them for Turks, took this means to draw attention to their religious belief; and from the number and ubiquity of the crosses, it is not improbable that a derelict old Turk or two were not above adopting a simple little life-and-property-saving device which could easily be rubbed off when all danger was past. High Town, Mustafa, fades off, very appositely, into a cemetery, where, under the shade of poplars and willows, a stone forest of obelisks lean and totter at every conceivable angle to earth and to one another. There is nothing in the world so respectably drunk-looking as a Turkish cemetery. It suggests all sorts of ludicrous fancies. Most of the tombstones are pointed at the upper end, of a rough triangular shape, and there is no inscription on them, nor is there any mound to mark the grave. The richer classes affect a neatly graven column, surmounted by a stone fez for the departed to wear in Paradise.

From the proximity of the stones one to another, the observer would deduce that owing either to the numbers of the population, or the profits to be derived from agriculture, land in Turkey fetched enormous prices; but it is hardly necessary to say that the observer would be wrong. Why the Turks really are so niggardly of space in their burial arrangements is a problem I must leave to wiser heads.

Beyond the cemetery there is a nice stretch of road, quite broad and reasonably smooth, flanked by cabbage-grounds beloved of the hungry soldier, who, after a brief divagation, marches on contentedly munching a huge round pale-green thing like a football, only very much harder.

On this stretch of road, which leads up to the yellow hill on which the barracks stand, all the drivers of ponies had tremendous fun. They seized their whips, flogged the animals, got up terrific speed, raced one another, and made uncomplimentary remarks to people and dogs who obstructed the course. It was but the natural reaction from the streets of Mustafa behind them. Away on the right turbid Maritza sped on through his bowing woods to meet and mingle with Tundja; and from the top of the yellow hill ridge after ridge, bare, gloomy, and grassless, stretched away to unseen Adrianople. Pryor and I walked about three miles towards the booming guns, and watched the dark serpentine battalions of reservists winding over the trackless hills. He found a pebble or two that he knew would please his little daughter; and I saw a poor solitary *Crocus speciosus* blooming forlornly amid the stones. Geologists may be interested to learn that all the stones in Turkey are

rounded, just as though they had been to the seaside.
I suppose this means that Turkey was only very recently
at the bottom of the sea; and I can't help feeling that
it was a most unfortunate circumstance that it ever came
up. At length we managed to locate the smoke of the
western Turkish forts, which were firing very rapidly;
but we could not determine whether the Bulgarians
were replying or not. Away to the south huge patches
of flame and coils of smoke showed where villages were
burning; and behind us Mustafa looked hypocritically
clean and virtuous in her autumn garb of gold.

It was (29th) a day of brilliant sunshine, still and
cloudless. As we got back to the racecourse road we
met two batteries of 6-in. guns, drawn by teams of ten
oxen, slowly moving towards the lines of the besiegers.
Then we met Mr. Philip Gibbs, the talented artist of
the *Daily Graphic*, whose interesting book on the war
was the first to appear. And that reminds me that the
whole posse of correspondents, and all the military
attachés, about eighty of them, had arrived in Mustafa
the previous night. It was clearly time to move on;
but then there was that terrible general to reckon with.
Our friend Lalage got us out of that difficulty—as she
got us out of so many others.

Our abode was a queer place. In a narrow street of
one-storeyed wooden houses there is a flat wooden door,
studded with nails, and very medieval-looking; this
protects from the outer world a considerable rabbit-
warren of ill-considered buildings. When one opened
the door one either fell, in the darkness, over a military
policeman asleep on the ground with the hood of his
greatcoat drawn over his face as though he were dead,
or blundered into the hindquarters of a horse, of which
there were generally half a dozen feeding in the gloom
of the passage. Then, if uninjured, one went on through
a horrid litter of rain-water and trampled hay and dung,

across the most feasible parts of which scraps of boarding had been set as bridges, and one came to a sort of little lodge, where one ducked one's head as one entered, and perceived a vast chaos of Indian corn. Then, down a step, one passed into what was the garden of the late Turkish proprietor.

A sickly vine trails over a meagre pergola outside the flight of stone steps leading to the front door—almost the sole floral survivor in the trampled mud, if you except a couple of mulberry trees which now serve as supports to cords from which depend the bloody skins of several sheep, and a few wilted stocks emerging from a malodorous sea of paunches and offal. In the house we were assigned a decent little room, with a row of cupboards running down one side. I peered into these one day, and found an incredible quantity of feminine trifles—bits of lace and silk, stockings, and all kinds of things. I was always under the impression that Turkish women dressed simply in yashmaks and sacks ; but apparently that is not the case.

The soldiery, who were perpetually cooking sheep in the garden, had removed as fuel a considerable portion of the wooden fence which separated our demesne from its neighbour ; and happening to wander there, through a whilom garden even more brutally defaced than ours, I found a house, the largest room of which struck me as being admirably adapted to the purpose of stabling our two cart-horses.

No sooner said to George than done. It is true that the fifteen-one horse demurred politely for a minute or two at entering a room with such dirty hoofs as he had ; or it may be that he considered the door inconveniently low. Whatever the reason for his hesitation he very soon bowed his head in token of submission and went in, followed closely by fourteen-two.

While we were thus engaged there was an unmistakable buzzing noise coming from nowhere, and we all, except the cart-horses, rushed out of the new stable to look at the aeroplane. It was a monoplane, high up, heading for Adrianople, laden with leaflets urging the garrison to surrender; and these, more dangerous than any bombs, fell like snow in the streets of the beleaguered city. Philip Gibbs has told us the story of the ending—the usual ending—of this plucky Bulgarian aviator: "After half an hour," he writes, "the aeroplane came back, flying swiftly away from the shot and shell which pursued it from the low-lying hills. Its wings were pierced, so that one could see the sky through them, but it flew steadily from the chase of death, and I heard its rhythmic heart-beat overheard. Its escape was certain now. It had mocked at the pursuit of the shells, the loud beat of its engine above us was a song of triumph. I watched it disappear again—to safety. So it seemed; but death has many ways of capture, and when I came back to Mustafa Pasha that day, I heard that the unfortunate aviator, after his escape from the guns, had fallen from a great height within sight of home, and that the hero's body lay smashed to pieces in the wreckage of his machine." *

Aeroplanes certainly played no very effective *rôle* in the Balkan War. The Turks left two behind them at Kirk Kilisse which they were totally incapable of using; and no aviator helped the Bulgarian cavalry to locate the enemy after his flight from that place. The man who died at Mustafa alone knew how to fly.

There is, after all, something in possessing a motor-car. When one does not want to use it oneself, and is perfectly persuaded that a horse, under the circumstances, is a very much better mode of conveyance, other people will give their ears for a thoroughly uncomfortable drive in it. This curious trait of human nature now redounded greatly to our advantage.

* *Adventures of War with Cross and Crescent*, pp. 108, 109.

M. Kostoff, Professor of the Art of War, and M. Arnaoudhoff, Professor of Comparative Literature, both of them of the University of Sofia, both full privates in the Bulgarian Army, and both detailed to act as Censors of the Press—a position which, in the Balkan War, was much more arduous than serving in the ranks, and very nearly as dangerous—had been allocated to the First and Third Armies respectively. Therefore, they had to get to those armies ; and it may be surmised that they did not want to walk, and that they could not ride. Consequently they cast longing eyes at our Lalage, and I am just a little bit surprised that they did not commandeer her privily by night. The probable explanation is that Alexander remained faithful, and that another chauffeur was not to be found. Correspondents in Bulgaria were, I have heard, treated with such uniform consideration that the seizing of a car which the censors knew would cause the correspondents a great deal of bother would undoubtedly have been regarded by the owners as rather a friendly act. But MM. Kostoff and Arnaoudhoff had perhaps patriotically determined to risk their lives in an attempt to rid the operations of two of the newspaper pests. When I saw the slimy precipices we had to negotiate I felt morally certain of it. At all events they very kindly asked us to come with them in our car.

Kostoff was a big, strong, open-faced fellow, with a moustache and imperial that recalled Napoleon III, and he was known and evidently liked by every single individual in the three Bulgarian armies. He was continually employed in waving his hand or returning a salute ; his right arm was never still for a second. He was the man who had taught the others the theory they were now putting into practice ; and every day the issue taught them that Kostoff's theory was very good theory indeed. It was no wonder that Kostoff was popular and admired. Besides, Kostoff was a man although he was a censor, and he would have loved to be shouldering a musket in the trenches. But high authority kept Kostoff vainly striving to understand English and French despatches translated into execrable German ; he was to be kept safe for the instruction of many future generations of officers. For Kostoff spoke only German to foreigners ; he had sat at the feet of the blood-and-iron men, and, if the Turks really carried out Von der Goltz' principles, Kostoff must have discarded most of the German ideas in favour of his own.

When I was thoroughly acquainted with Kostoff's kit I knew for certain that he was a great man. Only an organising genius of supreme capacity could have devised such a wonderful *multum* in so tiny a *parvo*. A greatcoat and a very small handbag wrapped in a waterproof sheet were all that Kostoff had, and as he always wore the greatcoat that oughtn't to count. And yet, with this exiguous equipment Kostoff had food to eat, and a bed to lie on, and bedclothes to cover himself withal, and books to read, and writing materials, hair-brushes, a very small mirror, a housewife, a comb, shaving materials, a flask, a toothbrush. But really I must stop, although the tale of Kostoff's cruse-like handbag is by no means told ; suffice it to say that many American women do not carry in ten Saratoga trunks a tithe of the things Kostoff could produce out of his fertile bag.

Arnaoudhoff was a very different sort of man. He was thin and pale and monkish. He was an ascetic and a book-worm, and told us that he worked for twelve hours a day until he broke down.

He had all the faults of the pedagogue, and laid down the gospel *ex cathedra* ; and naturally his lectures on English politics, literature, law, art, and commerce were listened to with the gravest attention. As regards his own country he was a megalomaniac ; when Bulgaria had beaten the Turks, she was, in rotation, going to attack, and, I need hardly add, defeat, Serbia, Montenegro, Greece, Rumania, and Austria-Hungary.   There was going to be a sort of Bulgarian millennium, and if Russia said anything it would be all the worse for her.

We were five men, and not by any means very small men, in a 10-h.p. car.   But that by no means represents the total congestion of our very congested district. There were bedding and benzine and bags and great-coats in mountainous excrescences all over the back and flanks of Lalage.   There was also a small wicker-basket with some tea and biscuits and a sardine tin or two ; and here I may remark, once and for all, that I was hungry the whole time I was in Turkey.

Maxwell had pointed out, not without reason, that it was necessary to travel light.   I accepted the position so loyally that I took nothing whatever except a Jaeger sleeping-sack.   It was extremely foolish of me, for the other four had all brought commodious bags, of which Alexander's was of course the largest.   Kostoff, the biggest man of the party, was given the best seat in front, and Maxwell, Arnaoudhoff and I sat upon one another by turns behind.

In brilliant sunshine on the afternoon of the 30th, we set off down the forbidden road to Adrianople, past the golden woods around yellow Maritza, and the bare brown hills rolling away interminably.   After about seven miles of the very fair metalled road, and when we were within ten miles of Adrianople, we came upon a merry bivouac of reservists, and were directed north-wards towards Iskudar over what appeared to be, in the fast-failing light, a trackless mountain.   Then began again the dreadful work of getting out and pushing, repeated every two minutes with such unfailing regularity that I fancy Arnaoudhoff began to think that driving in a motor was not such great fun after all.

The country was drab, bare, khaki-coloured, with hardly a bush to break the hideous monotony, and the adhesiveness of the mud was perfectly phenomenal. At last, having climbed high into the hills, we heard the murmur of ten thousand men, and in the twilight saw a wonderful scene. In front of us, silhouetted against the opaline glow of the eastern sky, was the broken outline of a village crowded with troops ; some were cutting down trees, some were sitting round the bivouac fires, and thousands were moving dimly to and fro. And as we turned a corner and faced the west the sun set in a blaze of blood-red splendour.

After a long wait in the freezing dark amid a welter of guns, horses, ox-wagons, and men, we were, at about nine o'clock, allotted a room in a typical Turkish house, for the broken windows were covered with sacking, and the stars twinkled merrily through the thatch of reeds. However, a grey-bearded veteran brought us plenty of wood for a fire, and spread chopped straw for us to lie on, and we made some tea, and ate a sardine, and lay down in a row, and watched the stars twinkling until we slept.

Travelling light in order to oblige a couple of censors is not a course to be recommended. To wake up in the morning with your back full of chopped straw, and to realise slowly the horrid truth that you have neither bath, nor sponge, nor brushes, no, not even a toothbrush, is a dreadful experience. Then there are lots of predatory insects in Turkish houses. Certainly people who are fond of comfort should not go campaigning with censors. Yet I cheerfully and gratefully admit that to-day (31st) they introduced us to some officers who were crammed into the smallest and dirtiest hovel I ever saw, and those excellent men gave us a breakfast of Russian tea and brown bread and cheese. This Bulgarian cheese is very white and soft and crumbly, and it has usually a very sour but not disagreeable taste, but occasionally you strike a brand which is terribly suggestive of the he-goat. I remember Segonzac called some we had at Ermenekeui *fromage de buc*.

Our objective being Kirk Kilisse our route this day lay in an eastern direction, following the northern line of investment which the Bulgars had drawn round Adrianople. All day we met and overtook howitzers and 6-in. guns, balks for emplacements, and all the paraphernalia of siege-work. It was very tantalising to be so near the positions and yet not allowed to go and see them; but this book is a record of the gentle art of baffling correspondents.

There was one very curious thing which I never saw before, and probably shall never see again. This was a sham gun, made of wood, which at night was attached to a donkey with a lantern hung on his neck, and then the poor ass was given a good smack behind, and sent off alone on his journey towards the Turkish forts.

Of course the Turks saw the lantern first, and then the donkey, and then the gun, and naturally opened a terrific fire on the unfortunate animal. Naturally enough, too, none of the shells hit either the donkey or the gun, or else I shouldn't have seen it. (There is a story that on Salisbury Plain, for purposes of gunnery, a flock of sheep were counted and then deliberately made the target. After the practice the flock was counted again, and the owner was more pleased than the gunners when it was discovered that, as a result of the deadly shower of shrapnel, there were two more sheep, or rather lambs, than when the cannonade began.) Naturally again, the donkey stopped to listen to the noise, and presently finding nothing happen, began to browse about, and eventually returned for breakfast to his battery.

What countless thousands of bullocks Bulgaria breeds! Our road that day, as we skirted the deadly zone enwrapping Adrianople, was moving with transport of every imaginable kind. We spoke to lots of people through the censors, and the chief topics were the battle of Kirk Kilisse, where the Turks were said to have left nine hundred dead on the field, and the massacres and mutilations perpetrated on Christian women and children.

This is a terrible subject, but the unreasoning liking for the Turks which seems to bias so many English minds—a liking which Mr. Gladstone's passionate denunciations appears only to have increased—is a good reason why the truth should be known.

Segonzac took a photograph of a dead woman and her unborn child. The woman had been ripped open, and the head of her child lay a yard away from his body, clean severed by a sword-cut. The Turks have been doing that kind of thing to Bulgarian women and children for four hundred years, and yet we English, as a nation, like them very much. Well, we are not Bulgarians, that is the great and essential difference, and, moreover, we are very ignorant of the facts.

God knows that feelings outraged by fearful cruelties have been the motive power which has driven the nations of the Balkan League to scatter their persecutors like chaff before the wind. And so we journeyed slowly on through the abysmal mud, over the bare, rolling, yellow plains, towards Pravodiya and the pointed mountains. Turkish villages are the most inconsequent-looking things in the world. In a Gloucestershire village called Coaley, near to which I once lived, a labourer, who was both an industrious and thrifty person and a good hater, built himself a cottage—red brick picked out with nice yellow Bath stone, and on a wide central plaque above the door he had engraved the name of his abode— " Neighbour's Enemy."

Turkish villages look as though every man hated his neighbour, and it is not a bit surprising that he should.

At all events the houses try to get as far away from one another as is decently consistent with the village theory, and the intervening spaces are filled in with offal, excrement, thorn-fences, and a little chopped straw. Savage dogs, of a large and hairy breed, keep up communication between the forts, and carry out their owners' conception of fraternity by biting every one but them.

Pravodiya is a picturesque spot. A steep yellow hill is dappled with crazy red and brown-tiled houses, and below in the valley, beneath a precipitous limestone escarpment, flows a clear stream fringed with poplars. This place, for the moment, was the Headquarters of General Tepavitcharoff, whom we found at the top of a treacherous wooden staircase, in a bare room with two huge maps hanging on the walls—a genial, grey-bearded, delightful gentleman, who showed us on the maps the position of the Turks at Lule Burgas, and the famous fort of Papas Tepe, to the south-west of Adrianople where such desperate fighting took place, it having been captured and recaptured no less than four times. Adrianople was now completely invested ; and as we sat on boxes chatting there came to us the sullen roar of the big guns close in front.

But it was soon time to be moving on, though Kostoff saw so many old friends with whom it was absolutely necessary to have a word that I began to fancy we should end our days on the dung-heaps of Pravodiya. The General was kind enough to send a soldier to find us something to eat, and presently he returned with a dozen eggs and two chickens, and would take not a sixpence for them, saying they were a present from the General. So we slid gingerly down the narrow, precipitous, boulder-strewn village highway, past dense groups of wondering women and bearded soldiers, and suddenly, far away in the south, out of the distant haze, loomed up the colossal dome and four great protecting minarets

of Sultan Selim's mosque in Adrianople. And other
minarets there were, four of them, satellites to the greater
four; and besides these eight aspiring columns, and the
dome of the great mosque, there was nothing. Somehow
there came a lesson in the sight; between us and those
buildings devoted to the worship of the Eternal Spirit
thousands of ant-like men were striving with deadly
weapons of their own devising to extinguish in their
fellow-men the life God gave; but they and their huge
engines of destruction alike were engulfed in a void of
nothingness, and only the towers they had raised in
honour of the Spirit pointed heavenwards in mute appeal.

Slowly we progressed, for to drive a motor-car slap
across Turkey in the rainy season requires a good deal
both of patience and push. Down to a stream, turbid
with the passage of countless vehicles, we would come,
and then we would all get out, except Alexander, who
sat at the wheel with his black eyes glinting very bright,
and his black hair getting longer and longer beneath his
rakishly cocked cap, and each would survey a riparian
section and seek out the best crossing, and then all four
would meet at the motor again, and each would assert
that he had certainly found the best place, and Alexander,
bored with a discussion in a tongue he understood not,
would suddenly clap spurs to his metalsome steed, and
drive it with magnificent determination at the very
spot in the river which his two masters and their two
masters had unanimously agreed was the one spot that
at all hazards must be avoided. And then, of course,
the car stuck in the middle of the stream, and we four
had to wade in and push, and seize the hind wheels and
turn them, or try to turn them, at imminent risk of getting
our arms broken if the car advanced, and all the time
Lalage would be uttering the most dolorous noises
in a loud voice, like some impotent pig on a bench striving
to escape from death. And then, when we, alone or

reinforced by good-natured soldiers (and how good-natured the Bulgarian soldier is I cannot tell you), had, with the utmost expenditure of muscle and wind, got the machine to the top of the sandy steep, and had thrown ourselves, panting and soaked, as much with our own sweat as with Turkish river-water, on the ground to rest, Alexander would quietly remove Lalage up a gentle rise which he afterwards protested was much too severe if we all got into her, and we would overtake him half a mile on, after swearing and shouting until we were hoarse, dripping, caked with mud—mud on faces, mud in hair, eyes, mouth, boots—serenely smiling in his placid Oriental way, and pretending to be utterly unconscious that he had done anything wrong. I had a pair of field-boots that galled my heels, and took the skin off so that they continually bled; I was a mass of insect bites; I had no change of clothes, not even at night; I had no sponge and no brushes: why was I ever born to come to this God-forsaken country, where all the sacrifices of comfort that one was obliged to make brought no compensating professional reward in the sight and knowledge of great deeds?

We lunched that day on the top of a great rock, out of which issued a beautiful pale-green spring of water, that not all the trampling of thousands of thirsty men and beasts could defile. But as a rule the water in Turkey was very bad, chiefly because the wells, naturally, were in towns and villages where, for hundreds of years, sewage had been percolating into them. Consequently the Bulgarians lost thousands of men from, at first, acute diarrhœa, and afterwards from dysentery and cholera. It was always easy to recognise the poor fellows who, despite their illness, still pluckily struggled on, though stricken with these fell complaints—the yellow, drawn cheek, the dull eye, the bent back, the dragging gait—these were the symptoms of those preventable diseases which the filthy habits of the Turks made more lethal to their foes than all the shells and bullets that they fired.

At six in the evening, in the dark, we reached Seliolo, and the burly, genial Kostoff was at once surrounded by a knot of friends, one of whom was a General, who spoke as one having authority, and not as a scribe. And immediately we were directed to push the motor from the midden in which it had stuck up a very steep muddy bank, and through a winding maze of narrow, thorn-fenced paths, until we reached, in the starlight, a house with a little verandah, quite uncommonly well-built and erect-looking, surrounded by countless white objects which seemed as though, like the Prophet's coffin, they were suspended between heaven and earth, and which gleamed and stank merrily in the moonlight.

Although his yard was full of it this was evidently the residence of no man of straw; a fellow who could have fifteen or twenty sheepskins hanging simultaneously up to dry must be a sort of Bulgarian Crœsus; or, horrid thought, was this all that the dear departed Turks had left him of his flock?

Our doubts were speedily resolved by the Mayor of Seliolo himself, for to lodge in the house of no less a personage were we come. He was a brisk young fellow of about thirty, with a very honest, cheery face, clad in the brown clothes of the Bulgarian soldier, and a sheepskin which had had time to dry surmounted his tunic. He seemed very glad to see us, and ushered us across the little verandah into one of the two rooms which composed his dwelling. It was about eight feet square, with mud walls and floor scrupulously clean, with a tiny glass window that wouldn't open because it couldn't, and beneath it, on the sill, some moribund geraniums in a tin of soil. Women, God bless them, are the same all over the world and in every rank of life;

and here was the Mayoress of Seliolo, with her mud floors and her sheepskins, trying to hear the divine note that all flowers strike. She came, a worn-looking but still young woman, carrying her tiny baby, and threw a lot of rugs on the floor for us to lie on. The other room was evidently the only one the family of four used; and it was four times the size of the one we were allotted. The most conspicuous objects in it were a huge pile of rugs—they reached from the floor half-way up the wall—a rifle, and a large fireplace with a jack and several large pots. There was also a little string hammock suspended from the roof, in which the baby was left to squall, which it did very conscientiously whenever its mother couldn't hold it in her arms.

The thing which struck me most of all in Turkey was the extraordinary difference between the life of the peasants there and the life of peasants in England. It is no exaggeration to say that peasants in England live in Heaven, and that Bulgarian peasants in Turkey live in Hell.

Whatever Government may be in power in England, men go about without fear of imminent murder, though of course they know that Mr. Lloyd George will rob them of nearly all they possess. But the Christian peasant in Turkey goes about in fear of his life, and, as in England, the taxes swallow up the best part of their scanty earnings. But the farther the comparison is instituted, the worse becomes the Bulgarian position. He has no weekly wage, paid regularly on Saturday, whether he does any work or not during the week. By genuine sweat of his brow he has to screw a pittance out of Mother Earth.

Towns and their shops and distractions are unknown to him; he buys nothing; he and his family make all they possess—clothes, boots, bedding, flour. Perhaps he buys, as perhaps his grandfather bought, a cooking-pot or so, and a picture of the Madonna; but that is about the extent of his purchases. If his wife is ill, or his child is dying, he has no material aid. There is no doctor within twenty miles, and he will not come out from the city to see a peasant, because the peasant cannot pay him, and so the peasant doesn't fetch him. Think of the diet of an English labourer, and compare it with the ever-recurrent bread of the poorer Bulgars. I do most heartily recommend any one (and he appears to be by no means rare) who takes a gloomy view of the present condition of England to travel extensively in countries like Turkey; and if he does not return a happier and a wiser man I shall be greatly surprised.

But we must return to the Mayor of Seliolo, Bulgarian village in Turkey in Europe. He did everything to make us as comfortable as he could; he brought in a brazier of charcoal, which, as the window wouldn't and couldn't open, ought to have asphyxiated the whole party; and would have, if the cracks in the door had not been so large. Then came his young-old wife, having handed over the baby to his sister, aged six, whom, to judge by his uninterrupted lamentations, he did not regard with unmixed affection. The Lady Mayoress, poor thing, had a picture in one hand, and a nail in the other. Somebody supplied a boot, which was the only kind of undressing we could do for dinner, and in a few moments we had a picture of the Holy Family, a gilt-framed oleograph of the very worst type, hanging devoutly over our heads on the mud wall.

I guessed the motive in that good woman's heart: we might be Englishmen and strangers, but Englishmen and Bulgars worshipped the same God, and that God was not the God of the Turkish oppressor; and here was the highest link that bound us all together.

Then she retired to the big room (although it was not really very big) to cook our two fowls for dinner; and Arnaoudhoff, who, as Professor of Comparative Literature, is compelled to talk to young and pretty women in warm kitchens, when his male friends are all in a freezing outhouse, presently followed her on the flimsy pretext of wishing to take down a folk-song ; and though he very considerately returned to our outhouse for dinner, the folk-song was so long that he had to return after dinner to the warm kitchen to take down more of it ; and when he finally rejoined us we were all in bed, that is to say, on the floor, and half-asleep.

The little six-year-old girl, who nursed the ungrateful baby and dusted the floors and porch with a grass broom, was a very pretty little creature, very prettily dressed. Her fair hair was done in two plaits, which escaped from a red coif bound with fillets of blue. Her plain black dress was fringed with a deep border of red, white, and then again black, and below it showed a snowy-white petticoat of woollen material, embroidered with red. Her mother wore a black sleeveless sheepskin Zouave jacket, with the wool inside ; on her arms were loose white linen sleeves ; on her head a white wimple, fastened with green fillets, and the dark hair loose below. Her black dress, cut low in front, was embroidered with red, and she wore two gold bracelets set with turquoises. Like some Biblical figure she took down the beautifully curved notched stick, and came back from the well balancing the heavy jars upon her shoulder with the easy grace that only Easterns know. The Lady Mayoress had an oven in the yard, close to the wood-stack where the hens lived. I watched her and the little girl and the Pope's daughter one day—all hard at work filling up the mud oven with wood, and bringing out round doughy things on platters, which were transferred to a long-handled bath-stirrer and popped skilfully into the very bowels of the earth.

That evening, before we went to bed, I said to Alexander, " Is the motor safe out there ? "

" Safe ? " ejaculated Alexander, in surprised French, " are there not four dogs in the garden ? "

One dog was quite enough to scare the Armenian out of his seven senses ; and so I presume he argued that no body of men, however well armed and courageous, would ever dare to attack a position guarded by four.

But now it is the day when fox-hunting begins in England, that dear old England which seems so extremely remote when one has spent the night with one's clothes on in a rug on the floor of a Bulgar hut in Turkey, and wakened in the small hours at feeling something in one's hair, and been horrified to grasp the fat and bestial body of an enormous parasite, and then to arise and find that all the dressing one can do is to put on a pair of field-boots that gall one's heels like anything.   Oh, it was a filthy, awful experience that I will never go through again.   Maxwell very kindly lent me one end of his towel and a razor, and knotted the end of the towel I was not to use, because that was his particular end, and I was so particularly dirty.   So at six we turned out into the cold and slushy yard, and thought, perhaps, of all the lads at home hard at work on glossy, well-bred skins, and of the nice new pink coats laid out for the first time by dressing-room fires, and of that ham on the sideboard—but no ! that was too awful ; the remains of two chickens which had constituted the inadequate dinner of four hungry men was all they were going to get for breakfast.

We had about twenty miles to go to get to Kirk Kilisse.   It was a cold, bright day ; there was ice on the puddles ;   the sun shone with invigorating brilliancy. Be it here interpolated that, so far as I know, November in Turkey is a very pleasant month ; the only pleasant thing about Turkey in November is the weather.   Towards the end of the month my Fahrenheit thermometer stood at 74° day and night ; I thought there was something wrong with it, but discovered it was the weather. There was hardly any wind, and very little rain. But, all the same, I should not recommend anybody to go to Turkey in preference to the Riviera: the houses are not quite so clean as at Cannes, and the scents are not the scents of Grasse.

The dear little six-year-old came out to wish us good-bye, with a bright flower stuck jauntily behind her ear. So we rolled away, with flags flying, down the steep midden into the brook and up the dirty hill beyond, seeing the unfinished, roofless white church away to our right—evidence, if evidence were needed, which it is not, that this perennially young disagreement between Christian and Turk is not by any manner of means the result of religious intolerance on the Turk's part. The Christian could worship openly in any Turkish village. But a handful of Turks have had to rule Christians who outnumbered them greatly, and so a massacre, from time to time, was regarded as a valuable adjunct to a naturally high Christian death-rate. At last what the Turks always feared has happened: the Christians have united, and the Turks have gone.

For about ten miles we drove mainly due south, skirting the willow-dotted banks of the Hasi Dere, and getting nearer and nearer to Adrianople. Fortunately for us there was a lot of rising ground between us and the forts, for if we had been seen we should undoubtedly have been bombarded.

This was quite a nice bit of sandy road, with an extraordinary absence of the usual brand of glutinous mud, and there were lots of little round hills dotted about, which the Professor of Comparative Literature asserted to be artificial *tumuli*, the burying-places of the ancient Thracians, who inhabited these parts before the Pelasgi.

We got to a village with a beautiful slender minaret

aspiring over it heavenwards; and the filthy lanes between the thorn-fences were full of dirty, ragged old women and blear-eyed children. These aged cronies found a motor a fine object for the exercise of their senile curiosity; and with a great show of intelligent appreciation they asked Alexander where the horse was. "In here, of course," replied Alexander, gravely pointing to the bonnet. The cronies gravely inclined their heads in comprehension as our invisible horse-power wafted us away.

Soon afterwards we got to the village of Haskeui, on the road between Kirk Kilisse and Adrianople. This was really a road, good, like the curate's egg, in parts, but with great white heaps of stones all along it which the Turks had been too lazy to put down. When Alexander saw it he got Delage on to top speed for the first time for a month, spat on his hands, cocked his cap, and looked round grinning at us. But his joy was speedily turned to sorrow. Beside us, on either hand, great black arable fields, in which the winter corn was just sprouting, stretched away for miles to the horizon. And there were other things in the fields besides corn, things which Alexander had to look at against his will. They were like scarecrows which had fallen down and got covered with mud; their arms were thrown wide apart, and their black faces stared up into the sunshine. Others, again, had fallen on their faces, and curious dark stains appeared on their greenish clothing. And every few yards there was a dead horse blocking up the roadway, and Alexander could only use one hand to drive with, because the other was employed in pressing a very dirty handkerchief very tightly over his nose and mouth. Once a bluebottle got in beside him and buzzed about under his legs; and I really thought the man would have a fit, and that we should all be upset and perish. He made frantic passes and terrific dashes at that inoffensive insect; and in his heart he was certain that it had come expressly, ptomaine-laden from a corpse, to infect him to his death. We were passing over the line of the Bulgarian advance on Kirk Kilisse—the advance of the enveloping right wing; and there was plenty of evidence that the Turks had retreated in a great hurry. All along the road were overturned ammunition wagons, and thousands of unfired shrapnel littered the ground. We told Alexander that if he drove over one of those big cartridges it would go off (as indeed it would have) and blow us all sky-high; and for the first and only time that I can remember the insubordinate Armenian paid attention to his instructions, and would pull up dead ten or twelve yards away from some obstructive shells, and wait quite patiently, with pallid face and haunted eye, until the gallant Kostoff had removed the danger.

That road to Kirk Kilisse, a straight white streak across the black and greasy plain, seemed as though it would never end. Often we had to leave the so-called road and navigate a difficult course over the bogged plain, and the motor stuck frequently, and only the help of passers-by enabled us to get her out. Surely war correspondents were never in sorrier plight? Miles behind the armies, under the jealous eye of two censors, one apiece, all in a motor meant to hold one less than it held, with no baggage, filthy, lousy, mud-bespattered, hungry, the acme of human misery seemed to have been touched.

At last we came to a steep descent, cut out of an apparently precipitous cliff with considerable engineering skill, and found ourselves suddenly in the village of Yenidje, round which had raged a terrific fight but a few days before. The place was crammed with wounded and medical corps, and in one of the groups Kostoff descried Captain Gueshoff, the son of the Prime Minister, and got out to have a chat with him. We then learnt, but not in any detail, that the Turks had made a very poor resistance at Kirk Kilisse itself; as usual, our censors were the reverse of communicative as to military affairs. But, as usual, the atrocities committed by the Turks were dilated on, with an eye to the English papers; when the Greeks entered Ellasona they found a huge pile of Christians butchered in the church, and on the top of the pile the body of the priest; and the Turks had put their Christian subjects at all the posts of danger on the frontiers, hoping to get them killed off without scandal by their co-religionists.

So we passed on through crowds of sallow, bearded, tired-looking men into the orchard-swamps, on to a ploughed-up track screened by tall poplars, inconceivably impassable, the joint result of much rain and traffic. But the journey over the interminable rolling prairie was nearly over; presently the road was bordered with great vineyards dotted with almond trees—black sticks a foot long speckling the black earth in serried rows. And there, at last, ahead, Kirk Kilisse clung to her twin hills, and wandered into the cleft between the two—a white and yellow city dotted with the green of mimosas, set against the purple of the jagged and ferocious outline of the Istrandja Dagh beyond.

The Turks call the city Kirk Kilisse, and the Bulgarians call it Lozengrad. The Turkish name is a product of what grammarians call false analogy. Kilisse is the same word as *ecclesia* and *église*, and once on a day there was one church here, in a swamp, for which the Turkish word is Kir; and so the place got the name of Kir Kilisse, or the Church in the Swamp. But somebody who couldn't spell, or who wished to exaggerate the Christian proclivities of a Turkish town, altered Kir to Kirk, which means forty, and so the place is now the City of Forty Churches, when, as a matter of fact, it has only got one. The Bulgarian name means the

City of Vineyards, and is much the more sensible name of the two, because undoubtedly the circumambient vineyards are the distinctive feature of the place. Good wines, both red and white—the latter a full-bodied, dark wine of the Marsala type, and the former a heavy Burgundy—are made of these grapes.

The Bulgarian is a very moderate drinker.

Of wine in Turkey, Busbecq wrote in 1552: "To drink wine is considered a great sin among the Turks, especially in the case of persons advanced in life; when younger people indulge in it the offence is considered more venial. Inasmuch, however, as they think that they will have to pay the same penalty after death whether they drink much or little, if they taste one drop of wine they must needs indulge in a regular debauch, their notion being that, inasmuch as they have already incurred the penalty appointed for such sin in another world, it will be an advantage to them to have their sin out, and get dead drunk, as it will cost them as much in either case. These are their ideas about drinking, and they have some other notions which are still more ridiculous. I saw an old gentleman at Constantinople who, before taking up his cup, shouted as loud as he could. I asked my friends the reason, and they told me he was shouting to warn his soul to stow itself away in some odd corner of his body, or to leave it altogether, lest it should be defiled by the wine he was about to drink, and have hereafter to answer for the offence which the worthy man was about to indulge in." *

Kirk Kilisse is a picturesque place. Little acacia trees fringe little awful side-walks, and nondescript, ramshackle, brown-tiled houses lean against one another in sympathetic attitudes. To the incredible filth of the roads and alleys one soon became accustomed, and splashed through the bogs with the calm *sang-froid* of men who

* Forster and Daniell's translation.

could not get any dirtier if they tried, and could not get any cleaner for the same reason. And, sometimes, when you had emerged from a narrow slum of glass-fronted dens, where many shuttered shops proclaimed death or exile, the sun would flash on the white walls and emerald dome of a mosque perched high on the hillside; and the filth was forgotten.

But it was a sad place, for it was crammed with wounded. Every other building was a hospital, and the streets were densely packed with soldiers with blood-stained bandages, most of them on the hands and arms, but some on feet that could not be put to earth, while their owners hobbled about with their rifles for crutches. The extraordinary number of men wounded in the hands and arms is easily explained. In well-constructed trenches (in which at Lule Burgas the Bulgarians lay for days) only a man's head and arms are exposed to the enemy's fire. Most bullets through the head finish the business at once; the bullets through the arms and hands do not.

The hospitals were eternally besieged by crowds of " out-patients " who came to get their diurnal dressing from the overworked surgeons; in the filth of the street, muffled in their brown overcoats, the lean, tired, hungry-eyed men sat for hours patiently, diffusing around a horrid stench of gangrene and iodoform.

On November 2nd we woke up after our first night in Kirk Kilisse, which had not been a particularly peaceful one. The bed that I had tried to sleep on may have accommodated itself to the anatomy of Greeks, but it must have resented the intrusion of a Britisher. The rain had come down in sheets, incessantly; and as there appeared to be a corrugated iron roof above the apartment that Maxwell and I shared, the noise can be imagined, but not described. The wind was extremely high, and banged the open window about with a din

that appeared emulous of the performance of the roof;
while it killed two birds with one stone, or very nearly,
by blowing us off our beds on to the floor, which was
certainly the softer resting-place. About one o'clock in
the morning, just as I had fallen into an uneasy slumber,
there was a great banging at the door, and in walked
Arnaoudhoff, in his greatcoat instead of a night-shirt,
shouting like a silly schoolboy that there was a great
fire, and really we ought to come to see it.

In my haste I devoutly wished that Arnaoudhoff
was spending the night in the burning building, and
that the Fire Brigade had business elsewhere; but
there was nothing to be done but to turn out and shiver
at a leaky window, watching the great tongues of flame
rise and fall like the tongue of the Wild Worm in *Siegfried*,
for it was a really good fire; and it was so cold in our
house that I wished it had occurred next door, instead
of half a mile away; besides, there would have been
a better chance of disposing of Arnaoudhoff. Never
was on this earth such a pandemonium as then. In
addition to the noises already enumerated, the wind
was banging the doors all over the house; and outside
every bell in the town was ringing, and every dog in
the town was barking, and live cartridges were exploding
by the dozen. Whether the bullets were let off by the
fire, or whether the sentries were firing at an incendiary,
or whether they were playfully attracting the attention
of the neighbours to their danger, or whether they were
putting victims of the flames out of their misery, I know
not, and shall never know. At all events the firing
(not the arson, if it was arson, but the bullets) lasted
far into the morning, and agreeably impressed us new-
comers with a sense of the security and peace of Turkish
towns in war time.

It was so delightful to get off that Greek (I had nearly
written Greecy) and Procrustean bed, and have none

of the bother of shaving and bathing and dressing and hairbrushing; on with the muddy field-boots, and there you are, equipped *cap-à-pie*, something like Venus Anadyomene rising in all her perfect beauty from the sea. I felt that if the cart with the baggage did not turn up soon I should go mad; for the fleas in Greek houses, to say nothing of allied carnivora, are very large, and as the sand of the seaside for multitude. That morning we made a new acquaintance, a certain M. Mateeff, a Bulgarian who spoke perfect English, and who had been for some time with George Smith, the distinguished Assyriologist. He told us he had been Minister at Athens, and represented Bulgaria at the St. Louis Exhibition. He also told us a story about the great mosque at Adrianople which Sultan Selim had had built by the greatest architect in his dominions.

The Sultan ordered the architect to put in a thousand windows; and that bewildered artist did his best to comply with the decree of his august lord. But at the last moment, when, indeed, by dint of making the interior exceedingly light, he had managed to get in 999, he discovered that another would ruin all. I do not mean that the mosque would have tumbled to pieces— it was far too well built for that; but merely that the whole effect would have been marred. The architect was a great artist, as any one who has seen his mosque, even from afar, will admit; and so, rather than spoil his handiwork by that impossible thousandth window, he resolved to die. He did not intend to commit suicide; but he meant to refuse to put in that absurd window; and he knew his Sultan Selim intimately. One day the Sultan sent for the architect, and told him it was high time that the mosque was finished. The architect, somewhat mendaciously, replied that it was. "Take me to see it," commanded the Sultan. The architect's slippers quivered a little as he led the way. Arrived in front of the mosque, the Sultan at once began counting out loud. He had had an excellent grounding in arithmetic, and he was a very fair pedestrian, so that the mental and physical strain involved in perambulating the mosque, which is a very big one, and looking up at the windows, some of which are very high, to say nothing of the counting out loud, did not unduly distress him. It took him an hour and a half to make the complete circuit, and then, with a very red face, the Sultan turned to the architect and shrieked, " There are only nine hundred and ninety-nine ! " " I beg your Majesty's pardon," replied the latter, after an awkward pause, for he was more at home with fabrics than with fabrications, " but I think your Majesty must inadvertently have omitted to count one of the windows." " Me ! " roared the Sultan, getting redder and redder—" me miss out a window ? When I've got as good eyesight as any man in Turkey, and won the prize for arithmetic at Owens College before the premature deaths of my fifteen Elder Brethren brought me to the throne ! Is it likely, you dog, and son of a dog, and grandson of a dog ? I'll pay you out for that insult ! " The architect saw that the game was up. There would be a great deal of bastinado, followed by a very little rope. He fell on his knees and confessed. The Sultan was considerably mollified when he heard that his arithmetic was correct, for he had had very little practice since he counted the corpses of his Elder Brethren.

Besides, it was such a relief to know that he would not have to walk round that beastly mosque all over again, as he had severely resolved to do if the architect stuck to his guns; though of course after the architect's demise.

" Well, now you'd better go home and get bastinadoed," genially remarked the Sultan, " and if you are able to walk you can come round and see me about five, and

I'll give you further instructions." This was horrible; the architect made a final effort. " Your Majesty, I carried out the spirit, and not the letter, of your august commands; for in the minds of the people nine hundred and ninety-nine seem more than one thousand; and they will say that any sultan could build a mosque with a thousand windows, but only the great and puissant Sultan Selim could build one with nine hundred and ninety-nine." " By Jove," said the Sultan musingly, " not a bad idea, that; something in it, I do believe. And, after all, it's not half a bad mosque. Took me a jolly long time to get round it; and another window would have given me a stiffer neck than I've got already. Yes, on the whole, I think I'll let you off this time. Don't do it again. By Gad! how late it is! I shall miss that suffragette meeting in the Harîm if I don't look sharp. Ta ta, old boy! and thanks very much for building me such a damned good mosque."

The above, taken down in shorthand from M. Mateef's recital, shows that there are Bulgarians who combine both a sense of humour and a command of English.

What a filthy, stuffy, rambling place that Greek house was—all linoleum and falling plaster and chintz blinds; where you seemed to be going up and down stairs all the time. The only refreshing touch in the whole sordid picture is the little fair-haired lassie who brings in the plates, and helps Alexander to wash up, and generally acts as housekeeper in this deserted ramshackle abode, whence, from the back windows, you see tier upon tier of brown-tiled flat-roofed houses climbing up into the sky.

The enigma of the house was the biggest, ugliest, and far and away the dirtiest man I ever saw. His face was nearly black with the accumulations of ages; his huge protruding eyes looked dully into vacancy; the general effect was that of a Brobdingnagian pug who has got dyspepsia. He never spoke, and he never did anything. Outside the house, in the little courtyard where the chrysanthemums were wilting, there was an old pointer bitch, and a little wizened crippled man who spun all day with a distaff.

We were told stories of wounded Bulgarians whose lives were spared by the Turks if they had enough money to buy themselves off; but this applied only to the rank and file. No officer was ever spared; his nose and ears were cut off first, and thereafter he was butchered.

The black caps of the Bulgarians told against them; they were much more conspicuous than the green khaki caps of the Turks. People said that the Turks fired away about five times as much ammunition as the Bulgarians. To-day we heard that the 29th and 32nd Regiments marched from the sector north of Adrianople at 3 P.M. yesterday, and got here—a distance of sixty kilometres—at 7 P.M. It rained the whole time, and the troops went straight across country. Verily these Bulgarians are splendid fellows !

November 3. Sunday. Thought of a certain dear creature going to church in her pretty frock across the autumn-coloured garden, and how peaceful and beautiful life in England is compared to life in these wild, ferocious climes ! Went through the wounded-crowded streets to the stinking post-office, which apparently has intimate relations with the Cloaca Maxima of Lozengrad, and wherein the briefest sojourn calls up unpleasant prognostications of imminent typhoid. And yet here men work like horses all day and half the night, and take no steps to mitigate the nuisance ! Sanitation is the one thing the Bulgarians are Laodicean about.

At the post-office I encountered for the first time the excellent Russian Captain Mamontoff, a sturdy fellow of twenty-eight, who had commanded a mitrailleuse in the Russo-Japanese War. He was in uniform, looking exactly like a Bulgarian officer, and was sending off reams of copy about Lule Burgas. He kept me waiting for the operator such an unconscionable time that I vowed I would never come back to the post-office without a bottle of eau-de-Cologne and a very large bandanna.

In the afternoon we walked to the northernmost of the two forts which were intended to defend Kirk Kilisse. They are both very much alike—huge semicircular mounds of earth protected by terrific ditches, with barracks and store-houses behind the shelter of the ramparts.

The country in front had been carefully denuded of trees, but the Turks had forgotten the rather essential matter of guns. The Bulgarians had got nine old Krupps into position at the north fort by this time. The fort is about a mile and a half from the town, and the track to it goes down a precipice into a ravine, and up the other side, through a jungle of vines and almond-trees, on which great bunches of mistletoe were growing.

November 4. The baggage question now superseded all others as far as I was concerned. For days I had not changed my clothes, or had a bath, or brushed my hair; and wild horses should not keep me from my kit. The scoundrel Alexis had returned, riding on my saddle on one of the horses, with some lie about the cart having stuck miles away back, which was not unnatural considering that he'd taken away the best horse! He was the most useless scoundrel I ever encountered; but he was a favourite of M.'s, who resented my importunities that he should be dismissed. M. Mateef kindly consented to accompany me with his Humber car in order to get all the baggage back if possible; and of course there was the inevitable censor in charge, which I managed to arrange should be Kostoff.

At 8.30 A.M. we started for Seliolo. It was a fine day, but previous rains, and the passage of thousands of bullock-wagons, had churned the tracks into indescribable morasses. Gleaming pools of dirty water, chance protruding ruts, and then a few yards of black greasy wheel-turned hills and valleys,—a mazy mountain system more erratic and difficult to pass than the Pennine Alps, —this was the charming landscape we motorists looked on for forty weary miles. I had managed to secure a spade at the fort on the previous day (I did not steal it), and this proved invaluable. Half a dozen times we literally dug the car out of the dirt, and with chance strips of wood and made-up ramps, built little causeways for the wheels.

A détour to avoid a hopelessly impassable lake outside Yenidje nearly ended in disaster. There was a choice between a lane full of water and a ploughed field with a narrow passage between two trees in a ditch. Alexander, of course, wanted to go on down the lane, in which he had already stuck five times. I cut a ramp up into the ploughed field, we pushed the motor up, and then I filled in the ditch, and told Alexander to go slowly on between the trees. He gesticulated and swore that it was impossible; but I had taken measurements, and knew what a beautiful steerer was our poltroonish Armenian.

He went at it at last; there was a slight brushing of the hood, and a bump down the far side, but the car got through. And then Alexander smiled his ineffable smile, as of one who had engineered the feat from the very beginning. The road was crammed with men and transport coming from Adrianople to reinforce the Lule Burgas armies; and the number of carts we saw stuck and derelict defy enumeration. The worthy Mateef, whose chief failing is not a lack of self-confidence, was emphatic on the point that the Bulgars were retiring from Adrianople in order to let the Turks out, and then smash them up in the open. At length, *post tot pericula*, we arrive again at the Mayor of Seliolo's house, still girded with its zone of malodorous sheepskins, still echoing to the howls of the latest scion of the mayoral stock.

The poor tired-looking, prematurely-aged Mayoress had a terrible ear-ache, which the excellent Kostoff tried to relieve with eau-de-Cologne. What Kostoff really carried in that inexhaustible case of his will ever remain a mystery. Short of a white elephant, I firmly believe he could have produced anything out of it.

We were very hungry; we were always hungry in Turkey. The Mayor looked at his flock of hens, and they disliked his expression, and scattered to the four winds of heaven. One of them, less cunning than her sisters, took seeming asylum in the midst of a wood-stack—apparently a most excellent place of refuge. But not from the Mayor of Seliolo—I suppose he is the most expert hen-catcher on earth. It took him about five minutes to worm his way into the bowels of that wood-stack; but at length a terrified gallic scream was heard, and the hinder parts of the Mayor were observed to be in motion backwards. At length the complete Mayor emerged, hot, but triumphant, holding aloft a hen. She and another, smitten to earth with a pole, were speedily decapitated, and allowed to flutter into the very filthiest liquid-manure puddles to be found in the whole farmyard.

At 6 P.M. the excellent Mayor provided two white oxen and a youth to go to Pravodiya and fetch the cart. They were to start at once and march all night.

November 5. About 7.30 A.M. I observed a black sheep running about the yard. The Mayor also observed it, and suddenly seized it unawares, as deftly as though it had been a mere hen. He then pulled his knife out of his belt, and plunged it into the neck of the sheep. As though fallen from the skies another man appeared, who skinned the sheep in a marvellously short space of time, pulling its hide off over its head as a man is divested of his sweater.

The greedy chauffeurs, watching vulture-like the process of gralloching, make away with the kidneys, the liver, and the best chops, which they grill privily over a wood-fire in the frosty dawn. Any old joint will do for those fools their masters, who consumed a portentous quantity of very fresh mutton, and felt like giants refreshed.

At the corner of the farmyard, hung about with sheepskins, to which gory collection the dripping trophy of our late black friend had been already added, was a little wattled patch of desolation a kind heart would have called the garden. In it were a few moribund specimens of artemisia, prickly pear, and snapdragon, and in the midst a wild datura was giving up the ghost.

A Turkish village is a garbage-ridden chaos of straw stacks, thorn fences, brown tiles, and cur dogs. Many of the seeming stacks are wooden frames covered with thorns and straw, in which is kept chopped straw, the fodder of the kine. The white oxen and black buffaloes live inside similar sheds at night; and to-day our Mayor produced from his pocket so unlikely an object as a comb, and proceeded to groom with it a favourite buffalo cow. The stream which flows through Seliolo is now only a series of muddy pools, fringed with limestone rocks, and bordered by hacked and mutilated poplars, willows, elms, and aspens. A couple of unfinished or ruined bridges project themselves uselessly half-way across the sandy flats. We came across an unfortunate soldier doubled up and groaning in all the fearful agonies of colic, or was it cholera? From subsequent events I suspect it was the latter. We found a doctor, who rather ostentatiously pronounced it to be colic.

Then we visited the really immense farm of Delaver

Bey, a progressive Turk who has been Mayor of Adrianople but who has had the sense to refuse office under the Young Turks. Several months ago, foreseeing war, he sold all his grain and stock and took his family away.

His farm-buildings are entirely surrounded by a wall ten feet high, flanked by a peel-tower loopholed for musketry, whose walls are three feet thick. This tower is only eighty years old, but it is in a ruinous state, the centre being choked with the huge stones used in the walls. Within the curtain-wall are two yards, each about eighty yards square, with roofed sheds for cattle, two threshing machines, an engine, granaries, a living house (now being used as a hospital), and a wrecked and ruined garden. The huge vine that a few weeks ago trailed over the long pergola lies, hacked and dying, in the filthy mud ; the pergola itself has served for fuel. It is possible to recognise the stumps of what were once geraniums. Everywhere are strewn the dirty rags and indescribable litter of a Turkish camp ; with heaps of spent machine-gun cartridges, and all the evidences of men making haste to flee. Here was fought one of the most important actions which paved the way for the evacuation of Kirk Kilisse.

In this village of Seliolo, in 1903, many Bulgars tried to sell their property and emigrate. They were prevented by the Turks from selling, but nevertheless emigrated ; and in their houses Turks were installed by a paternal government. These Turks have now fled, and the woodwork of their purloined houses is being vigorously converted into firewood by their Bulgarian neighbours.

All day long the dogs bark, answering the boom of the big guns thundering round Adrianople. There is an unfinished white church on the side of the hill above the stream ; and the Papas, or Pope, or Pastor thereof is a dark-bearded man who wears a cassock and a miniature top-hat of silk.

M. Mateef is full of information, and his portmanteau is full of food. He plucked a plant and extracted the seeds, and gave them to me to eat, saying they were sesame and very good. When we got back he gave me some nougat-like stuff called sesame hulvar, which was quite nice, and reminiscent of "You shall each have a cake of sesame—and ten pound," Ruskin's immortal book, and Ali Baba.

In the afternoon we walked in the direction of the cart, and we had not gone more than a couple of miles over the oak-scrub-covered plain before Kostoff put up his glass and said, "Sie kommt." I could have sung a Te Deum for very joy; there were fresh raiment, and a bath, and sponges and towels and soap in that approaching cart!

Yes, at length the little flags hove in view, and all doubts were at an end. I could have hugged the mud-stained form of George. That evening I discovered on the wall a cartoon representing a huge John Bull holding a duck in both hands, while a diminutive Greek on one side and a tiny Turk on the other tugged violently at his flowing yellow whiskers. I suppose it had some reference to Crete. We went to bed about nine, and the lice and fleas were perfectly awful. Even Alexander, who must have had a comprehensive acquaintance with such gentry, complained in the morning of the ravages of the " petits enfants."

November 6. We sent off the cart at 5 A.M., and got off in the motors at 9, after bidding farewell to the Mayoress and her little Irene. Mateef was furious because I put a modicum of baggage on to his car; he said I should break the springs, and altogether made himself very unpleasant. The drive back to Kirk Kilisse was not agreeable; Mateef was sulky because his predictions as to the springs of his motor were not fulfilled ; the farther we went without broken springs the sulkier he got.

We got safely back to Kirk Kilisse by one o'clock, and learned the glad tidings of the departure of Arnaoudhoff. In the afternoon we went shopping in the crowded, acacia-fringed, narrow little streets, where proud little ponies with blue beads on their harness jostled ox-carts full of bandaged men, sallow-visaged, bearded, and dull-eyed.

After ten days of filth what a joy to have a bath ! Then dinner at the Officers' Club with three colonels, two of whom talk French, and one English ; and all are very agreeable. They tell us they captured forty guns at Lule Burgas, and fifty elsewhere, and 150,000 rounds of ammunition. Back down the cyclopean-stoned alley, sliding and slipping, and through the massy door, and so to bed in my own camp-bed, where I sleep as in a palace, with the stove blazing by my head to the accompaniment of Maxwell's snores.

November 7. Last night there was another fire, and the usual concomitants of frenzied firing and bell-ringing. Little Irene, our small but efficient housekeeper, comes and helps us to pack up, wearing a pair of Maxwell's stockings that he had burned a great hole in by putting them too near the stove chimney. Poor little Irene has hitherto been used to bare legs and feet, even in the coldest weather, and a miserable little cotton frock, much too small for her ; so to-day she surveys her nether garments with great pride, regardless of the large patch of pink leg surrounded by its circle of burnt stocking. With her black satin bow stuck jauntily on one side of her flaxen head she is quite a dainty little creature.

Then there is benzine to be sought for the motor, and Kostoff, for to-day we are off to the front, to see a battle at all hazards. I seek the benzine, and am refused it ; it is all to be kept for the military. Fortunately we have a fair supply in hand. Mateef has left in a huff, doubtless because his motor did not break down when he said it would. So, after the appallingly difficult task of getting all our baggage and ourselves into the motor, we bid farewell to little Irene and depart. Kostoff is nowhere to be found; and the dirty, pug-faced person is fortunately absent. The road to Yenno is one dense, black mass of soldiers, 15,000 at the least, and the huge, serpent-like trail winds for miles up hill and down dale, men, guns, and transport moving to the south and east. An officer comes galloping by; he brings a report that Adrianople has fallen, and a great wave of cheering runs down the huge column. Probably this report was deliberately invented to hearten up the men.

Finally the road, such as it was, ended where a great mass of shrapnel and broken ammunition-wagons lay in the mud, and we emerged upon a boggy upland incredibly muddy, and dotted with pools of black water. The agonies of getting the motor over that abandoned Serbonian bog!

If it stuck once, it stuck fifty times, and at last, close above the village of Yenno, violent concussion against rocks knocked the bottom-plate into the fly-wheel, and the handle would not turn when we tried to restart the car.

If the exterior of Yenno was remarkable for its rocks, the interior was, even in Turkey, and that is saying a good deal, remarkable for its filth. The streets were so narrow that the motor could hardly get through them, and all alike were decorated with sheeps' heads and feet, paunches, and blood. We put up at the house of M. Kostaki, a very hospitable Greek gentleman, whose house was particularly clean and well furnished, and arrived very soon at the conclusion that in future the splendid little motor would be useless to us.

November 8. The house of M. Kostaki is blue-washed, and blue-washed also are the paraffin tins in the little garden, in which oleanders, stock, and geraniums flourish.

The first business was to get horses. Of course we were told that there were none to be had. How could there be ? First the Turks had carried off all those above ground, and then the Bulgars had searched the cellars. But it is unwise ever to believe natives ; horses we must and would have. So at length we were conducted, by devious sewage-channels, to the house of a certain horse-coper, with Alexander in attendance as interpreter.

When the wicket in the huge door was opened we saw three woe-begone Rosinantes hanging their heads in the mud, and two wretched women sitting listlessly on their doorstep. When Alexander spoke to the elder one she burst into tears ; all her belongings have been pillaged, first by the Turks, and then by the Bulgars. There is nothing left but the three horses, which they managed to hide underground. For two of these half-starved crocks the wily Greek wants £40. We realise that he will eventually take £20, and depart, with well-assumed indignation, for the house of the excellent M. Kostaki. As we sit in the little garden drinking black coffee provided by our kind hostess and her daughters, there is a knock at the garden door. A poor, broken-down, emaciated woman is admitted. She asks for bread ; she has absolutely nothing, and is starving. We give her a little food and some money. But will that provide her with food in this sacked and pillaged village ? I doubt it. There is a terrible sadness in such scenes as this. Such is war : mutilated men and weeping women, and children crying for their bread.

The haggling with the horse-coper dragged on, while I looked at the ivy on the wall, and the carnations in buckets, and a few meagre chrysanthemums ; it was delightful to see a flower again. At last a white-haired professor took a hand in the chaffering, and I strongly suspect he hinted at the bastinado if a bargain were not speedily struck—a bargain in which he appeared to take rather more than a Platonic interest; for when the coper finally came down to ten guineas per horse we closed, and the professor very kindly suggested that we should hand the money over to him, and that he would pay the coper. We smelt a rat here, and I at once handed my ten guineas to the coper in English gold, but whether the professor ever got any of it I am unable to say. I think he must have been a Professor of Political Economy, specially versed in the Theory of Exchange.

My purchase was a little bay stallion, about 13.3, called Harriet. Harriet is the Turkish for liberty; and so the name seemed doubly inappropriate; for there is no liberty in Turkey, and Harriet is a lady's name. However, I waived all that, and continued to address the stallion as Harriet. And then a horrible thing happened. I went to the cart for my saddle; it was not there. That scoundrel, Alexander the coppersmith, *alias* cook, had done me much evil. He had ridden on my saddle to Kirk Kilisse when he deserted the cart, and now he had left it behind by mistake. So he said. The villain, of course, had sold it. Without wages he was dismissed to return to Kirk Kilisse, and to fetch back the saddle. He burst into tears, and fawned on us like a dog; but I was in no mood to be placated. I had to borrow an old Turkish abomination from our host, the stirrups of which were so small that I could not get my feet into them. Stirrupless, then, I rode a couple of hundred miles; and every mile I rode I cursed Alexander the coppersmith with bell, book, and candle.

The village was full of burnt houses, and as we rode on our way southwards blazing villages were seen everywhere. At length we got to the now famous village of Bunar Hissar, the northernmost point of the long fighting-line which had extended thence to Lule Burgas ten days before. No correspondents had been allowed to escape from Kirk Kilisse until all was over.

Bunar Hissar was a filthy medley of burnt houses and mud, and our jaded, ill-fed mounts stumbled horribly amid the rock-strewn pools of the main street. Close to the church, about half of which is built below the level of the ground—a symbol of Christian inferiority,—was a long line of fresh graves ; each had its rough, stick-like wooden cross. These were all officers. One of them, called Gregoroff, had four or five crosses, all jumbled together, large and small, some painted, some inscribed, and surmounted by a kind of miniature umbrella.

We were given some bread by a kind soldier (bread was a luxury for us !), and luncheoned without the village on a white stone, which stood solitary in a sea of mud in which a few tobacco-plants were eking out a miserable existence. A Greek priest came by, with a servant, both riding, and M. went off with them, and was seen no more.

I thought it my duty to stay with the cart, and that day's and night's work I shall never forget as long as I live. The huge mounds on the plain that marked the graves of 10,000 Turkish and Bulgarian soldiers were a melancholy sight enough, but the jibbing cart-horses affected me more. The going was incredibly bad—ruts two feet deep, and black mud of a tenacity that defies description. The climax seemed reached when, in the dark, we stuck midway across a stream, against a boulder. The horses jibbed ; George flogged ; it was all no use. At last the brilliant idea occurred to me of dismounting and attaching Harriet to the cart, by means of a spare pair of traces I had providently bought in Kirk Kilisse. It was great fun wading about up to one's middle in that river, but Harriet was a good puller, and managed, with Alexander and me pushing behind, to get the cart off the boulder.

Here we passed some trenches, and saw a soldier skinning a not recently dead horse. Then we got lost. It was nearly pitch-dark ; there was no track, and there was a steep ascent in front of us, and the horses were dead beat. So were we. It was a charming situation. We had very little food, and no idea of the direction to take. With fearful exertions we got the cart to the top of the bank, and then, to our intense delight, we felt ourselves on a hard road—quite a good road for Turkey.

One of the grey cart-horses—he who had jibbed and kicked so lustily in the stream—was so done that he had to be taken out and led. Alexander and I walked behind the cart, he dragging the horse along. Suddenly I heard Alexander stop George, and saw the wily Armenian clamber up the back of the wagon and lean drowsily over the top. Thus precariously perched, for a fall backwards would have killed him, Mr. Alexander the chauffeur went fast asleep like a stork, still dragging his horse behind him. The road and the darkness got worse, so I lit a candle-lamp and walked in front. It was lucky I did so, for soon I came on a chasm in the roadway that would have engulfed ten of our carts, horses and all, and assuredly broken everybody's neck. It was a terrific hole, over ten feet deep. We got past this obstruction with great difficulty, and then both men seemed inclined to chuck it. They sat down by the roadside and groaned. I also sat down and groaned. I gave them a drink of wine and some chocolate, and they felt better.

About half-past ten, after twelve hours of incessant hard work, we came on flickering bivouac fires, and the steep hill that leads up to Visa. At the top of the hill, just where the village begins, the road was completely blocked with medical transport. The carts were parked there for the night; the oxen had gone to bed. No chance of getting our cart through. It was the kind of thing that makes one swear. I got a stable for the horses, and the cart was put behind the great door of the yard, in a spot which had been used for all sorts of purposes. There I had to get out our scanty supper and eat it. I shall never forget the horrors of that meal. But some excellent doctor got wind of my misfortunes, and sent an orderly to fetch me down to the house where he was quartered. As we passed along the silent and deserted street, suddenly, above our heads, rang out the most appalling shriek I had ever heard up to that day. I heard others like it later on. Then came groans and ejaculations and mutterings. "Turkish hospital," said the orderly. Cholera, sure enough. That shriek is unmistakable when you've heard enough of them; but at the time I supposed it was a wounded man, deserted and left to die alone. What a day! Every note of suffering seemed to have been sounded: women's tears; men's groans; dogs tearing madly at the bloody entrails of horses in the juniper-bushes.

The orderly took me down the village; and at about half-past eleven I was accommodated with a window-seat by the kindly medicos, and slept the sleep of the utterly worn-out.

November 9. We marched from Visa to Serai—the Palace—and overtook the headquarters of the Third Army, commanded by General Radko Dimitrieff. The day was chiefly remarkable for the sight of the evidences of the encounter at Tatarli, where guns, a motor-car, with two dead men inside, and the chauffeur dead beside it, and hundreds of corpses lay inextricably jumbled in the black mud. One of the ghastliest of sights. But not so ghastly as the sight at one of the sacked and burnt villages we passed that day, where a correspondent took a photograph of a disembowelled Christian woman, with the fœtus beside her trampled underfoot.

Children were hacked to pieces by these dastardly Turks, particularly at Ivalli, near Lule Burgas. These brutalities have excited in the Bulgarians the spirit of vengeance. In the oak-scrub which surrounds Serai we found poor women hiding in rude shelters made of boughs.

What they had lived on, God knows. They looked like skeletons. As the Bulgarian troops came up they returned, a mass of muddy rags, to their houses. In one village I passed through, where the Turks had first outraged the women and then killed them, there was a large pig with its head cut half in two. The fanatics ! There is no room in Europe for a religion which lays down what people and what animals are accursed in God's eyes.

We dine at the club (*sic*) in Serai, and drink coffee and listen to a prosy politician of a doctor. At dinner there were four French, three Russian, and two English correspondents crowded at a table hardly big enough for four. The food was perfectly odious : onions covered with vinegar, and black, greasy olives, with tough cold mutton. That was the first meeting of all the correspondents— nine then, and ten when Fox came—who, out of 150 who left Sofia, managed to see the battle of Tchataldja.

November 10. At Kirk Kilisse we had laid in two glorious Rehoboams of generous yellow wine, excellent stuff ; and yesterday, apparently, George and Alexander drank most of it. Our new censor-in-charge, a dark, pale-faced, quiet man, who talks English, hears us rebuking the servants, intervenes, and tells the guilty pair in their native language that he will give twenty-five lashes to any one who steals the smallest thing. At this Alexander turned pea-green.

We get the order to march 20 kilometres to the village of Istrandja, at the foot of the mountains of the same name.

The country now improves ; we get on to undulating ground, covered with oak-scrub, and in the dry, sandy soil grow heather and rock-roses, bracken and brambles. We came on two dead Turks, head to head in the roadway, and scores of dead horses. There is a tree hereabouts with foliage of a gorgeous apricot colour ; and against the purple hills I noted a patch of vivid crimson, in front of which a white minaret lifted up its slender head. A really pretty spot, and such a relief after the *triste* drab monotony of the past fortnight.

Near Istrandja there are clumps of fair-sized oaks—all that remains of the great forest that once clothed this country. The village lies well against the furrowed hillside; there are green grass, and red scrub, and yellow leaves, and a stream meanders through the lower fields. Two little white streamers float over a newly-dug grave. Here is collected mile upon mile of ox and buffalo transport. The architecture of this Greek village is picturesque and peculiar. For about ten feet up the houses are built of stone, in which there are no windows; above this the second floor is composed of thin red bricks set herring-bone-wise in mud.

We were given rooms at the house of the village priest, Papas Pandeli by name, where we were very hospitably received. The tall-hatted, bearded, dignified old man gave me the run of his kitchen; and I soon had ready a savoury meal of onions and macaroni.

November 11. Have just returned from an interview with General Dimitrieff—a most amiable and courteous man, beloved by his troops; middle-sized, dark, a black moustache, hair drooping Napoleonically over a square forehead, and an alert, direct expression. Amongst other things he said : (1) Tchataldja will be attacked. (2) The Nizam army there consists of about 105,000 men, already demoralised. (3) He has enough men to take the lines. (4) He has about 120 guns captured from the Turks, but no horses to draw them. (5) In the big fight at Bunar Hissar—Lule Burgas Turks probably lost 40,000 men, since the Bulgars lost about 6000 (6) Every available Bulgar is in the field, and the wounded keep returning to their corps; boys and girls do the postal work in the towns. (7) The attackable part of the Tchataldja position is 20 kilometres wide, and defended by old guns. He feels

certain he will take it.   General Kutincheff commands the
First Army, with which Dimitrieff will co-operate.

November 12. Perhaps the most tiring day I ever spent
in my life. Got up at six, and felt pains in legs, back, and
head. This due to the stenches and water of Istrandja,
incomparably the dirtiest place on earth. We marched to
Ermenekeui, close to Tchataldja. The track baffles
description. The country is a series of oak-scrub-covered
undulations, with narrow valleys holding streams of
varying depths and impracticability. The previous
passage of guns had churned the ground into ruts a foot
deep. The headquarters' baggage was drawn by plucky
little ponies, whose efforts were magnificent. I saw three
of them down within fifty yards of one another. First one
wheel is high in air, then the other ; how the carts retain
their equilibrium is a mystery. The soldier lying atop
must have a rather shaky time of it.

The cavalcade is guided by a bare-headed, curly-
headed, black-avised ruffian in a brown coat and red sash,
mounted bareback on a pony. The type of gentleman I
should distinctly avoid on a dark night.

From 8 A.M. to 9.30 P.M. we laboured over the awful
track. At 5.30 it was dark, and thenceforward life
became almost unendurable. My pony fell several times,
and then I got off and fell myself ; after that he knocked
me down, and a cart all but went over me ; and then I got
off the track and was tripped up in the oak-scrub, until at
last I found salvation on the tail-board of a cart, to which
I tied up Master Harriet, and so bumped and jolted on,
until the ascents forced me to get off and help push. My
long field-boots were covered with clay up to their very
tops. De Segonzac, who has travelled all over Morocco,
says that he never in his life saw such bad roads.

At 9 P.M., as we stumbled on in the dark, it was a
splendid sight suddenly to see, far below us, the dancing
bivouac fires of 50,000 men. Roueski, our censor-in-

charge, was half afraid it was the Turks; but he was so done that he said he did not care whether he was killed or not.

The country we passed through to-day was far and away the most interesting of any yet seen. On the north the rolling hills faded into the Black Sea, of which I caught two glimpses; and under the ubiquitous oak-scrub grew heather and rock roses and hellebore. At one point we got into quite a respectable wood of good oaks, like a pheasant cover at home; and there wild roses grew tall, and a herd of white cattle roamed about with their tenor bells tinkling musically. We passed several villages, with the usual litter of maize and sheep's paunches, but not a solitary inhabitant was to be seen. Here and there were bright emerald patches of grass and young corn, and occasionally a patch of tobacco. It was interesting to cross the great wall of the Roman Emperor Anastasius, now the home of the oak-scrub, and levelled almost to the ground, yet with the remains of a flanking-tower or two still discernible.

How glad I was when, at 10 P.M., I found my quarters, had a glass of water, and lay down in my clothes on the floor, feeling very ill, and soaked with sweat and mud!

November 13. One of the most perfect days imaginable. A bright sun, as hot as May in England, tempered by a breeze. We all feel too hot; and this is the campaign in which we were to be frostbitten! There are two regiments here (one Bulgarian regiment contains 4600 men), and one of them goes tomorrow into the hills.

Ermenekeui is a small village of about a hundred detached houses, prosperous because of its tobacco, now hanging up to dry in every hall, and permeating the whole house with its heavy pungent smell. The streets are muddy, but not the V-shaped drains of Istrandja; and the air is bracing and healthy. The village lies in a hollow, surrounded by low oak-scrub-covered hills.

The cart, with all that makes life worth living within it, turned up before noon ; and Alexander almost wept as he recounted the horrors of the march. The poor fellows spent the night out in the open with hardly any food. When the baggage came in, our room was a curious medley of East and West, of the retreating female and the advancing male. Rugs, pillows, valises, and a rubber bath jostled native-painted trunks, and a brand-new pair of stays, which Maxwell averred did not belong to him. From the walls looked down the Greek and Austrian royal families, and a curious " mausoleum " of the heroes of the war of Greek independence—blue-uniformed gentry ascending by steps into Heaven. The soldiers sit, naked to the waist, mending their washen shirts, and revelling in the sunshine. This village is a packed congeries of bandit-like soldiers (not their fault, brave lads !), cavalry horses, hairy pigs in wattled enclosures, and great wind-screens of tobacco stalks.

There is a large and excellent spring of water on the confines of the village, ever thronged with natives and soldiers. Nobody here will drink unboiled water, except myself : *Kismet*. There is a day fixed for the death of every man. The big guns at Tchataldja keep up an intermittent fire all day.

November 14. Night, and day too, for that matter, is made hideous in this house with the incessant wailing of children ; and the odour resulting from a combination of drains and drying tobacco is not conducive to health. Again a lovely day, and my little thermometer stands so persistently at 74° F. that I fancy that it must be out of order. The Papas is walking round the village with holy water, a sprig of hyssop, and a crucifix, blessing the troops before they go into action. Regarding the scene with the impartial eye of the Protestant, I suddenly find myself confronted by the good Papas, the hyssop is dashed into my face, willy nilly, and I did not dare to wipe my face with my handkerchief. So, half-blinded and streaming, I stood in the sun, and told myself that I was now a Catholic. Close by, a lady, instead of opening a window, poked out her head through the aperture caused by a broken pane, and, thus aureoled, conversed at length with a friend in the street below.

This was a day of adventures. M. had two friends, a captain and a lieutenant, who offered to take us to a village called Kurdkeui, where lived a strange race of half-savage Kurds—men who say they left Bulgaria four hundred years ago, and eighty years ago became Moslems.

We rode to the village, half-hidden in an oak-wood, with a meadow of green grass stretching in front of it. The inhabitants were assembled in two groups for our inspection ; the men in one group, the women and children in another. A more miserable-looking set of savages I never saw. They have the long black hair, hooked noses, and pale complexion of the Afghans ; the women's noses are more hooked than the men's. They wear white homespun clothes, with a red sash, and no headgear. Most of the women's clothes were falling off them in rags, and the children were nearly naked, and covered with foul sores. They live by charcoal-burning, cattle, and a little cultivation. Their huts are tiled, and their bakehouses are in the open. All were terribly emaciated ; a sickening sight.

Presently the two officers disappeared, and all of a sudden two revolver shots were heard, and shouting in the lower part of the village. I told Maxwell they must have found some Turks, and ran round a house to get a better view. There I saw our big captain, with naked sabre, slashing at the back of a man who was running for dear life with a sack behind him. The lieutenant was similarly engaged. When they had had enough running, they came back, and told us they were punishing looters out of their own army ! This is the way the Bulgarians understand discipline! This is how they have made their army invincible!

As we rode back to Ermenekeui, M. asked the captain if he would ride with us in the afternoon to the top of a certain hill, from which is obtained a good view of the lines of Tchataldja, and both the Black Sea and the Ægean. After much importunity General Dimitrieff had given M. leave to go there. The captain refused point-blank, and said it was far too dangerous, as the hill-sides were full of lurking brigands, looking out for a stray Bulgar or two. (Certainly suspicious rifle-shots were heard at frequent intervals in the woods round Ermene-keui.)

M. now asked the lieutenant to go, and he also refused, alleging the same reason as the captain. M. was now on his mettle; he had so frequently declared his determination to get to the top of that hill that nothing could deter him. He went off to lunch with the lieutenant; and his arguments prevailed. The lieutenant consented to come, and would bring his sergeant. I was riding the big grey cart-horse that day, and not the inadequate Harriet, and very glad I was when we had finished.

Our way lay at first through young corn, and then on to the hill slopes, where vines grew under fig and other fruit trees, and boys were herding cattle. There was no track; we could see the mountain; I took the lead and went straight for it. Presently we got out of the region of cultivation; the boys and tinkling cows were far behind; the sandy uplands were dotted with heather and dwarf arbutus. Then there loomed in sight a precipitous descent into a ravine, covered with brambles and rose-bushes and other obstructions.

To get up the mountain we must cross that ravine. I got off and led the good grey down that horrid declivity, with the brambles and rose-bushes doing their best to stop us. M. followed me, but the lieutenant and his sergeant made off to the left, and the last I saw of the lieutenant was at the top of a path leading down into the ravine, down which his sergeant had preceded him, and joined us at the bottom. It was now fairly plain sailing to the top of the mountain, though the going was none too good, owing to large stones and tough arbutus scrub. I pushed on as fast as I could, with the sergeant beside me, but M. dropped back, his horse not being quite as good as ours. Presently I heard him shout, and stopped and shouted back what was the matter. He replied, " I see a man lying down on that hill ! " As he had a telescope, and was using it, and the top of the hill was only 400 yards from us, I thought it was no time for the sergeant and me to be doing nothing, and offering pot shots. I motioned to the sergeant to draw his sabre, and myself drew and cocked my revolver ; and side by side we galloped as hard as we could go in the direction of the enemy. We saw no man ; he had probably retired when M. shouted.

The view from this hill was very lovely in that clear yellow evening light. Rolling moorlike country stretches away to the north until it falls down to the Black Sea, covered with tinkling herds, and dotted with lone villages. In front a great plain rises into the misty undulations of Tchataldja ; and to the south lie the marshy flats which border the inlet of Boyuk Tchekmedje. We could see a Turkish war-ship in the little landlocked inlet ; and in front of it a village was in flames.

Down below us long sinuous lines of Bulgarian infantry were marching northwards to take up their positions. But we had to cut short the pleasure of gazing at that historic panorama, for it would soon be dark, and we had a longish way to go.

We now began to get anxious about the lieutenant. Where was he ? Had he gone quietly back to camp ? Or had a marauding Turk snaffled him ? We got back to the gorge; and still no sign. Then we went up the steep path by which the sergeant had come down. I was leading, and suddenly I saw a sight which gave me a shock. There was the lieutenant's cap, lying by the side of the path. I turned and went back to the others, with the cap in my hand.

When the sergeant saw it I thought he would go mad. Evidently he was very fond of the lieutenant. He turned his horse, and dashed at full gallop into the ravine, and up the far bank, and along the slope, shouting as he went. M. and I were left to examine the spot where I found the cap. There was no blood, no sign of a struggle, and the bushes had not been broken. I walked on and found the track of a horse going upwards. That settled it; the lieutenant had quietly ridden home to tea. I told M. this, but he jeered at the idea of an officer going home without his cap: *non bene relicta parmula* kind of idea.

When I said I was going home to find the lieutenant, M. was most indignant, and reproached me for my unfeeling conduct. But when the sergeant, who, like myself, had done a little tracking in his time, had come on the returning horse-tracks, and galloped past us up the path, with me in hot pursuit, M. eventually changed his mind about stopping out to look for the lieutenant, for when, ten minutes later, the sergeant and I ran into our quarry, coming back in a very battered cap to look for his new one, M. was not very far behind us, and not in the least disconcerted at the upsetting of all his theories. When I handed the lieutenant his cap he was very grateful, for in it he had hidden some valuable documents.

Our house is a veritable Inferno of noise and stench. The children yell continuously; the drying tobacco exudes its heavy, sickly smell; the hall is full of garlic-diffusing soldiers; upstairs No. 15 contributes its terrible quota to the poisonous compound. Garlic is eaten in huge quantities by everybody, from the general downwards, because of its microbe-destroying properties. It is held to be a prophylactic against cholera. The house is of wood, with plastered walls covered with a blue distemper which comes off on to one's clothes, bedding, and pyjamas; added to the yells of half a dozen children is the exasperating tick-a-tick of M.'s typewriter; outside cocks crow, asses bray, horses neigh, and oxen bellow; next door officers get up and go in and out at all hours of the night. Every banging door shakes the place to its rotten foundations. Outside are a few stunted acacia trees, a wooden belfry surmounted by a cross, not far from the little church; an open space, now walled in for cavalry horses; everywhere the reek of fires, and little groups of squads squatting round the central pot, into which each man thrusts his spoon in turn, and ladles out not undelectable soup.

November 15. Wake up feeling very ill; turn to the invaluable Burroughs & Wellcome, whose tabloids are a real boon to travellers. I stated my complaint, through the medium of the eyes, to Messrs. B. & W.; they had already printed my prescription; it was salol. I took salol, and was cured. Wonderful telepathic, not homœopathic, doctors are Messrs. B. & W.! See Von Dreyer, who says Angus Hamilton,* correspondent of the *Daily News*, was taken prisoner by the Bulgarians at Tchorlu; and as he was in Turkish dress they manacled him.

Saïd Pasha, the Turkish commander at Tchataldja, has sent a flag of truce to the Bulgarian outposts to discuss terms. The Turks will surrender with the honours of war. The Bulgarians want unconditional surrender. It is still 74° F. in the shade.

In the evening all the bands play gaily, for General Savoff, the Commander-in-Chief, is expected. However, he does not come.

The men of the Seventh Regiment hold a great sing-

* Angus Hamilton died in June last.

song, and stirring patriotic airs draw hundreds of poor homesick fellows to the open doors and windows. Brave as lions as they are, the tears run down many a bearded cheek.

In the mess to-day a medico told the story of a man of twenty-five who lost his way in a wood. The Turks took him ; cut off his nose, ears, and tongue ; and then conducted him back to his parents' house. There he lingered three days and died.

The most celebrated doctor in Sofia went on active service. He had just dressed a Turk's wounds. The Turk raised his rifle and shot him dead.

November 16. At 7.30 A.M. the temperature is 60° F. Slept well, and feel all right again. A glorious day ; what a pleasure to see so much of the sun ! The Pomaks in the woods have cut up ten men close by here ; and a lot of Macedonians are being sent to wipe them out. We were lucky not to meet them the other day. I walked with the Frenchmen to see the blown-up railway bridge at Karabachkeui, and the pace set by Segonzac was terrific. On the way we met a cavalryman sitting on his saddle by the roadside, and in the road was his dead horse. We had to jump a fairish brook, which Puaux cleared in grand style. He told me that yesterday he was watching some troops march in, and saw an officer knouting a soldier over his face, from which the blood ran down in streams. The poor fellow was so done that he could hardly struggle along. And this was the gentle persuasion ! Verily iron is Bulgarian discipline.

The bridge at Karabachkeui is the ordinary iron structure, built on girders, and it has been most thoroughly demolished. Its loss is of little strategic importance to the Bulgars, since stores can be brought up by rail to Sinekli, a very few miles in rear of Karabachkeui.

The following were dictated to me by Colonel Asmanoff, chief censor at Ermenekeui :

"*November* 3. To-day at Bunar Hissar the following *procès verbal* has been addressed by the Commander of the First Brigade of the Fifth Division—Colonel Abadjieff —to the Commander-in-Chief of the Third Army. ' After the battle which, during four days, took place to the south of Bunar Hissar, when we began to bury our dead, we found among them some on which we saw traces of mutilation and atrocity, as well on the dead as on the wounded who had remained some time in the enemy's zone. The fate of thirteen men of the Twentieth Regiment of infantry—His Royal Highness Prince Cyril of Preslav's Own—was particularly atrocious. These soldiers, being wounded, had received first aid from Bulgarian doctors, and had been grouped in a position, but for want of time had to be left in the hands of the enemy, who then atrociously murdered them. In proof of which, etc., etc.' "

" BUNAR HISSAR, *November* 4. After the battle to the south of this place, among the dead we found soldiers whose heads had been cut off, others who had been murdered with picks ; other had their ears cut off ; among them Captain Tzanikaramad-Drakoff ; others had their tongues cut out, etc.

(Signed) *Dr.-in-Chief of Second Regiment*, ISKER.
Dr. Major, TODOROFF.
Dr. of Battalion, MIOLUCHEFF.
Dr., ASCHER.
Dr., ASTROOK.
Papas, RAITCHEV."

November 17. The day of days has arrived and passed ; we have seen the first episode of the battle of Tchataldja.

We correspondents, whose number has now been increased to ten by the arrival of Mr. Fox of the *Morning Post*, an Australian who has made a plucky ride with a craven servant across a dangerous country in order to see the battle, were assembled under the command of M. Tcheprachikoff, the King of Bulgaria's secretary, and filed off into the hills about 7 A.M. The ground rose gradually until at length, after about an hour and a half's ride, we came down into the white village of Arkalon, clinging to its steep brown hill across the stream. Then we climbed a steep flank above the village, and found ourselves at the Bulgarian headquarters. In front of us was a deep valley, with a village to the north, and the dressing-station in front of us; in front of these again loomed big hills, on which the Bulgarians had disposed their batteries; to north and to south gleamed the seas; and in front, ridge after ridge culminated in the peaks of the distant mountains of Asia Minor.

It was a grey, cloudy day, with some rain. At 9.30 the artillery cannonade began; at eleven the machine guns joined in the fray, and by 11.30 the rifles were speaking. When the concert achieved its fortissimo the noise was splendid. The whole heaven was white with the little shrapnel clouds; below us the ground was torn up with ineffectual bullets. It was soon apparent that this was a reconnaissance, in order to test the lines of advance; and before the day closed, it seemed equally obvious that the Bulgarians were massing their men to the north, in order to force the Turkish right. I cannot give any details; none of us saw any. The King's secretary occasionally moved us a few yards to the right or left, as the shrapnel moved him; but to see anything more than a great twenty-mile panorama of warfare, with all the broad outline and none of the detail, was of course impossible.

All of us felt that we had witnessed one of the most magnificent spectacles, in a magnificent setting, it is given to mankind to see. Going home to Ermenekeui our censor, Rueski, a banker of Rustchuk, lost his way; and we had to find a way through the oak-scrub before it got dark, which was no easy matter. Fox was on a borrowed cavalry horse, which bolted with him at every opportunity.

November 18. Last night there was a terrific wind, which broke a branch off a tree near the house, and it fell into the window of the room Fox and I now inhabit. The crash woke both of us up at 3.15 A.M., and subsequently we had rather more ventilation than we deemed essential to health.

At eight we ride out again to the battlefield, carefully shepherded by the King's secretary and Rueski, over the road across the hills, now being corduroyed in the worst places. The rain falls fast, and there is a driving mist which obscures everything. At Arkalon the houses are full of sick and wounded; dysentery and cholera are playing havoc with the army. There is no forage for the horses, and food for the men is getting short. In my humble opinion it is a thousand pities that this misguided attack was ever made.

It was absolutely impossible to see anything at all of the fight, owing to the fog. I saw one sight I do not want to see again, and that was a soldier rolling on the ground in the agonies of cholera. As the day wore on, the lines of ox-wagons taking back the wounded grew ominously long. One thing was evident: the Bulgarian attack on the north was being pressed with the utmost determination.

The Bulgarian guns have advanced a little since yesterday, but not very much. These French guns are infinitely superior in every respect to the Turkish-German guns—in length, in accuracy, and in the fusing of their shrapnel.

The rain of bullets that their *rafale* poured down upon the unfortunate Turks must have done fearful execution. At one moment of the fray a huge vulture, as large as a condor, hovered greedily high in air.

One of the French officers calls this " une bataille sur

une digue " (breakwater or jetty). The comparison is apt. There is a front of 20 kilometres, and neither side can effect a turning movement; it must be all straight slogging. As for the greater part of the day we could see absolutely nothing, most of the correspondents spent their time lighting fires in trenches, at which to warm their hands and dry their handkerchiefs. It was raining all the time, and the cold was awful. I had a thick fur coat on, and shivered in it. Headquarters very kindly gave us lunch; and the grilled mutton and hot tea was decidedly refreshing. Then the slightly wounded began to stream past us to the rear. One fellow, fearfully bloody about the head, was led tenderly by the hand, like a little child, by a wounded comrade; another was carrying his long boot, and limping along with his gaiter a mass of clotted gore; others went on one leg, and used their rifles as crutches. There was that uncanny battle-tired look in the eyes of them all. One beardless lad had an expression on his face that I cannot describe and shall never forget.

At the outskirts of Arkalon, as we returned to camp, we passed two stretchers being carried reverently into the town. They held the bodies of the colonel and major of the Fourth Regiment. We none of us were in very good spirits as we rode back; evidently the decisive attack had failed.

These Bulgars are such splendid fighting-men that a repulse will only tend to make them more than ever determined to get through.

9 P.M. Have just returned from mess, and sit down to write out statement spontaneously given by Colonel Jostoff, Chief of the Staff of the Third Army, which practically amounts to a confession that the Bulgarians have bitten off more than they can chew.

" 1. Dysentery is accounting for thousands.

" 2. Cholera has appeared.

" 3. To-day the Fourth Regiment, in the fog, got

between two Turkish forts, and was nearly wiped out: the colonel, a major, and several captains killed.

" 4. We hoped to cross this wall, but we didn't expect to have to reckon with sickness.

" 5. To-morrow we shall do nothing, and you correspondents will remain at home."

How sorry I am for the gallant Dimitrieff! It is said that the country between Tchataldja and Constantinople is a seething mass of refugees, and that the epidemics originated there. Altogether not a very bright outlook. There were 450 Bulgarian guns in action to-day.

November 19. I left London exactly a month ago : how much has been crowded into it! Everybody is dejected about the repulse, and a good many are frightened about cholera. The precautions against it in the mess are rather amusing. The mess, by the way, is in the former inn of the village—a brown wooden two-storeyed house ; and the long arm of Britain appears in the legend, " British America," over the door. I suspect it is an insurance company.

The room on the left of the door is the kitchen, the room on the right the mess. Upstairs are the censors' offices ; but as no news whatever is allowed to get through, both they and the correspondents may be said to be *functi officiis*.

The mess-room is quite a small place and is always most uncomfortably crowded. It is full of flies and smells, and a couple of canaries are hung up in a cage near the roof. In the middle is a fearsome lamp, which is pumped up with air, and then emits a flare which would put the biggest acetylene head-lamp to shame. In fact, there is rather too much light. On the wall is a coloured print of a bloodthirsty character, all overturned guns and slaughtered blue-uniformed Italians ; while the majestic equestrian Turks drive the remnant of the invaders through the palm-forest into the sea.

The head cook is an officer of sorts : an obese gentleman in a blue frock-coat, who wears his hair long, and his cap on the back of his head. If the food is not up to standard he can be court-martialled and shot. I cannot for the life of me understand why he is still alive. But General Dimitrieff is universally beloved for his kindly nature.

The first operation is the solemn disinfecting of knives, forks, and spoons. Several large bowls full of boiling water are brought in and passed round ; and into the bowl each man dips his cutlery, holds it there a second or two, and passes the bowl on to his neighbour. The only logical outcome of this system would appear to be, that if one man's fork should chance to have the cholera it would give it to all the others.

After the aseptic treatment of the cutlery, boiled water, nice and hot, is brought, and each man's glass filled. I always had a suspicion that the water which went out after the knife-disinfecting reappeared to appease our thirst ; but this may be doing the head cook officer a cruel injustice.

The food is frankly horrible—greasy, ill-cooked, nauseating. Brown gritty bread and the goat-scented soft white cheese are about the best things on the menu.

November 20. Horses' backs in very bad state, especially M.'s, which has a hole two inches deep. I doctor them as best I can. Read *Turkey in Europe*, by Odysseus, who is really Sir Charles Elliot—an excellent work, which, though nearly twenty years old, would not be out of date to-day if there were any Turkey in Europe left. I cooked a chicken in butter for lunch, and it was much approved of. The Frenchmen are going to Jamboli, they say. Saw Dimitrieff, who says the two days' cannonade of Tchataldja was a reconnaissance, which has fixed the Turkish position. " It is a fortress which must be reduced by siege operations." He is sending for siege-guns. Sickness very greatly retards things. Of peace negotiations he has heard a rumour, but nothing official. " Il faut de patience." Walk in afternoon with Fox and M., and discuss question of staying or going. Fox, in his khaki suit, putties, Sam Brown belt, and enormous furry gloves and cap, looks like a Territorial under orders for the Arctic. We finally decide to go, and return if any developments occur.

November 21. A beautiful day, sunny and hot, and the cart is loaded up, and the jaded nags got out and our leave taken of Ermenekeui. We marched to Karabachkeui, and past its broken bridge to Sinekli, and as we crossed over the high ridges above the latter place we looked back and saw the last of Ermenekeui, nestling in its green hollow amid the fulvous woods.

Sinekli is the rail-head, and it is also a cholera camp. There is a dingy brown house, with some clothes hung out to dry from a window, about sixty yards from the line, and round it walks a sentry with fixed bayonet. We have to wait for our train and load up our baggage within a hundred yards of this plague-spot. The fourgon we are given holds baggage in ordinary times, but to-day it holds twelve men, including the Frenchmen's four servants, and all our baggage, which produces a state of congestion impossible to exaggerate. Just before the train started, at 7 P.M., there broke out the ghastly, oft-repeated, blood-curdling screams of a soldier struck down with cholera. They lasted about three minutes, and during that time not a soul in our wagon spoke.

Segonzac and Puaux have got a bed of straw, but I find my camp chair, close to the great open side of the fourgon, very comfortable. It is a delight to watch the dark clouds scurrying across the brilliant moon, and the great cumuli of engine-steam trying to imitate the clouds. The Man in the Moon smiled broadly all night.

November 22. When the train stopped in the early morning at Baba Eski—a featureless place on a drab

plain, with only barrack-like buildings in sight beside
the new red-tiled station, terrible scenes took place,
quite indescribable. Suffice it to say that we were in the
same train with the cholera and dysentery patients. One
poor fellow, wounded in the hand, and suffering from
dysentery, dragged himself back to the train, and hung his
head on the footplate of the engine, tired of everything.
It was a pathetic sight. Even the tops of the tall fourgons
are covered with white-robed figures getting by hook or
by crook to Lozengrad.

There we arrived about 11 A.M., and found our old
quarters, where nice Irene and the dirty, pug-faced man
live, now tenanted by two generals; and we have to apply
to the Municipality for lodgings.

The Mayor is apparently a deaf-mute; he never opens
his mouth, or even moves in his chair; but, huddled up,
consumes an appalling number of cigarettes, and watches,
with lack-lustre eye, his subordinates at work. While we
were in the august abode of the Mayor—the Town Hall,
I suppose I should call it—a row broke out in the hall,
and a sentry with a long bayonet in his rifle burst into
tears, while his unarmed opponent made off laughing.

November 24. After threading the maze of dirty little
rat-runs that call themselves streets we found the Municipality again, and in front of it was waiting a cart and
two ponies, driven by a Turk—a brown-faced youth from
Anatolia, as most of these *arabajis*, or drivers of carts, are.
A lusty fellow, as strong as a horse, and very good-
tempered. Then we got half a barrel of benzine for the
motor, and some hay to sit on, and were off. The road
to Yenno is as dull as it was before—burnt villages, drab
thorn-fences, and yellow mud, with the Istrandja Dagh
lit up by fitful gleams of light far away on the left. The
corpses have had rough mounds of earth heaped over
them; and into these the lean dogs are burrowing and
tunnelling.

The grey-backed crows flock together near the car-
casses, and some dogs loiter near the remains of a horse,
of which everything has been eaten except the bones and
the hoofs. The brown boy flogs his ponies with a thick
stick, and they trot on gallantly. The springless cart
jolts terribly, and the wooden sides heave and sway as
though tenanted by a tortured soul.

We met some fellows with ox-wagons bringing round
water-worn stones to repair the road, and two great oxen
were dragging about ten stones in each wagon. They
do not consider economy of time in the East. Alexander
bandies jokes with the roadmen over what he calls " cinq
kilos de pierres." At last we gain the ridge, and look
down on the stony, undulating valley, backed by the
Istrandja Dagh, in which lies brown-tiled Yenno. There
are a few, a very few poplars—that is the whole extent
of the vegetation—with here and there a patch of green,
which means young corn. The Kostaki family are very
pleased to see us again, and are most kind and hospitable ;
they kiss our hands, give us bread, wine, cheese, and
cherries, and put us into an excellent clean room. There
are six daughters and one son ; one of the daughters,
married, is a revelation of Parisian modishness in her
Sunday gown. I have to read the Greek essay of one of
the younger ones ; I can understand it all right, but my
Etonian pronunciation excites some laughter. The Greek
girls gave us large posies of chrysanthemums, daisies, and
carnations, and the scent of these perfect creatures, after
all the stenches we have endured, is a breath from heaven.

A crowd watches us start out of the dirty yard, and
into the dirtier streets, as we wave farewell to the good
Kostakis. The car travels excellently, and only once do
we have to invoke the aid of our *arabaji* to pull us out of
a bog. At 3 P.M. we were back at Kirk Kilisse, and
Alexander was very proud of himself. We overtake some
English-looking youths near the hospitals, and find that

they are part of the English Red Cross detachment, consisting of thirteen surgeons and twenty-two dressers. Our return with the car to the house of Michaelis where we lodge is quite an event for the neighbourhood, the small boys of which tire not of blowing the hooter.

November 26. The streets are incredibly clean, and flags wave everywhere; everybody talks about peace, but nothing is known. Savoff, Daneff, and Fitcheff are said to be negotiating at Tchataldja. Puaux tells me that Dimitrieff was dressed down by Fitcheff because he let us see the Tchataldja fight.

November 27. Beautiful day. Walked the streets, and suffered more than ever from the awful feeling of boredom and weariness which the place seems to engender. Saw a dead man, eyes staring, hands clenched, being drawn uncovered on an ox-wagon. The crowds of waiting wounded round the hospital greater than ever. Segonzac and Puaux say they are going home at once. Found a notice on Fox's door: " In this house lived Mr. Fox: he leaves a horse for the English nurses." How very perspicuous ! Is the horse in the drawing-room, or upstairs ?

The censors can tell one nothing; Lyon knows no more than we do; people say that at noon to-day we shall know whether there is peace or not. The best thing to do is to go back to England; there is nothing to be done here. So bored that we eat no lunch. The eating-house in the town is too filthy for words.

November 28. Walk out with M. to the eastern fort, where there are huge earthworks but no guns. From the great mound of yellow earth you see both the fantastic, serrated peaks of the Istrandja, and the saddle-like white, brown, and blue town of Lozengrad, with many a league of purple plain stretching away southwards.

We meet two soldiers in ragged overcoats and battered black slouch hats—a queer uniform ! They were coal-mining at Denver, Colorado, when the war broke out. They are gunners of the reserve, but beneath their great-coats they still wear their blue working overalls. They came back in twenty-five days *via* New York and Havre, the fare costing them £22 apiece.

" Ja, we come back fight. When the war over we go back again, unless we dead. Plenty dead this war. Not Turkish-Italian war; Bulgarian-Turkish war." The patriotism of such fellows is splendid, and shows what stuff the people are made of.

A wireless telegraph is thrumming and buzzing in front of the fort, and our friends tell us it is in communication with Tchataldja.

As we return through the high upper part of the town we find 103 Turkish guns stretched in long lines in front of the barracks, and a great crowd of wounded waiting to be attended.

An epidemic of cleanliness, probably pursued with so much zeal because of its novelty, seems to have seized on all classes and sexes and ages of the population. Yesterday we found small girls with large shovels in the kennel of the roadway bespattering passers-by with filth, while demurely pretending to be removing garbage.

To-day an aged Papas, white-haired and black-gowned, is to be seen resolutely grappling with the ordure outside his dwelling, while a few paces away a small boy brushes up clean dust with a grass-broom ; and across the street a tiny girl draws down upon her head the imprecations of an adult male relative by removing the grass that grows on the outer limit of the footpath.

And as the aged and the infants toil at the dirt problem, robust youths sit on their hunkers regarding them curiously ; even as critics at a new play of which the plot is undecipherable.

We meet Fox again, who is always going and yet never goes ; and the Frenchmen, who are really going ; and

Beaumont of the *D.T.*, who has just returned from Tchataldja, and is also going; in fact, if we stay we shall be the only correspondents left in the town. We go for lunch to the eating-house, where the grimy waiters skip about with almost supermanlike agility, and the food is greasier and nastier than it is possible to conceive. There is yellow, gleaming, wicked-looking grease on everything; vinegar in all the soups, dirt and grit in all the rice, and the table-cloth, and the knives and forks and spoons—oh! And then, suddenly, into the swarm of unshaven, dirty men, into the dark reek of that unsavoury den, comes the blue-clad figure of a young girl, with a white handkerchief over her hair and a Red Cross on her arm—a dark, pretty, fresh-looking creature. Thank you, Miss, whoever you are! We are all the better for the sight of you.

November 29. I go to censor's office to send a wire to *The Times* about the capture at Dedeagatch; M. remains outside. There are three telegrams for him: he reads them and hands them to me. They all say the same thing: "Come home at once." In the afternoon we go to the Attaché's and play bridge.

There were Lyon, and Lewis the Swiss, and Romanoffsky the Russian, and the Dutch attaché. Puaux and Segonzac come in; this is said to be the twelfth time they have come to say good-bye. "À la gare comme à la gare," says the Dutchman as he shakes hands.

Then we visit Mrs. Stobart's excellent hospital, entirely organised by herself, and entirely run by women doctors —a notable achievement in a strange land. M. cruelly says that their uniform is a cross between those of a policeman and a rifleman.

Then we visit Major Birrell's hospital on the road to Yenno, and are shown all over the place by that enterprising and able officer. It is a model of cleanliness and order, and there is a strong staff of thirteen surgeons and twenty-two dressers, besides an *X*-ray expert.

We were spared nothing. There was the man with a hole in his face, caused by shrapnel, so large that you could see right through his jaws ; we were shown a man actually undergoing an operation of a terrific kind, but we did not stay long there ; we came on a girl dressing the back of a poor fellow who was groaning with pain. Birrell said the worst thing was the gangrene set up by dirt and neglect : lots of them came too late.

It was good to see British method and cleanliness here ! Piles of dirt had been thrown out through the windows and used to fill up holes ! the paths were neatly marked with white stones—you might have been at Aldershot.

November 30. Leave Kirk Kilisse, I hope for ever, after giving superfluous stores to Lyon. The Bulgarians have done more for the road in three weeks than the Turks have done in three hundred years. Alexander takes a wrong turn out of Seliolo, and lands us at Timurjeli, where we find a delightful N.C.O.—an enormously powerful, black-bearded fellow, 6 ft. 2 in. high.

The evening star is, as usual, taken for a fire-balloon over Adrianople. The cannonade continues. M. says the Ladysmith people also fancied the stars were balloons. Our giant friend then held his roll-call of dirty, red kummerbunded, blue-turbaned old Turks, who are shepherded into the precincts with bayonets, and driven like oxen into a stable till the morning.

The giant visits his posts at 4 A.M. He has a lot of forage under his care, for he is on the main road between Mustafa Pasha and Kirk Kilisse.

December 1. Early this morning there was a great hubbub outside, and the giant and his two myrmidons sprang out. The unfortunate gentleman with a bayonet, whose business it had been to guard the superannuated Turks last night, had counted his prisoners and found one missing. So he came screaming to the sergeant, as one anticipating a speedy doom. " He didn't like work ! "

he yelled. I never heard a man make such a row. The sergeant took it philosophically, and the guard departed, with still within his bosom a spark of hope that his life will be spared.

It is a day of much pushing of the car. At 1 P.M. we arrive at Provadya, where a pretty little stream runs under green hills topped with horizontal limestone outcrop, which is perforated with holes in which thousands of birds have made their nests. The village, perched on the steep flank of an opposite hill, is one of the most picturesque we have seen. We run across an excitable and loquacious Swiss correspondent, who tells us that the remarkable amount of information he has secured is due to the two facts that he walks and knows the language. " In your motor you see and hear nothing. Now yesterday I found scores of women crying because the Serbians had stolen the wood out of their houses. The names of the places are all wrongly spelt on your map." And so on.

We managed to buy eight eggs, boiled them, and had a royal lunch. Swiss gentleman infallible in the matter of wine also. " There is a house below where splendid wine is to be got : I send a boy for you." Our last precious Rehoboam is despatched per boy ; but it never returns. We tire somewhat of the Swiss gentleman, and depart. We expected George and the *charrette* to be at Provadya, or at all events to get news of him ; but none is forthcoming, and our ill-luck culminates in three punctures.

Dusk comes on, and with it an appalling place to cross—a muddy stream at the bottom of a deep gully. We wait for a bullock-wagon to come up, and then compel the boy in charge to unharness his bullocks and drag the motor across.

A soldier with fixed bayonet throws down his musket and helps. There is a burning village a hundred yards away, and the leaping flames give us a good light to work by. Presently Alexander, in conversation with the soldier, turns the greenest green : " It is a cholera village, and this man is the sentry ! " Good Lord ! What are these fires ? They are burning the corpses in the houses. The two bullocks are no good ; their iron-shod feet slip on the greasy bank, and they fall down helplessly. We manage to get two more, and the cholera sentry is invaluable, or the sight of his bayonet. With four bullocks we get Lalage up to the top in triumph, and pay off the boy. But silver does not console him ; he cries bitterly, and will not be comforted. Why ? I fancy it was the sight of his dearly beloved bullocks straining and falling in the mud.

Farther on darkness overwhelms us ; Alexander cannot see to drive ; we stick helplessly. We commandeer a third team of oxen, but the devil is in one of the pair, who gallops, kicking, away, when brought near the inoffensive Lalage. Finally the attempt is abandoned ; we get into the ox-wagon, and, tired to death, eventually arrive at Sekun. There the Serbians, with 50,000 men, hold the north-west sector of the siege-lines.

The officers we found in a hovel were decidedly suspicious at first. They stared at us with hostility, and took our papers to be examined by the general. At last our identity was established, and after some talk on the threadbare subject of when Adrianople was going to surrender, we were taken to the abode of the surgeon-general, who received us most hospitably in his tiny room, and gave us cakes to eat. There was just room for the three of us to sleep on the floor. The room was terribly hot and stuffy, for the gallant surgeon-general had pasted paper over the windows and fireplace, and hermetically sealed himself against fresh air.

December 2. At breakfast the surgeon-general talks of nothing but cholera. He is very gloomy about it, and says the shadow of it is over the whole force hereabouts. Enter then, hurriedly, a pale, distraught-looking officer, who begs for medicine. The panic is on him. Soon the

patients outside, all with the fear of the plague written
on their faces, number a score or so. Sekun is nothing but
a dung-heap; I never saw a filthier place, and apparently
no effort whatever is made to improve matters. Under
such conditions can they wonder if they get cholera ?

In the surgeon-general's garden, or dung-heap rather,
soldiers are engaged in killing a sheep and several hens
not three yards from his door. Truly life in Sekun is
barbaric. It was with joy that we said farewell to the
good Serbian doctor and departed.

Up and down we went over the black mud—a greasy
wilderness. We crossed the Tundja by a wooden bridge,
and found ponies very useful in hauling us up the steep
banks beyond that stream.

At last we struck what Alexander calls the *chaussée*, and
the sight of it was too much for him ; his emotion brought
on a stomach-ache, for which whisky was the only cure.
We gave him some, and he then drove so furiously that
we burst a tire.

It is good to see the yellow Maritza once more, now in
full flood, as when it bore down the head of Orpheus, and
its thickets of tall poplars standing out against the low
blue hills. Mustafa Pasha knew what he was about when
he selected this spot for his town.

The Turks captured at Dedeagatch have brought the
whole population into the streets ; but we are thinking of
food, and at a new restaurant—new since our day—we
simply gorge bacon and eggs. I have been hungry for
three weeks.

At dinner at the restaurant—surely Lucullus never ate
such food as this ?—a merry Dutch lad who talks excellent
English gives us a graphic description of the hanging of
two Bashi-bazouks in a garden in the city, and how the
crowd hung on to their legs to assure themselves that it
was thoroughly done.

The correspondents had the execution transferred from

one garden to another, because in the first the light was not good enough for photography. When the men let go of the dead men's legs they were cut down, and women and children came and pulled their ears.

December 3. Walk out to the station, and see the old sights—burning houses, filthy roads; the kennel a mass of liquid mud bordered by huge irregular stones, on which two men passing each other balance and then one of them falls prone into the morass. The surrounding country is a mass of floods, out of which the pollarded mulberries, hacked and mutilated, rise forlornly. There are belts of silver-boled poplars still faintly yellow, and on the huge plain the ploughmen are getting to work again. The streams of bullock-wagons are as thick as ever; in one a dead Turk, with bloated red face, as though recently hanged, is carried by uncovered. At the station the hospital camp is surrounded by bullock-camps; hardly sanitary.

At night the cannonade round Adrianople becomes terrific.

At the censor's office one gentleman is full of M. Isvolsky and his power in Europe: he rules the Tsar; he made the Anglo-Russian *entente*, the Franco-Russian alliance. He is now engaged in turning Rumania into the ally of Russia, and winning her help for the great war which is to be fought against Austria and Germany. He planned the Balkan War; he is the arbiter of Europe; if he is made Foreign Minister, and M. Delcassé returns to his old office in France, let Germany and Austria beware!

Correspondents pleasantly inform us that we shall be kept six days in quarantine at the frontier. Possible, but hardly likely. If so, why send all these Turkish prisoners into Bulgaria? The truth is, these immured correspondents have got into such a state of quidnuncism that every rumour is a certainty, and every possibility a scare.

December 4. Spent all last evening packing and getting ready for the start, which took place in heavy rain at 1.30 A.M., when all the house was asleep, and our shutting of the massy front door made a hideous row. We plodded on through rain and slush, past the bayoneted sentries and the mouldy shops, over the atrociously paved bridge. And then I could not keep up with the striding grey, so I turned George out, and balanced on a pile of boxes for an hour and a half.

The parting with the servants was very affecting. Alexander gave me a note for his wife; and after we had shaken hands (poor old George's horny fists all covered with disgusting ulcers) they both kissed our hands before we knew what they were doing. And then Alexander came back round the corner of the carriage, weeping, his face all puckered up, like a child's, and managed to stammer out: " You'll not be long before you send for us to Sofia, will you, M. le Colonel?" Pathetic, very.

I felt a brute to be plotting fresh adventures at Adrianople for the peace-and-comfort-loving Mr. Mamegonian, who is to await a telegram telling him what to do.

Timed to start at 3.40, the train did not go till 6.30 A.M. Rain and colder. Interminable waits at roadside stations. A Bulgar doctor combats M.'s assertion that there is cholera in both camps with that venerable, if now discredited, argument: " Oh, but it can't be cholera; the proportion of deaths is only 2 per cent. and *those are the official statistics*!" This would be an excellent joke, if the doctor had any sense of humour, but he has not. Had a wait of a couple of hours at Tirnovo Semen, where a battalion of boyish recruits go by singing, and the rain comes down in sheets. At 6 P.M. we got into Philippople; train besieged by crowds. Von Dreyer and Mamontoff, and a wounded corporal educated for the law at Grenoble, in same carriage. Sofia at 1 A.M.

December 5. Jolly to see Bourchier again, who has had

the narrowest squeak for his life. His pony slipped on the cobbles just as a tram was passing, and the tram went within two inches of B.'s head as he lay on the ground!

His escape is a sort of national event in Sofia, where a street has been named after him.

Get a small boy as interpreter. He has been at Robert College, Constantinople, and speaks excellent English. His pastime is base-ball. Sofia appears a city of the dead. Snow is falling; there is a weird silence; and hardly a soul stirs in the wide streets. Lunched at Union Club. Noel Buxton and his brother there, and had a long talk. N. B. a person much and rightly respected in the Balkans. He is by no means the Little Englander he is sometimes depicted. It is a happy time for him. He tells me that he has to look after the finances of the English hospitals at Lozengrad, and finds the ladies much more economical than the men.

Leave Sofia, after long chat with Bourchier, at 10.30 P.M.

December 7. In the dead of night we reach the Serbian frontier. There an exhaustive examination for cholera suspects is made. I was had out twice, but they were finally satisfied, after asking a lot of very embarrassing questions as to where I had come from, to which I had to reply in a diplomatic manner.

Next morning found that we were four hours late, due to the fact that the doctors had nosed out a suspicious case in the person of a Serbian captain, who had refused to be detained in quarantine. So a squad of infantry had to be sent for, to remove him by force, and that had taken time.

Delighted to see Segonzac and the Russians on the train. If we are four hours late at Vienna we shall miss the Orient Express, and that is a calamity not to be contemplated, so we subscribe seventy-five francs, and tell the engine-driver it is his if we catch the express. The gallant fellow imperilled all our necks and did it.

CHAPTER IV

THE LITERARY ASSOCIATIONS OF THRACE

ADRIANOPLE has a long literary history. Hadrian's city was Roman before it was Turkish, and the Thracian Orestia before it was Roman; and its original inhabitants seem to have set up a standard of senseless brutality very faithfully adhered to by its late possessors. Placed at the wedding of Maritza, the ancient Hebrus, and Tundja, it has ever drunk of a stream immortalised by Virgil.

No passage in that wonderful poet is more beautiful than his description of the death of Orpheus (*Georgics*, iv. 515-527):

> Nulla Venus, non ulli animum flexere hymenaei;
> Solus Hyperboreas glacies Tanaimque nivalem
> Arvaque Rhipaeis numquam viduata pruinis
> Lustrabat, raptam Eurydicen atque irrita Ditis
> Dona querens; spretae Ciconum quo munere matres
> Inter sacra deum nocturnique orgia Bacchi
> Discerptum latos iuvenem sparsere per agros.
> Tum quoque marmorea caput a cervice revulsum
> Gurgite quum medio portans Oeagrius Hebrus
> Volveret, " Eurydicen " vox ipsa et frigida lingua,
> " Ah miseram Eurydicen ! " anima fugiente vocabat;
> " Eurydicen " toto referebant flumine ripae.

I have been rash enough to attempt a translation:

> No love that's carnal dalliance his purpose could prevent;
> Alone across the icy wastes by Tanais he went.

The snows eternal clinging to Riphus' flank he crossed,
Seeking the fruitless gift of Dis—Eurydice the lost.
The Thracian dames he'd slighted, when Night to Bacchus yields,
Rewarded Orpheus with his doom, and strewed him o'er the fields.
Then did Oeagrian Hebrus whirl down upon his stream
A head torn from a neck that shone like marble in a gleam.
" My poor, my poor Eurydice ! " his fleeting spirit cried.
" Eurydice ! Eurydice ! " the river-banks replied.

In Plato's *Republic*, Book x. p. 620, Er has a vision of the soul of Orpheus. Jowett translates the passage thus :

" Er sees the souls choosing their lot in the next life from samples submitted to them by Lachesis, the daughter of Necessity. There he saw the soul which had once been Orpheus choosing the life of a swan, out of enmity to the race of women, hating to be born of a woman, because they had been his murderers."

Distant connections of the ladies who did Orpheus to death were not always so ambitious of a reputation for the undivided affection of a lover's heart. When their husbands died they took particular pains to make it appear that their husbands and they had never really quite hit it off. This mental attitude was the outcome of their peculiar customs.

Herodotus (*Terpsichore*, v. 5) wrote : " The up-country Crestonians do as follows. Each man has many wives. And when a man dies, his wives hold a great trial ; and the deceased's beloved take tremendous pains to find out which of them really was the man's best beloved. And she who is adjudged to have been so, and is honoured and applauded by both men and women, is slain at the tomb of her husband. And when she is slain she is buried with her husband. And the rest of them have a great meeting. And the thing has become a perfect scandal."

The Crestonians inhabited a district of Macedonia between the Axius and the Strymon, near Mount Cercine ; their chief town was Creston, or Crestone, founded by the Pelasgians. This is no doubt the modern Kustendil.

" Doriscus," wrote Herodotus, " is the seashore of
Thrace, and a great plain.   Through it runs a great river,
the Hebrus.   On it was built a royal castle, called Doriscus,
in which Darius had kept a guard of Persians since the
time when he was fighting the Scythians.   And it seemed
to Xerxes a convenient place in which to set in array and
number his army, and he did so " (*Polymnia*, vii. 59).   The
old historian goes on to tell us that the host amounted to
2,641,610 fighting men.   With this vast army Xerxes
marched, in the spring of 480, through Macedonia and
Thessaly against Greece.   Thermopylæ was won by the
invaders, and Leonidas and his Spartans fell, but at
Salamis the Greek fleet saved Europe from Oriental
domination.   Doriscus is no longer Doriscus, but Enos ;
well known to-day as the line, with Midia, once proposed
by the Powers as the boundary of the New Bulgaria.

On July 3, A.D. 323, there was a great battle at
Adrianople between Constantine, the Emperor who built
the city of Constantinople, and his rival Licinius.   Gibbon
thus describes it :

" . . . The prudent Licinius expected the approach of
his rival in a camp near Hadrianople, which he had fortified with an anxious care that betrayed his apprehension
of the war.   Constantine diverted his march from Thessalonica to that part of Thrace, till he found himself stopped
by the broad and rapid stream of the Hebrus, and discovered the numerous army of Licinius, which filled the
steep ascent of the hill, from the river to the city of
Hadrianople.   Many days were spent in distant and
doubtful skirmishes ; but at length the obstacles of the
passage and of the attack were removed by the intrepid
conduct of Constantine.   In this place we might relate a
wonderful exploit of Constantine, which, though it can
scarcely be paralleled either in poetry or romance, is
celebrated, not by a venal orator devoted to his fortune,
but by an historian, the partial enemy of his fame.   We

are assured that the valiant emperor threw himself into the river Hebrus accompanied only by *twelve* horsemen, and that by the effort or terror of his invincible arm he broke, slaughtered, and put to flight a host of one hundred and fifty thousand men. . . . Thirty-four thousand men are reported to have been slain. The fortified camp of Licinius was taken by assault the evening of the battle; the greater part of the fugitives, who had retired to the mountains, surrendered themselves the next day to the discretion of the conqueror; and his rival, who could no longer keep the field, confined himself within the walls of Byzantium."

Later on, on August 9, 378, " a day," says Gibbon, " among the most inauspicious of the Roman calendar, there was another battle at Hadrianople. Thence marched the Emperor Valens to attack the Goths, and was defeated and killed.

" The Roman cavalry fled; the infantry was abandoned, surrounded, and cut in pieces. The most skilful evolutions, the firmest courage, are scarcely sufficient to extricate a body of foot encompassed on an open plain by superior numbers of horse; but the troops of Valens, oppressed by the weight of the enemy and their own fears, were crowded into a narrow space, where it was impossible for them to extend their ranks, or even to use, with effect, their swords and javelins. In the midst of tumult, of slaughter, and of dismay, the emperor, deserted by his guards, and wounded, as it was supposed, by an arrow, sought protection among the Lauccarii and the Matiarii, who still maintained their ground with some appearance of order and firmness. His faithful generals, Trajan and Victor, who perceived his danger, loudly exclaimed that all was lost unless the person of the emperor could be saved. Some troops, animated by their exhortation, advanced to his relief; they found only a bloody spot covered with a heap of broken arms and mangled bodies, without being able to discover their unfortunate prince either among the living or the dead. Their search could not indeed be successful, if there is any truth in the circumstances with which some historians have related the death of the emperor. By the care of his attendants Valens was removed from the field of battle to a neighbouring cottage, where they attempted to dress his wound, and to provide for his future safety. But this humble retreat was instantly surrounded by the enemy; they tried to force the door : they were provoked by a discharge of arrows from the roof; till at length, impatient of delay, they set fire to a pile of dry faggots, and consumed the cottage with the Roman emperor and his train."

Thirty years later the tables were turned, and Claudian was enabled exultingly to write the lines chosen as a motto for this book :

> Unoque die Romana reprendit
> Quotquot ter denis acies amisimus annis.

> And in one day the Roman line regained
> All we had lost in thirty long sad years.

At Lule Burgas, and at Salonika, and at Kumanovo, old civilisations also regained from the barbarians what they had lost in more than thirty long sad years.

Adrianople has, indeed, been a place chosen by the Almighty to lay life's riddles before the human mind. There the Germanic barbarians put their heels on the neck of Roman law, Roman civilisation, and Roman despotism, and, as it seemed, gave the world over to confusion and to savagery. At Adrianople John Hunyady was foiled at the very moment when to all appearance he had saved the Byzantine Empire, and had thrust back the Ottoman power into the Asia whence it sprang. His failure meant in the end four centuries of Turkish tyranny.

But who knoweth the ways of Wisdom, and who can search out her paths ? It may be that the defeat of Valens saved individualism, and has prevented Europe from being dragooned into a more than Chinese uniformity, a uniformity in which all that means Progress would have been stifled in the cast-iron mould of Roman Order and Roman Law.

Constantinople might pass under the crescent, and the sacrifice might cease in Santa Sophia, but the precious leaves of her libraries were swept over Europe by the fierce Eastern gale, and freedom of the intellect sprang from the soil whereon they fell. On the other hand, Austria was called into existence as a bulwark against the Turkish onrush westwards.

Germany in the sixteenth century had been on the point of becoming one of the greatest colonising powers in Europe; but German thought and German civilisation dwarfed the individual.

The desolation which the Catholic Reaction, in the main the work of Austria, brought on Germany gave England and France space in which to develop and expand; and the colonisation of the New, and the conquest of the Old, World fell to those who could give the individual mind a plot in which to grow and to blossom. And the fruits of that tree are the United States of America, and all that the British Empire stands for.

Ogier Ghiselin de Busbecq, Signeeur of Bousbecque, knight, and Imperial Ambassador in the middle of the sixteenth century, tells us more about Turkey, in his admirable letters, than perhaps any other author.

" We cannot turn to our gardens without seeing the flowers of Busbecq around us—the lilac, the tulip, the syringa. So much was the first of these associated with the man who first introduced it to the West, that Bernardin de Saint Pierre proposed to change its name from lilac to Busbequia "! * Gardeners will be profoundly thankful that his proposal was not adopted.

* Forster and Daniell, Introduction.

Old Busbecq wrote in 1554 : " In order to descend to the level country in front of Philippopolis it is necessary to cross the mountain by a very rough pass. This pass the Turks call Capi Servent—that is to say, the Narrow Gate. On this plain the traveller soon meets with the Hebrus, which rises at no great distance in Mount Rhodope, which stood out cold and clear with its snowy covering. The inhabitants, if I am not mistaken, call the mountain Rulla. From it, as Pliny tells us, flows the Hebrus, a fact generally known from the couplet of Ovid :

> Qua patet umbrosum Rhodope glacialis ad Haemum,
>   Et sacer admissas exigit Hebrus aquas.

In this passage the poet seems to refer to the rivers want of depth and its scant supply of water, for though a great and famous stream, it is full of shallows.

I remember, on my return, crossing the Hebrus by a ford close to Philippopolis, in order to reach an island, where we slept under canvas. But the river froze during the night, and we had great difficulty next day in recrossing and regaining our road.

There are three hills which look as if they had been torn away from the rest of the range. On one of these Philippopolis is situated, crowning the summit with its towers. At Philippopolis we saw rice in the marshes growing like wheat. The whole plain is covered with mounds of earth, which, according to the Turkish legends, are artificial, and mark the sites of the numerous battles which, they declare, took place in these fields. Underneath these barrows, they imagine, lie the victims of these struggles.

Continuing our route, we followed pretty closely the banks of the Hebrus, which was for some time on our right hand, and leaving the Balkans, which ran down to the Black Sea, on our left, we at last crossed the Hebrus by the noble bridge built by Mustapha, and arrived at

Adrianople, or, as it is called by the Turks, Endrene. The name of the city was Orestia until Hadrian enlarged it and gave it his own name. It is situated at the confluence of the Maritza, or Hebrus, and two small streams, the Tundja and Arda, which at this point alter their course and flow towards the Aegean Sea. Even this city is of no very great extent, if only that portion is included which is within the circuit of the ancient walls ; but the extensive buildings in the suburbs, which have been added by the Turks, make it a very considerable place.

After stopping one day at Adrianople, we set out to finish the last stage of our journey to Constantinople, which is not far distant. As we passed through these districts we were presented with large nosegays of flowers, the narcissus, the hyacinth, and the tulipan (as the Turks call this last) . We were very much surprised to see them blooming in midwinter, a season which does not suit flowers at all. There is a great abundance of the narcissus and hyacinth in Greece ; their fragrance is perfectly wonderful, so much so that, when in great profusion, they affect the heads of those who are unaccustomed to the scent. The tulip has little or no smell ; its recommendation is the variety and beauty of the colouring.

The Turks are passionately fond of flowers, and though somewhat parsimonious in other matters, they do not hesitate to give several aspres for a choice blossom. I, too, had to pay pretty dearly for these nosegays, although they were nominally presents, for on each occasion I had to pull out a few aspres as my acknowledgment of the gift. A man who visits the Turks had better make up his mind to open his purse as soon as he crosses their frontier, and not to shut it till he quits the country ; in the interval he must sow his money broadcast, and may thank his stars if the seed proves fruitful.

But even if he gets nothing else by his expenditure,

he will find that there is no other means of counteracting the dislike and prejudice which the Turks entertain towards the rest of the world.   Money is the charm wherewith to lull these feelings in a Turk, and there is no other way of mollifying him.   But for this method of dealing with them, these countries would be as inaccessible to foreigners as the lands which are condemned (according to the popular belief) to unbroken solitude on account of excessive heat or excessive cold.   Half-way between Constantinople and Adrianople lies a little town called Tchourlou, famous as the place where Selim was defeated by his father, Bajazet.   Selim, who was only saved by the speed of his horse Caraboulut (*i.e.* the dark cloud), fled to the Crimea, where his father-in-law exercised supreme power.

Just before we reached Selimbria, a small town lying on the coast, we saw some well-preserved traces of an ancient earthwork and ditch, which they say were made in the days of the later Greek emperors, and extended from the Sea of Marmora to the Danube.

These fortifications were intended to defend the land and property of the people of Constantinople which lay within their defences against the inroads of barbarians. They tell of an old man in those days who declared that the existence of these works did not so much protect what was inside as awe the surrender of the rest of the barbarians, and so encourage them to attack, while it damped the spirit of the defenders.

At Selimbria we stopped a while to enjoy the view over the calm sea, and pick up shells while the waves rolled merrily on to the shore.   We were also attracted by the sight of dolphins sporting in the waters ; and, in addition to all these sights, we enjoyed the heat of their delicious clime.   I cannot tell you how warm and mild the air is in this charming spot.   As far as Tchourlou there was a certain amount of cold, and the wind had a touch of the north about it; but on leaving Tchourlou the air becomes extremely mild.

Close to Constantinople we crossed over bridges, which spanned two lovely bays (Boyok Tchekmedje and Kutchuk Tchekmedje). If these places were cultivated, and Nature were to receive the slightest assistance from Art, I doubt whether in the whole world anything could be found to surpass them in loveliness. But even the ground seems to mourn its fate, and complain of the neglect of its barbarian master. Here we feasted on most delicious fish, caught before our eyes.

While lodging in the hostels, which the Turks call Imaret, I happened to notice a number of bits of paper stuck in the walls. In a fit of curiosity I pulled them out, imagining that there must be some reason for their being placed there. I asked my Turks what was written on the paper, but I could not find that they contained anything which could account for their being thus preserved.

This made me all the more eager to learn why on earth they were kept; for I had seen the same thing done at other places. My Turks made no reply, being unwilling to answer my question, either because they were shy of telling me that which I should not credit, or because they did not wish to unfold so mighty a mystery to one outside the pale of their religion. Some time later I learned from my friends among the Turks that great respect is paid to a piece of paper, because there is a possibility that the name of God may be written on it; and therefore they do not allow the smallest scrap to lie on the ground, but pick it up and stick it quickly in some chink or crack, that it may not be trodden on. There is no particular fault, perhaps, to be found with all this; but let me tell you the rest. On the day of the last judgment, when Mahomet will summon his following from purgatory to heaven and eternal bliss, the only road open to them will be over a red-hot gridiron, which they must walk across with bare feet. A painful ordeal methinks. Picture to yourself a cock skipping and hopping over hot coals! Now comes the marvel. All the paper they have preserved from being trodden on and insulted will appear unexpectedly, stick itself under their feet, and be of the greatest service in protecting them from the red-hot iron. This great boon awaits those who save paper from bad usage.

"On some occasions our guides were most indignant with my servants for using paper for some very dirty work, and reported it to me as an outrageous offence. I replied that they must not be surprised at such acts on the part of my servants. What could they expect, I added, from people who are accustomed to eat pork?

"This is a specimen of Turkish superstition. With them it is a fearful offence for a man to sit, even unwittingly, on the Koran (which is their Bible); in the case of a Christian the punishment is death. Moreover, they do not allow rose-leaves to lie on the ground, because they think that the rose sprang from the sweat of Mahomet just as the ancients believed that it came from the blood of Venus. But I must leave off, or I shall tire you with these trifling matters." *

The vivacious and encyclopædic Lady Mary Wortley-Montagu travelled to Constantinople in 1717, by way of Buda-Pesth (or Buda as it was called then), Belgrade, Sofia, and Adrianople; somewhere about as long after Busbecq as the author of *Eothen* went after her ladyship. She writes:

"We came late to Belgrade, the deep snows making the ascent to it very difficult. It seems a strong city fortified on the east side by the Danube and on the south by the river Save, and was formerly the barrier of Hungary. It was taken by Solyman the Magnificent, and since by the Emperor's forces, led by the Elector of Bavaria, who

* Forster and Daniell, pp. 106–111.

held it only two years, it being retaken by the Grand Vizier, and is now fortified with the utmost care and skill the Turks are capable of, and strengthened by a very numerous garrison of their bravest janissaries, commanded by a pasha seraskier, *i.e.* general. This last expression is not very just; for to say truly the seraskier is commanded by the janissaries, who have an absolute authority here, not unlike a rebellion, which you may judge of by the following story, which, at the same time, will give you an idea of the admirable intelligence of the governor of Peterwaradin, though so few hours distant. We were told by him at Peterwaradin that the garrison and inhabitants of Belgrade were so weary of the war, they had killed their pasha about two months ago, in a mutiny, because he had suffered himself to be prevailed on, by a bribe of five purses (five hundred pounds sterling), to give permission to the Tartars to ravage the German frontiers. We were very well pleased to hear of such favourable dispositions in the people; but when we came hither, we found the governor had been ill-informed, and this is the real truth of the story. The late pasha fell under the displeasure of his soldiers, for no other reason but restraining their incursions on the Germans. They took it into their heads, from that mildness, he was of intelligence with the enemy, and sent such information to the Grand Signior at Adrianople; but, redress not coming quick from thence, they assembled themselves in a tumultuous manner, and by force dragged their pasha before the cadi (judge) and mufti (priest), and these demanded justice in a mutinous way; one crying out, Why he protected the infidels? Another, Why he squeezed them of their money? That (*sic*) easily guessing their purpose, he calmly replied to them that they asked him too many questions; he had but one life, which must answer for all."

Kinglake begins *Eothen*, the record of his travels in 1835, as follows:

" At Semlin I still was encompassed by the scenes and the sounds of familiar life ; the din of a busy world still vexed and cheered me ; the unveiled faces of women still shone in the light of day. Yet, whenever I chose to look southward, I saw the Ottoman's fortress—austere, and darkly impending high over the vale of the Danube— historic Belgrade. I had come, as it were, to the end of this wheel-going Europe, and now my eyes would see the splendour and havoc of the East.

" The two frontier towns are less than a gunshot apart, yet their people hold no communion. The Hungarian on the north, and the Turk and the Servian on the southern side of the Save, are as much asunder as though there were fifty broad provinces that lay in the path between them.

" Of the men that bustled around me in the streets of Semlin there was not, perhaps, one who had ever gone down to look upon the stranger race dwelling under the walls of that opposite castle. It is the plague, and the dread of the plague, that divide the one people from the other. All coming and going stands forbidden by the terrors of the yellow flag."

Lady Mary Wortley-Montagu wrote of Adrianople :—

" I went, two days after, to see the mosque of Sultan Selim I., which is a building very well worth the curiosity of a traveller. I was dressed in my Turkish habit, and admitted without scruple ; though I believe they guessed who I was, by the extreme officiousness of the doorkeeper to show me every part of it. It is situated very advantage- ously in the midst of the city, and in the highest part, making a very noble show. The first court has four gates, and the innermost three. They are both of them sur- rounded with cloisters, with marble pillars of the Ionic order, finely polished and of very lively colours ; the whole pavement being white marble, the roof of the cloisters being divided into several cupolas or domes, leaded, with gilt balls on the top. In the midst of each court, fine fountains of white marble; before the great gate of the mosque, a portico, with green marble pillars. It has five gates, the body of the mosque being one prodigious dome.

"I understand so little of architecture, I dare not pretend to speak of the proportions. It seemed to me very regular; this I am sure of, it is vastly high, and I thought it the noblest building I ever saw. It had two rows of marble galleries on pillars, with marble balusters; the pavement marble, covered with Persian carpets, and, in my opinion, it is a great addition to its beauty that it is not divided into pews, and encumbered with forms and benches like our churches; nor the pillars, which are most of them red and white marble, disfigured by the little tawdry images and pictures that give the Roman Catholic churches the air of toy-shops. The walls seemed to me inlaid with such very lively colours, in small flowers, I could not imagine what stones had been made use of; but going nearer, I saw they were crusted with japan china, which has a very beautiful effect. In the midst hung a vast lamp of silver, gilt; besides which, I do verily believe, there were at least two thousand of a lesser size.

"This must look very glorious when they are all lighted; but that being at night, no women are suffered to enter. Under the large lamp is a great pulpit of carved wood, gilt; and just by it, a fountain to wash, which you know is an essential part of their devotion. In one corner is a little gallery, inclosed with gilded lattices, for the Grand Signior. At the upper end, a large niche, very like an altar raised two steps, covered with gold brocade, and, standing before it, two silver-gilt candlesticks, the height of a man, and in them white wax candles, as thick as a man's waist. The outside of the mosque is adorned with four towers, vastly high, gilt on the top, from whence the *imaums* call the people to prayers. I had the curiosity to go up one of them, which is contrived so artfully, as to give surprise to all that see it. There is but one door, which leads to three different staircases, going to the three different stories of the tower, in such a manner, that three priests may ascend, rounding, without ever meeting each other ; a contrivance very much admired.

" Behind the mosque is an exchange full of shops, where poor artificers are lodged *gratis*. I saw several dervises at their prayers here. They are dressed in a plain piece of woollen, with their arms bare, and a woollen cap on their heads, like a high-crowned hat without brims. I went to see some other mosques, built much after the same manner, but not comparable in point of magnificence to this I have described, which is infinitely beyond any church in Germany or England ; I won't talk of other countries I have not seen."

Lady Mary Wortley-Montagu to the Abbé Conti.

" CONSTANTINOPLE, *May 29*, O.S., 1717.

" I have had the advantage of very fine weather all my journey ; and the summer being now in its beauty, I enjoyed the pleasure of fine prospects ; and the meadows being full of all sort of garden flowers and sweet herbs, my berlin perfumed the air as it pressed them. The Grand Signior furnished us with thirty covered waggons for our baggage and five coaches of the country for my women.

" We found the road full of the great spahis and their equipages coming out of Asia to the war. They always travel with tents ; but I chose to lie in houses all the way.

" I will not trouble you with the names of the villages we passed, in which there was nothing remarkable, but at Tchiorlu we were lodged in a *conac*, a little seraglio, built for the use of the Grand Signior when he goes this road. I had the curiosity to view all the apartments destined for the ladies of his court. They were in the midst of a thick grove of trees, made fresh by fountains ;

but I was surprised to see the walls almost covered with little distiches of Turkish verse written with pencils. I made my interpreter explain them to me, and I found several of them very well turned; though I easily believed him, that they lost much of their beauty in the translation. One was literally thus in English:

> We come into this world; we lodge, and we depart;
> He never goes that's lodged within my heart.

"The rest of our journey was through fine painted meadows, by the side of the Sea of Marmora, the ancient Propontis. We lay the next night at Seliorla, anciently a noble town. It is now a very good seaport and neatly built enough, and has a bridge of thirty-two arches. Here is a famous ancient Greek church. I had given one of my coaches to a Greek lady who desired the conveniency of travelling with me; she designed to pay her devotions, and I was glad of the opportunity of going with her. I found it an ill-built place, set out with the same sort of ornaments, but less rich, than the Roman Catholic churches. They showed me a saint's body, where I threw a piece of money; and a picture of the Virgin Mary, drawn by the hand of St. Luke, very little to the credit of his painting; but, however, the very finest Madonna of Italy is not more famous for her miracles. The Greeks have a most monstrous taste in their pictures, which, for more finery, are always drawn upon a gold ground. You may imagine what a good air this has; but they have no notion either of shade or proportion. They have a bishop here, who officiated in his purple robe, and sent me a candle almost as big as myself for a present, when I was at my lodging.

"We lay the next night at a town called Bujuk Checkmedji, or Great Bridge; and the night following, Kujuk Checkmedji, Little Bridge; in a very pleasant lodging, formerly a monastery of dervises, having before it a large court, encompassed with marble cloisters, with a good fountain in the middle. The prospect from this place, and the gardens round it, are the most agreeable I have seen, and show that monks of all religions know how to choose their retirements.

" 'Tis now belonging to a *hogia* or schoolmaster, who teaches boys here; and asking him to shew me his own apartment, I was surprised to see him point to a tall cypress tree in the garden, on the top of which was a place for a bed for himself, and, a little lower, one for his wife and two children, who slept there every night. I was so diverted with the fancy, I resolved to examine his nest nearer; but after going up fifty steps, I found I had still fifty to go, and then I must climb from branch to branch, with some hazard of my neck. I thought it the best way to come down again."

CHAPTER V

BULGARIA—ANCIENT HISTORY

ULGARIA is in one sense the oldest, in another sense the youngest, of the Balkan States. At a time when the names of Servia and Montenegro were yet unknown the Byzantines trembled before the on-slaughts of the Bulgarian hordes, from whom Constantinople itself was only saved by its strong walls. Yet Bulgaria was the last of the Balkan States to be freed from the Turkish yoke. Until the time of the Crimean War Western Europe had scarcely realised the existence of the Bulgarians.

A race of Finnish origin who at the end of the seventh century had migrated from the Volga across the Danube to rule amongst the Celts, the Slavs, and the relics of Roman colonies who dwelt in the wide plains of the ancient Moesia, the Bulgarians had soon become Slavs in habits and in language. Whilst still heathen under their Kings Crum and Cok, they had in 809 driven the Greeks from Sofia, captured the Greek Emperor Nicephorus, who sought to recover the city, and used the skull of an anointed and consecrated Cæsar as a drinking-cup at their banquets.

In 810 Omortag, one of Crum's immediate successors, laid aside his designs on Constantinople, and made a truce for thirty years with the Emperor Leo.

Under Omortag Christianity was introduced into Bulgaria, and spread rapidly despite barbarous persecution, but it was not until the time of Boris (862) that Cyril and Methodius made Christianity the dominant religion, and first reduced a Slavonic tongue to writing. Boris became a Christian for political reasons, for he saw that only thus could he maintain his kingdom amongst such powerful neighbours as the Frankish, the Moravian, and the Byzantine Emperors; but he was far from being wedded to the Greek Church, and quickly entered into negotiations with the Latins, who were then parting for ever from Byzantium. In August 866 his envoys appeared at Rome before Pope Nicholas I., but want of tact on the part of that Pope and of his successor, Adrian II., lost Bulgaria, and with Bulgaria the great mass of the Slavonic peoples, for ever to the Church of Rome, and in 869 a Council decided that Bulgaria was subject to the Patriarch of Constantinople.

Simeon, the son of Boris, was the greatest of all the Bulgarian rulers, and brought the old Byzantine Empire to the verge of destruction.

In 913 Simeon's army appeared under the walls of Byzantium; in 914 he held Adrianople for a time; in 917 the Greeks were finally crushed in a great battle fought within sight of the Balkans.

At that time the boundaries of the Bulgarian realm extended from Mesembria on the Black Sea past Adrianople to Mount Rhodope.

In the south the boundary went from Olympus to the mouth of the Kalamas, opposite Corfu, from sea to sea. The Albanian coast, with a few exceptions, was ruled by Simeon as far as the Drin. Towards Servia the Bulgarian border was formed by the Drin, the White Drin, and the Ibar; from there it reached to the Save. Belgrade was under Bulgarian dominion. Beyond the Danube, before the Magyar invasion, Wallachia and perhaps also parts of Hungary and Transylvania seem to have belonged to Bulgaria.

In the terms of modern geography the first Bulgarian Empire comprised Bulgaria proper, the northern and western parts of Eastern Rumelia, with a boundary extending from the Black Sea at Misivri north of Bourgas, but not including Adrianople itself, to the Despoto Dagh, with the greater part of Macedonia, excluding, however, Salonika, Epirus, though without Janina, and Albania and the eastern portion of Servia down to the river Ibar, whilst Servia comprised but little of the present kingdom, and extended chiefly over Bosnia, Herzegovina, and Montenegro. Nor did Skutari in Albania form a part of Simeon's dominions.

Simeon's residence was at Preslav, in a beautiful mountainous district, near a village now called by the Turks Eski-Stambul (Old Stambul), lying ten miles south-west of Shumla. Like the Kremlin at the present day it was a fortress, a palace, and a sanctuary. " When the stranger crosses the threshold," writes John the exarch, " he sees buildings on both sides ornamented with stones and covered with different sorts of woods. And when he goes farther into the court, he sees lofty palaces and churches with countless stones, woods, and frescoes, their interior inlaid with marble and copper, silver and gold, to such an extent that he does not know with what to compare it, because in his own land he has never seen the like, but only poor huts of straw. Wholly beside himself he will sink down in bewilderment. But if by chance he catches sight of the prince, sitting in a robe embroidered with pearls, with a chain of coins about his neck, with bracelets on his arms, girded with a purple girdle and with a golden sword at his side, and sees his boyars sitting on each side of him in golden chains, girdles, and bracelets, then, if any one on his return home asks him, ' What hast thou seen there ? ' he will answer, ' I know not how to describe it. Only your own eyes could be able to comprehend such magnificence.' Once again the charm of captive Greece had taken captive the fiercest of her European conquerors. 'Now there is nothing left of all this splendour but a few stones.'

"The ruler of such a monarchy could not be satisfied with the simple title Prince, which Boris and his predecessors had borne, but took the Imperial title Czar of the Bulgarians, and Ruler of the Greeks. Such an Emperor could not be imagined without a patriarch at his side; the Archbishopric of Bulgaria was elevated to a patriarchate. Simeon received the Imperial Crown from Rome, not from Constantinople. He died on May 27, 927, after appointing his younger son Peter his successor." *

A curious memorial of the transitory connection between the Slavonic peoples and the Chair of St. Peter still exists at Rome. On the Forum, facing the Coliseum and the ruins of the temple of Venus and of Rome stands the Basilica of St. Clement, the third successor of St. Peter, who died a martyr at Kertch in the Crimea. This church was restored about 866 by a wealthy devotee, and contains frescoes recording the deeds of St. Cyril and St. Methodius.

But the first Bulgarian Empire was brought to an end in 1018 by the Greek Emperor Basil the Bulgar-Slayer, and became subject to the Greeks, who had been called into the country to expel the Russians.

Byzantine supremacy lasted from 1018 until 1186, an epoch during which the country was ravaged by barbarian invaders and plundered by its nominal protectors. A trivial incident led to the expulsion of the Greeks. "Two brothers, Peter and Ivan (John) Asen, descendants of the old family of Shishman, made the tour to Constantinople which sons of good family were expected to do. They asked, like well-bred youths with ambition, for what they probably deserved—a grant of certain lands, this in right

* *Historians' History of the World*, vol. xxiv.

of their descent. They expressed a desire also for an official appointment if the Emperor should be so disposed. Both demands were refused, and a high court functionary emphasised the refusal by slapping the younger of the two brothers on the cheek. It is due to this event that the Empire staggered still more feebly ; that the Turk, who was strenuously encroaching from the south, received fresh encouragement, and that there was a second Bulgarian Empire." *

This Bulgarian Empire lasted from 1186 until 1398. Its history is not altogether unimportant even to-day, since it is upon the memories of this second Empire that modern Bulgaria has been in part built up.

Amongst its chief sovereigns were Kaloyan (1197–1207) and Ivan Asen II. (1218–41).

Kaloyan was an implacable enemy of the Greeks, and allied himself with their enemies whether political or religious. He remained friends with the Bogomils (Bulgarian dissenters), and yet established himself on a friendly footing with the Pope. That Pope was Innocent III. (Giovanni Lothario Conti, 1198–1216), who raised the Papacy to the height of earthly power. Kaloyan (Joannice) allied himself with the fierce Kumani by marriage, and in conjunction with them made inroads into the Byzantine Empire as far as the very walls of Constantinople. Finally (1201) the Byzantines were obliged to conclude peace with Kaloyan. All the territories he had captured were left in his power, and his Empire extended from Belgrade to the Black Sea, from the mouths of the Danube to the Struma and the Upper Vardar. Kaloyan, however, saw how necessary it was for him to have a confirmation of his title from the Pope. Three times the embassies he sent to Rome were detained by the Hungarians or Byzantines. The report, however, reached Innocent III., and in 1199 a Papal messenger, a

* *Historians' History of the World*, vol. xxiv.

Greek priest from Brindisi, arrived in the Bulgarian capital, Tirnovo, wholly unexpectedly. He brought Joannice a letter from Innocent stating that he had heard of the King's descent from a Roman family (a statement which may quite possibly have been true), and admonishing him to manifest his allegiance to the Papal throne. The fierce Bulgarian seized this opportunity with pleasure. He was delighted that God had reminded him of the race and of the fatherland from which he had sprung, and he asked the Pope to bestow upon him the Imperial Crown and to receive him into the Roman Church (1202). In order to obtain his wish more quickly he conferred his land in perpetuity on the Pope.

It is interesting for Englishmen to remember that Innocent III. was the Pope who received from our own King John the gift of the English kingdom, which but the year before His Holiness had bestowed upon Philip Augustus of France.

In 1204 Constantinople was taken by the Latins, and Count Baldwin of Flanders was placed on the Imperial Throne. Kaloyan offered to enter into a Treaty of Peace with him, but received the answer that he was not to treat with the Franks as a King with friends, but as a slave with his masters, since he was wholly unjustified in assuming dominion over the land which he had torn from the Greeks.

Kaloyan wrote later to Innocent III., " They proudly replied to me that they would have no peace with me unless I returned the territory which I had wrested from the Empire. I answered that I possessed this land more justly than they themselves possessed Constantinople." To Joannice's professions of descent from the Romans of Trojan the crusaders opposed their descent from Francus, son of Priam. " Troy," said they, " belonged to our ancestors."

The " King of Blaquie and Bouguerie " (Wallachia and

Bulgaria), as the Franks styled him, at once allied himself with the Greeks, who hoisted his banner over Adrianople. Baldwin hastened to recover it, but on April 14, 1205, was met before the city by Joannice with a host of Vlachs, of Bougres (Bulgarians), of Greeks, and of fourteen thousand unbaptized Kumani. The latter, fighting after the fashion of nomads, by a feigned flight attracted the French cavalry, whom they riddled with arrows. Baldwin after a brave resistance with his battle-axe was taken prisoner. He died in a Bulgarian dungeon. Two years later Joannice, who was known by the Greeks as *Skylojohannes*, " Dog John," laid siege to Salonika. He was found murdered in his tent. Report said he had been slain by St. Demetrius, the patron of the city. " His character is stained with blood, and it cannot be washed clean." Among the Bulgarians the memory of the " great and most pious Czar " is held in high esteem. He still figures to-day in the myths of the Thracian Bulgarians.

His successor, Ivan Asen II. (1218–41), raised the power of Bulgaria to its highest point. " For the first time since Samuel (974–1014), the Bulgarian Slavs were united under one sceptre ; Asen's Empire touched three seas. At Tirnovo he built a Cathedral in which an inscription records his victories as follows : 'In the year 1230 I, Ivan Asen, czar and autocrat of the Bulgarians, faithful to God in Christ, son of the old Asen, have built this most worthy temple from its foundations, and have completely decorated it with paintings of the forty holy martyrs with the aid of whom, in the twelfth year of my reign, when the temple was being painted, I fought in the war against Rumania and defeated the Greek army and took captive the Czar Theodore Comnenus himself with all his boyars (nobles), and I have conquered all lands from Odrin (Adrianople), to Drac (Durazzo), the Greek, the Albanian, and the Servian land. Only the towns around Carigrad (Constantinople) and that city itself did the Frazi

(Franks) hold, but these two subjected themselves to my
rule, for they had no other czar than me, and lived out
their days according to my will since God has so ordained.
For without Him is no deed or word accomplished. To
Him be honour for ever. Amen.' " *

His ideal was a Slavic monarchy with its capital at
Constantinople, and he bore the title of Tsar of the
Bulgarians and of the Greeks.

The Bulgarian national church was recognised by the
Greeks. An active commerce, splendid buildings, and a
rare religious liberty testified to the progress of civilisation.

When he died, Asen II. left an empire which touched
three seas ; within sixteen years all his possessions had
reverted to Greek, Macedonian, and Servian rulers, and
the Asen dynasty had come to an end with the murder of
Kaliman II. (1257), who in his turn had murdered his
cousin Michael, the son of Asen II., and successor of his
brother Kaliman I.

Bulgaria gradually broke up into independent states,
and the last shadow of a united kingdom vanished at the
death of John Alexander in 1368, whose sister had married
the great Servian ruler Stephen Dushan, and who had
tried to maintain an alliance between the Bulgarians and
the Servians. The Turks invaded the country. The
battle of Kossovo had sealed the fate of the whole Balkan
Peninsula, and in 1393 Bayazid I. (1389–1403) sent his
son Djelebi against Tirnovo. The city was suddenly
surrounded on all sides, but it was not taken until after a
three months' siege. In the absence of its Czar Shishman (Shishman III., 1365–93), who was trying his
fortune elsewhere against the Ottomans, the patriarch
Euthymius was the chief person in the city. He went
manfully out to the Turks to soften the anger of the
barbarian prince. Bayazid's son, when he saw the

* *Historians' History of the World*, vol. xxiv.

patriarch approaching, " undaunted and serious, as though all the terrors of war were only paintings on a wall, stood up, received him kindly, offered him a seat, listened to his petition, but followed up his promises with few deeds." *

In 1396 Widdin passed into the hands of the Turks after the defeat of Sigismund of Hungary at Nicopoli, and Bulgaria sank into Turkish slavery.

Of the cities many were destroyed, but others received new protection through Turkish privileges. The boyars maintained themselves for a long time chiefly by accepting Islam. The villages were terribly depopulated, for the Turks transformed whole regions into deserts, and everywhere burned cloisters and churches.

The inhabitants of the plains fled to the mountains and founded there new cities. A large mass of the people, together with boyars and clergy, escaped to Wallachia.

Bulgaria sank into Turkish slavery, but the mass of the population remained Christians, and some trace of freedom survived amongst the outlaws who carried on a guerilla warfare in the mountains for centuries.

It was only in the eighteenth century that the literary revival began with the writings of the monk Paisii and Bishop Sofronii. In 1835 the first Bulgarian school was opened at Gabrovo. Such schools spread over Bulgaria, and a vigorous effort was made to break down the rule of the Greek clergy who had dominated the intellectual life of the country since the Turkish conquest. In 1870 the Turkish Government established the Bulgarian Exarchate with jurisdiction over fifteen dioceses, to which other dioceses could be added in case two-thirds of the Christian population so desired. The first exarch and his followers were ex-communicated by the Patriarch of Constantinople in 1872. It is to the decree establishing the Bulgarian Exarchate that all the troubles between Greeks and Bulgarians in Macedonia owe their origin.

* *Historians' History of the World*, vol. xxiv.

In 1876 a rising, inspired by fears of a general massacre of the Christians, broke out in the Sanjak of Philippopolis. It was put down with terrible atrocities. The report of these massacres reached London. The tale was treated by Disraeli as " coffee-house babble." Mr. Gladstone was fired by his cynicism and took up the cause of the Bulgarians, although his first efforts were but coldly received; he himself has told us that he had all but desisted from them when he saw a report of a meeting organised by working men to denounce the Bulgarian massacres. He wrote a pamphlet : that pamphlet roused the indignation of Europe. Russia vanquished Turkey in a war which was suspended by that Treaty of San Stefano which called Greater Bulgaria into life. England put her money on the wrong horse, and sprang into the breach to defend the Turk. A Congress was held in June 1878 at Berlin, and by the Treaty of Berlin Macedonia was once more handed over to Turkish tyranny, and a greatly diminished Bulgaria was formed into a principality for Prince Alexander of Battenberg. In 1885 a revolution united Eastern Rumelia with Bulgaria, from which it had been severed by the Treaty of Berlin. A war with Servia followed. Russia, seeing that Bulgaria was now grown too strong for her purposes, deprived Prince Alexander of his throne. He was succeeded by Prince Ferdinand of Coburg, who in 1896 was named by the Sultan Prince of Bulgaria and Governor-General in Eastern Rumelia, and was officially recognised by the Powers. Bulgaria in 1909 became a Kingdom ; its ruler took the old national title of Tsar ; and it was as a Kingdom that Bulgaria entered into war with Turkey on October 17, 1912, Turkey having declared war on Bulgaria and Servia.

The object sought was to force the Porte to apply to the Turkish Provinces in Europe the reforms instituted by Article XXIII. of the Treaty of Berlin, which provided for the introduction into these of organic laws, the details of which should be settled in each province by a special commission containing a large representation of the native element, and which were to be put in force by the Porte, after consulting the European Commission instituted for Eastern Rumelia. Nor did Bulgaria, doubtless, forget that by the Treaty of Berlin she had been deprived of large territories which had been granted to her by the Treaty of San Stefano, extending from the Black Sea to the Albanian Mountains, and from the Danube to the Aegean, enclosing Ochrida, the capital of her ancient Tsars the Shishmans (1186–1398), Dibra and Kastoria, as well as the districts of Vranya and Pirot, with a port on the Mediterranean at Kavala, Adrianople, Salonika, and Chalcidice being left to Turkey. Of the districts named, the Berlin Treaty gave Vranya, Pirot, and Nish to Servia, the others, which included the greater part of Macedonia and part of the vilayet of Adrianople, being replaced under Turkish rule. The reforms promised to these provinces under the Treaty had never been carried out. Such had been the outcome of the interference by England with the work of the Tsar Liberator.

CHAPTER VI

THE ORIGIN OF THE WAR

" Come over into Macedonia, and help us."—Acts xvi. 9.

> Through midnight gloom from Macedon
> The cry of myriads as of one,
> The voiceful silence of despair,
> Is eloquent in awful prayer,
> The soul's exceeding bitter cry,
> " Come o'er and help us, or we die."
> *Hymns Ancient and Modern* (Rev. S. J. Stone).

PAUL, when slumbering at Troas, in the land which Rome was proud to hail as the birthplace of her greatness, saw that vision of the man of Macedonia whose bitter cry for help in the end brought Europe and all the lands through which her influence has spread to the foot of the Cross. King Ferdinand, the descendant of princes who had done much to save Christianity and Western civilisation in Europe, heard the cry of Macedonia. Like St. Paul of old, he lent his ear to that cry, and the outcome of his daring has been the liberation of that land which was the first in Europe to hear Christ's name, and which has been the last to groan under the tyranny of the Moslem.

Montenegro, it is true, rushed into the fray without waiting for her allies, but the formation of the Balkan League, which alone saved her from perishing, the victim of her rashness, had not been the work of the little mountain state. That League, as Mr. Bourchier, *The Times* correspondent in the Balkans, has shown in his articles on " The Balkan League,"* was the work of Bulgaria and of Greece. His modesty forbids him to add that his own name will live in history as that of the man who inspired the sovereigns and prime ministers of the two states with the thought of laying aside the differences which for so long had kept them apart, and of working together for freedom and for the Faith with one heart and one soul. It was nought to the Balkan nations that they jeopardised the lives of their sons, perhaps their very existence as free peoples, that they poured out like water the modest wealth which they had accumulated by their labours during the short space since they had themselves been redeemed from Turkish slavery, if at the price of their blood and of their treasure they could end the misrule and murder which was turning Thrace and Macedonia into blood-soaked, fire-blackened deserts. " Greater love hath no man than this, that a man lay down his life for his friends."

But Divine Providence has brought these nations and their rulers a rich reward for their sacrifices for their brethren.

When, under the influence of that righteous anger which arms even the weakest with the strength which overcomes the strongest foes, Bulgaria, Servia, and Greece flew to arms to support Montenegro, they little thought that a few short months would see them the masters of Epirus, Macedonia, Old Servia, Thrace, and Candia, with the Archipelago; or that five great cities, Adrianople, Salonika, Yanina, Skutari, and Prizrend, would have brought their keys to their conquerors. Such successes had never been foreseen when the Balkan League was founded.

* *The Times*, Wednesday, June 4; Thursday, June 5; Friday, June 6; Wednesday, June 11; Monday, June 16, 1913.

As Bourchier has shown, the idea of a Balkan League is not altogether a new one.   The conception dates from the time when, to the great and just dissatisfaction of the young Balkan States, the Great Powers at the Congress of Berlin, which followed on the Russo-Turkish War of 1877, remodelled the provisions of the Treaty of San Stefano, by which most of European Turkey had been liberated from the Turks, to suit their own supposed interests.   Many years afterwards Lord Salisbury, speaking as Prime Minister of England, owned that, at Berlin, England had put her money on the wrong horse.   M. Ristitch, the Servian statesman, suggested that the young states should combine to protect their own interests, and believed that a reformed, constitutional Turkey might find a place in such a scheme, an idea which apparently has only lately been abandoned by certain Balkan politicians. The idea was regarded with favour by King Charles of Rumania and by Prince Alexander of Bulgaria, but was frustrated by the revolt of Eastern Rumelia in 1885, which, as both Greece and Servia demanded compensation for the aggrandisement of Bulgaria, led to the war between Servia and Bulgaria, and, in the end, to the deposition of Prince Alexander.   In 1891, however, the idea was revived by the Greek statesman M. Tricoupis, who thought that the Balkan States might combine against Turkey, after having settled the division of the prospective spoils on the principle of *do ut des*.   His idea was received with favour at Belgrade, with courtesy at Sofia, but M. Stambuloff, the then Bulgarian Premier, thought that the still unstable position of Prince Alexander's successor, Prince Ferdinand, rendered it too great a risk to launch the country into such an adventurous policy, and declined to accept the proposal.   He is even said to have, at Austrian instigation, denounced the project to Constantinople, but the Porte had already got wind of it through the Turkish Minister to Servia,

Feridun Bey, thanks to an indiscretion committed at Belgrade.*

The project slept during the next twenty years, mainly because Bulgaria wished to constitute Macedonia as an autonomous state under Turkish suzerainty, whilst Greece and Servia desired its partition. Indeed, Greece preferred a *rapprochement* with Rumania in place of one with Bulgaria, and even arranged in 1901 a Greco-Rumanian *entente* against her under the auspices of King Charles and the late King George, who met at Abbazia, but the combination proved a short-lived one. The long struggles between the Bulgarising and Hellenising elements in Macedonia, which date from the introduction of foreign " control " under Austro-Russian auspices, also kept the two races yet farther apart, and these internecine contests lasted up to the time of the Turkish revolution of 1908.

By that revolution the Young Turks came into power. By an ill-inspired policy of centralisation to be carried out by the destruction of all the varied nationalities and religions in the Turkish Empire, they endeavoured to make Turkey a nation. But it was owing to this ill-starred attempt, carried out by violence and cruel wrong-doing, that those nationalities, at least in European Turkey, were led to lay aside their secular feuds, and thus it gave the opportunity for the Balkan League to come into being. Readers of Macaulay may remember that we have had a similar experience in England, when during a few halcyon months all parties, united for a moment by the ill-judged policy of James II., joined in bringing about the Revolution of 1688, despite the threats of the over-whelming world-power France.

In the spring of 1910 Albania, where the Young Turks had endeavoured to abolish both the language and the

---

* Mr. Bourchier's articles, "The Balkan League, the History of a Memorable Alliance," are in *The Times* for Wednesday, June 4; Thursday, June 5; Friday, June 6, 1913, etc., etc.

peculiar institutions of the Albanian race, broke out in revolt. The rising was put down with merciless severity, and, though Macedonia had remained passive, the authorities determined to take the opportunity to disarm the Macedonian population. The Great Powers had withdrawn their military representatives from the country, and the horrors which then took place have, consequently, never been reported.

A community of suffering led the Christian races of Macedonia to forget their quarrels. " The reconciliation, which began from below—it would hardly be exaggeration to say that Macedonian peasants laid the foundation of the Balkan Alliance—passed upwards and outwards." * The Greek Patriarch and the Bulgarian Exarch eventually began to exchange amenities, and to make joint representations to the Porte ; friendly conversations passed between Balkan statesmen.

The position of affairs in Macedonia became known to Bourchier through a chance conversation with Apostol, the famous Bulgarian *voyvode* or guerilla leader, who had for some time been sheltered from the Turks in the houses of the Greek peasantry of southern Macedonia. " The Greeks had always regarded Apostol as their worst enemy ; he was now their friend, but the fact brought home the conviction that a wonderful change of sentiment had taken place." * In the autumn of that year King Ferdinand and the Heirs-Apparent of Servia and Greece met at the Jubilee celebration of King Nicholas of Montenegro, and the fact showed the growing harmony of the Balkan States. It was increased when it became known that Rumania, as the humble servant of the Triple Alliance, had offered the support of her army to Turkey in case she went to war with Bulgaria. The Balkan statesmen believed also that Austria, but a few years before, had offered Rumania, in such an event, a liberal

* Bourchier, in *The Times.*

share of Bulgarian territory. Such at least is the story told by a Vienna correspondent. The Austrians forgot, perhaps, that the Rumanian population in Bulgaria only numbers some forty thousand; in Hungary, in Transylvania, and in Bukovina, some millions.

The foreign policy of the Young Turks also did much to consolidate the Balkan League. Austria had become an empire under the pressure of the Turk, when the Sultan was the most dreaded potentate in Europe. The pressure of the Turk in his decay was to consolidate the populations of his European possessions into a power which was to expel him from them for ever. Pressure misapplied by Austria may yet unite the Balkan League into an Eastern Empire.

During the autumn of 1910 the relations of Turkey with Greece and Bulgaria became exceedingly strained, and shortly before the offer of Rumanian military help was made to the Porte, large bodies of troops had been brought from Asia Minor and distributed along the Greek and Bulgarian frontiers. Doubtless, these troops included some of the savage Lazes, and the Kurdish Hamidieh cavalry. We have seen the excesses of which these warriors have been guilty during the present war. The constant refusals of Turkey to consent to the construction of the railways needed to connect the Bulgarian network with Salonika, and the Greek railways with Europe, added fuel to the fire; whilst by the persistency with which Turkey asserted her shadowy rights of suzerainty over Crete she gave continual pin-pricks to Greek feeling in Greece, a country which was greatly injured by the boycotting of her goods organised by the quay porters of Salonika.

Unfortunately, too, for Turkey, the leading statesman in Greece was himself closely connected with Crete. Early in 1910 the Military League had brought M. Venezelos to Athens to champion their cause, and in

October of that year he undertook to form a Government. In his speech on taking office he advocated a complete understanding with Turkey, and by a curious coincidence, M. Gueshoff, the late Bulgarian Premier, who was then in opposition, in the same week made a speech advocating a similar policy in the Bulgarian Sobranye.

In March 1911 M. Gueshoff became Prime Minister of Bulgaria, and at once prohibited the formation of bands for Macedonia in the kingdom. Already the announcement of the Rumanian offers to Turkey had led to negotiations for an understanding between Athens and Sofia, but on the advent of M. Bratiano in January 1911 to power at Bukarest, these negotiations were put a stop to.

M. Venezelos, however, was cordially detested by the Young Turks, and their conduct towards Greece became so aggressive that Count Aehrenthal, the Austrian Foreign Minister, hinted to the Grand Vizier, during his visit to Vienna in the autumn of 1910, that he ran a grave risk of driving Greece to conclude an understanding with Bulgaria. Instead of following his advice the Young Turks continued their policy of repression in Macedonia, whilst asserting the existence of a Greco-Turkish *entente*. Their efforts were in vain. So grave was the situation in Macedonia that M. Venezelos proposed to the Bulgarians to enter into an understanding with Greece which might develop into a defensive alliance if Turkey attacked the two states. The offer, which Bourchier modestly refrains from stating was entirely due to his own exertions, was transmitted to Sofia in April 1911. Five months later negotiations were also commenced with Servia, where a Serbo-Bulgarian Alliance was suggested as a counterpart to that between Greece and Bulgaria, the proposed objects of which were, firstly, to secure an *entente* with a view to common action for the defence of the Christians in Turkey, and, secondly, an eventual defensive alliance to provide against a Turkish attack.

Bulgaria did not, at first, reply. King Ferdinand, indeed, was supposed to be in favour of some such plan being adopted, but a war between Turkey and Greece seemed likely to break out about Crete, and the Bulgarians were, perhaps, no very great believers in the military value of the Greek army. Still the matter was not lost sight of. The heads of the four great Christian communities in the Ottoman Empire, the Greek, Armenian, and Chaldean Patriarchs, and the Bulgarian Exarch, for the first time acted together in approaching the Sultan, and soon an opportunity for intervention seemed to be afforded by the outbreak of the war between Turkey and Italy. King Nicholas wished the Balkan Powers to declare war against the Turks forthwith, but Italy had agreed to respect the *status quo* in the Balkans, and M. Venezelos thought that the Greek forces needed three years' further training under their foreign instructors before they could take the field. Hence nothing was done for the moment, but the events of the war in Tripoli inclined Servia to join the alliance, and in April 1912 Bourchier was sent from Sofia by M. Gueshoff to Athens with a verbal message asking the Greek Government to transmit definite proposals on the lines already sketched out. Formal diplomatic negotiations were, therefore, begun through the sole medium of M. Panas, and, as it was very desirable that it should be ascertained whether the Greek and Bulgarian Churches would agree to act in harmony, Bourchier was despatched to Constantinople to consult the Greek patriarch, Joachim III., and the Bulgarian Exarch.

These two great dignitaries were evidently on very friendly terms, and the Greek Patriarch expressed himself as being ready "to abolish the schism," although he put forward conditions which the Bulgarians could not well accept. It was thought best, therefore, to leave ecclesiastical negotiations alone.

M. Panas finally succeeded in arranging a treaty consisting of four articles and a preamble between Greece and Bulgaria, which was signed in April 1912.

The objects in view were stated in the preamble to be the desire of the contracting states to secure equal civil and religious rights for the various Christian nationalities in the Ottoman Empire, and to strengthen the *entente* between the Greek and Bulgarian elements in Turkey. Their policy, however, was in no sense to be an aggressive one.   If in consequence of their adopting this line of action they were attacked by Turkey, they pledged themselves to defend one another.   They were to endeavour to induce their kindred in European Turkey to contribute to the peaceful relations of the inhabitants of the Empire, and to act together in defence of their common interests. The third article provided that the treaty should remain in force for three years, but that it could, on its expiration, be renewed for a year; the fourth, that it should be kept entirely secret.   In a declaration annexed, Bulgaria pledged herself to a benevolent neutrality should war break out between Turkey and Greece over the question of admitting the Cretan deputies to the Greek Parliament, and that she would not hamper the Greeks in their efforts to settle the Cretan question or any other arising out of the events in Turkey in 1908.

In the summer of 1912 the atrocities, which still continued in Macedonia, culminated in the massacre at Kochana, a town with a Bulgarised population in the province of Uskub, close to the Bulgarian frontier, and facing the Bulgarian town and garrison of Kustendil.* A cry for war arose all through the kingdom.   The time to act was come.

But before matters came to a climax in Macedonia, the Bulgarians had already come to an agreement with Servia. The Serbo-Bulgarian Treaty was signed on March 15,

---

* *Czar Ferdinand and His People*, by John Macdonald (London, T. C. & E. C. Jack, 1913; 1 vol.), pp. 330–331.

1912, whilst their treaty with Greece dates from May 29 —the 459th anniversary of the day on which Constantinople was entered by the Turks.*

The Serb element in Turkey was comparatively small, and although feeling was aroused by the Albanian outrages in Albania and in Old Servia, there was little hostility to Turkey in the popular mind. Indeed Turkey was sometimes, as in 1908, looked upon as the natural ally of Servia against Austria. However, ever since Bulgaria and Russia had become reconciled in 1895 Russia had cherished the idea of bringing about a Serbo-Bulgarian understanding as a counterpoise to Austrian influence in the Balkan Peninsula, and to block her advance ot Salonika, and at the same time to effect the union of the Serb race. On the other hand, Bulgaria was, as I have already said, anxious for an autonomous Macedonia, in order that the greater Bulgaria of the Treaty of San Stefano might some day be realised by its absorption in Bulgaria. It was believed that the dearest wish of Russia was to revive the Bulgaria of the Treaty of San Stefano, which so long kept Bulgaria and Servia apart. In 1908 the Revolution in Turkey brought the Young Turks into power, but the Young Turks favoured Servia in order to lessen the influence of Bulgaria in Macedonia, and the Servian propaganda, therefore, made headway amongst the Macedonians. Moreover, Austria had irritated Servian opinion by closing the frontier to Servian pigs in 1909, whilst Bulgaria made no objections when the Austro-Hungarian monarchy annexed Bosnia-Herzegovina. This increased the ill-feeling between the two countries, and it was not known at Belgrade that Tsar Ferdinand had declined certain offers which the Austrians had made him in order to subvert Servian independence.

In October 1909, however, M. Hartwig arrived as

* *The Times*, Wednesday, June 11, 1913, " The Balkan League," iv. " The Arrangement with Servia."

Russian Minister at Belgrade, and his first effort was to bring about a *rapprochement* between the two Slav states, and the plan was discussed between M. Isvolsky and M. Milovanovitch, the Servian Prime Minister, when the latter was with King Peter at St. Petersburg in March 1910. The proposals were not lost sight of, and when the Turkish-Italian War broke out in September 1911, M. Milovanovitch proposed a Serbo-Bulgarian *entente*, with a view to protecting the interests of the two states. M. Gueshoff was then in Western Europe, but on his way home had an interview with the Servian Minister, who agreed to set negotiations on foot. The coming of age of Prince Boris, King Ferdinand's heir-apparent, was celebrated at Sofia early in 1912—the year which the King at the New Year's Reception at the Palace had called an *année énigmatique* (an enigmatical year), and all the heirs-apparent of the Balkan States were present at the festivities. The gathering was, at the time, regarded as significant, but the only person amongst the guests who was acquainted with the negotiations was the Grand Duke Andrew Vladimirovitch of Russia. In a conversation with Mr. Bourchier M. Milovanovitch expressed his fears that a rupture with Turkey would lead to the commercial isolation of Servia, but the distinguished statesman was destined to die before he could see the triumph of the Balkan cause.

The treaty between Servia and Bulgaria was signed on March 13, 1912. Like the Bulgarian-Greek treaty it was a purely defensive one formed for the purpose of securing the political and religious rights of the various nationalities in the Turkish Empire without any aggressive action against Turkey. However, should this policy lead to a war in which the allies were victorious, it was arranged that any territorial acquisitions made by them should be divided between them according to a plan laid down in the treaty. This is said to have been done at the suggestion of M. Pashitch, who wished, as Servia was the weaker power, to secure her rights beforehand. Bulgaria was to take the whole of the territory south and east of the Rhodope range and the Struma river, whilst Servia was to take that north of the Shar range, including Old Servia and Kossovo. The remainder of the territory was to form the autonomous Macedonia which Bulgaria desired to see constituted. Should it prove impossible to form such a state, a line was drawn from the point at which the Bulgarian, Servian, and Turkish frontiers meet, a little north-west of Kustendil, to Struga at the north end of Lake Ochrida, leaving Kratovo, Veles, Monastir, and Ochrida to Bulgaria, whilst the Tsar of Russia was to act as arbitrator with regard to the rest of the region, including the Kazas of Kumanovo, Uskub, Krshevo, and Dibra, with the Nahié of Struga. Neither Adrianople nor Albania was named in the treaty.

By an annexe to the treaty signed on May 12, 1912, Bulgaria was to mobilise 200,000 men, and Servia 150,000. The idea was that Macedonia would, if war broke out in Turkey, be the seat of war so far as the allies were concerned, and that Russia would take the field farther east. If Austria threatened Servia, Bulgaria, under a clause couched in language in which Austria was not named, undertook to send 200,000 men to support Servia, whilst Servia, in her turn, undertook to lend 100,000 men to Bulgaria against Turkey.

These agreements were cancelled when it was found that Turkey was massing her troops in the Adrianople district, and by a convention signed on September 28, within three days after the Turkish mobilisation became known to the allies, they agreed to distribute their forces according to the needs of the situation.

The military convention between Greece and Bulgaria was signed on September 25, 1912. Under it Bulgaria engaged to place at least 300,000 men and Greece 120,000

men in the field. The two staffs were to inform one
another of their general plan of operations and of any
modifications which they might make in it. Bulgaria
undertook to send considerable forces into the vilayets
of Kossovo, Monastir, and Salonika, but should Servia
employ 120,000 men in those regions the Bulgarians
might be concentrated in the Adrianople district. The
Greek fleet was to control the Ægean and prevent any
communication between European and Asiatic Turkey by
sea. Such were the bases of the Balkan League so far as its
three chief members were concerned. It only remains for
us to deal with the accession of Montenegro to the League.

As early as 1889 King Nicholas had addressed a
memorandum to Russia suggesting that the Balkan
States should combine to expel the Turks from Europe.
Just before the Italo-Turkish War broke out in 1911, he
made proposals for joint military action with Servia,
Greece, and Bulgaria for that object, which he had previously mooted to the Russian Embassy at Constantinople.
Servia at first declined, but, after the visit of Crown Prince
Danilo to Belgrade early in 1912, changed her attitude.
Greece accepted the idea from the first, and in April 1912
a definite understanding was arrived at between Bulgaria,
Servia, and Montenegro, to which Greece subsequently
acceded, to take common action on behalf of the Christian
nationalities in Turkey. This action was to be diplomatic,
but it came to be seen after the massacres of Kochana and
Berane in the summer that military intervention would be
required. A formal convention between Servia and
Montenegro with this object was signed in September
1912. One of its articles stipulated that in no case should
any town or village occupied in Turkish territory be held
jointly by Servian and Montenegrin troops. This
measure rendered it possible to carry out the Servian
advance on Durazzo and Alessio without friction, although
it was by no means agreeable to the Montenegrins.

That King Nicholas was the first of the allied sovereigns to take up arms was due to the pressure put upon him by his ministers, General Martinovitch and M. Plamenatz. They pointed out to him that the expansion of her territory was an absolute economic necessity for Montenegro, which was cut off from the Adriatic by Austria to a very great extent, and could not hope to wrest an accession of territory from a reformed and regenerated Turkey if the reform of Macedonia were taken in hand by Europe. *Now or never* was the word, if the mountaineers were to win a fresh kingdom with their yataghans. Such were the motives why Montenegro plunged into the fray without waiting for the decision of her allies. There is no doubt that the Balkan League profited by her bold resolution, for had not the war broken out so suddenly they would have found the Turks far better prepared to meet them.

Such is briefly the history of the origin of the League which has driven Asia to the utmost bounds of Europe, and which may yet form an Eastern Empire which will be one more guarantee for the peace of the world, by removing from the arena that apple of discord Constantinople and the Straits.

CHAPTER VII

THE OUTBREAK OF THE WAR

THE mobilisation of all the Balkan States began about September 30, but the Bulgarians, who had shorter distances to traverse and a far better organisation, were able to complete their mobilisation long before the Turks. The Bulgarian infantry war units were formed at their depots in four days, the artillery in six. The strength of the cavalry is practically the same on a peace and on a war footing. As two Turkish army corps, the Third and the Fourth, had their headquarters close to the Thracian frontier in Kirk Kilisse and Adrianople respectively, they might easily have raided Bulgaria and disturbed the process of assembling these units in their concentration areas, especially as the Adrianople corps possessed some ten thousand free cavalry. To guard against this danger all the eleven Bulgarian cavalry regiments were, a few days before mobilisation began, despatched from their peace stations to the Thracian frontier, one regiment only being left with the 7th or Dubnitza Division south of Sofia.

The Bulgarian armies were organised for active operations as follows. The 7th Division, of which the headquarters in peace time are at Dubnitza, was told off to operate in Macedonia, the 2nd (Philippopolis) in the Rhodope, whilst the cavalry, on reaching the frontier, was so distributed as to guard it against all possible Turkish raids. The ten regiments were formed into two bodies, one of some 24 squadrons, or about 3500 men, under Major-General Nazlumoff, which had its headquarters at Kizil Agatch in the Tundja Valley, and watched the main approaches from Kirk Kilisse and the north of Adrianople, whilst the other of 9 squadrons, or about 1300 men, was at Hebibtchevo under Colonel Taneff to guard the Maritza Valley. At the same time the 7th (Dubnitza) Division occupied the passes south of Sofia, the 2nd (Philippopolis) held the Rhodope, and the 3rd (Sliven) supported the cavalry division in the valley of the Tundja.

Behind the screen thus formed three armies were rapidly concentrated. The First Army consisted of the 1st (Sofia), 3rd (Sliven), and new 10th Divisions; the Second Army, of the 8th (Starazagora), the 9th (Plevna), and the new 11th Divisions; the Third Army, of the 4th (Shumla), 5th (Rustchuk), and 6th (Vratza) Divisions. But until they had actually reached their concentration areas, even the divisional commanders did not know to which army they were allotted, and throughout their journeys units of divisions never knew their destinations for more than one day ahead.

The Turks, under the inspiration of Marshal von der Goltz, had carried out manœuvres in Thrace, from which they had derived the impression that the Bulgarians could only invade the country by certain well-defined routes, one of which passes Adrianople on the east and the other one by the west, both uniting on the line Hafsa-Dimotika, so that a Turkish army concentrated about Lule Burgas would completely protect Constantinople. Moreover, the country between the Tundja Valley and the Black Sea could be regarded as absolutely impenetrable by any regular forces. The only measure of special precaution taken was to construct a railway from Mandra to Kirk Kilisse. The Bulgarian Staff were well aware of the extent to which the Turks were influenced by these ideas, and, consequently, arranged to deceive them. Elaborate orders

were issued for the Second Army to assemble at Haskovo,
south of the Maritza, but as each train arrived at Seimenli,
the nearest station to that point, the troops were ordered
to keep their seats and despatched to Yamboli, a place
in the Tundja Valley north of Adrianople. The 3rd
(Sliven) Division was already on that river, and was soon
joined by the 1st (Sofia) and 10th Divisions, whose
headquarters were fixed at Kizil Agatch.

Thus the Turks were completely deceived. They had
every reason to suppose that they were faced by an
army in the Tundja Valley, another in the Maritza, and
a third farther west towards Dubnitza, which, however,
could easily be marched to cover either flank. In reality
the Third Army was in a very different quarter.

Directly the 3rd (Sliven) Division had arrived to support
the cavalry in the Tundja Valley, the latter marched eastwards and was distributed to protect the frontier between
Kaibilar and the Black Sea. The Third Army then concentrated east of Yamboli, with its headquarters at
Straldja. The 4th (Shumla) and 5th (Rustchuk) Divisions
marched to this area, as the railway from Starazagora to
Tirnovo was not then completed, but the 6th (Vratza)
was sent round by rail from Sofia, its commanders, until
they reached Seimenli, remaining under the impression
that they were on their way to Haskovo.

The 6th (Vratza) and the two new divisions were made
up of two brigades, the remainder all of three. Each
brigade includes 10,000 fighting-men, so that roughly
there were 300,000 rifles under arms. The field-guns
numbered 800, the cavalry 37 squadrons (four regiments
of four squadrons, seven regiments of three squadrons),
or 5500 sabres. Excluding the forces detached to Macedonia, and the 11th Division, which was not fully
mobilised until October 17, the Bulgarian forces destined
to invade Thrace consisted of 230,000 rifles, 5000
cavalry, and 600 guns.

The General Headquarters assembled at Starazagora. The commander-in-chief was nominally the King, but he delegated the executive command with a very free hand to Lieutenant-General Michael Savoff. The Chief of the Staff was his old assistant commandant at the Military School, Major-General Fitcheff.

The combination was said to be an admirable one— Savoff a man of great personality and determination, enjoying the full confidence of all ranks, ready always to accept responsibility, to take rapid decisions, and to run necessary risks; Fitcheff a deep student, a master of detail, and blessed with a placid temperament, enabling him to restrain on occasion the somewhat more impetuous disposition of his chief.

The command of the three field-armies was vested in the three Inspectors-General Kutincheff, Ivanoff, and Radko Dimitrieff, with Colonels Papabapoff, Jaykoff, and Jostoff, respectively the commandants of the Military School, the new Staff College, and the School for Reserve Officers, as Chiefs of their Staffs.

The concentration was completed, with the exception of the 11th Division, on October 17, the day on which the Turks declared war, although for four days afterwards they failed to make any move whatsoever. The Bulgarians knew that the Turkish forces were collecting about Adrianople, Kirk Kilisse, and Lule Burgas, whilst they had massed cavalry round Haskeui or Havsa between the two former places. The Bulgarians prepared to take the offensive. Their plans were, firstly, to surround and mask Adrianople, with the smallest possible force; secondly, to storm Kirk Kilisse even at the cost of the greatest sacrifices; and lastly, to meet the main body of the Turkish forces, wherever they might be, with every available man.

National sentiment in Bulgaria was unanimous. The population of 3,500,000 included 500,000 Moslems, yet when the National Assembly on October 5, 1912, voted the mobilisation, the Turkish deputies voted with their Christian colleagues, and it was opposed only by one deputy, and he was not a Turk.*   On the 16th, Tsar Ferdinand left Sofia for his headquarters at Starazagora, where on the 18th, at a great religious ceremony in the Cathedral, he published his declaration of war against the Turks.   I may, perhaps, quote its most impressive passages :—

   " The tears of the Balkan slaves and the groaning of millions of Christians could not but stir our hearts, the hearts of their kinsmen and co-religionists, who are indebted for our peaceful life to a great Tsar Liberator, and the Bulgarian nation has often remembered the prophetic words of the Tsar Liberator, ' The work is begun, it must be carried through.'   Our love of peace is exhausted.   To succour the Christian populations of Turkey there remains to us no other means than to turn to arms. . . .   Our work is a just, great, and sacred one. . . . I bring to the cognisance of the Bulgarian nation that war for the human rights of the Christians is declared. I order the brave Bulgarian army to march on the Turkish territory ; at our sides, and with us, will fight for the same object against a common enemy, the armies of the Balkan States allied to Bulgaria—Servia, Greece, and Montenegro. And in this struggle of the Cross against the Crescent, of liberty against tyranny, we shall have the sympathy of all those who love justice and progress. . . .   Forward, may God be with you." †

   The venerable patriot Archbishop Methodius then blessed the Bulgarian army, and the Tsar was deeply moved.   Well did he know what the liberation of Macedonia would cost Bulgaria in blood and tears.

   * *Czar Ferdinand and his People*, by John Macdonald (London, T. C. & E. C. Jack ; 1 vol.), pp. 331–334.
   † Mr. Macdonald quotes the translation published in *The Times*.

On the same day, October 18, the Bulgarian armies began to move. The Guard Regiment of Cavalry with the advanced troops of the Second and First Army Corps, to the former of which it was attached, crossed the frontier and seized Mustafa Pasha, where is the only bridge over the Maritza, a river about the size of the Thames at Hampton Court, for a stretch of 30 miles between Seimenli in Bulgaria and Adrianople town. This bridge is 17 miles north-west of Adrianople and was built by the Romans. Over it runs the great road from Constantinople to Europe. The Turks had tried to blow up the massive old Roman masonry, but had only chipped a chunk off its side. In advancing on Adrianople the Bulgarian army had only two slight skirmishes with the Turks, one at Hadikeui on the west and one at Fikele on the north, and by October 21 all the Turkish troops had withdrawn behind the outlying screen of redoubts, and the place was invested on all sides save the east.

It was impossible to foresee that the garrison of Adrianople, some 60,000 strong, would remain passive, and so the First Army Corps slowly moved southwards from Kizil Agatch to support the Second, and by the 21st had reached Tartarlar, about 16 miles to the north-east of the fortress.

The Third Army, in the meantime, moved slowly from Straldja to Kaibilar, which its advanced troops reached on the 21st. As its existence was unknown to the Turks, it was hoped that these forces would find an opportunity of attacking the Turkish garrison of Kirk Kilisse, should it expose its right flank by moving west-ward to attack the Bulgarians at Tartarlar. The advance was not an easy one, for as the frontier is approached the terrain becomes hilly and very rough and broken, forming part, as it does, of a chain of low hills which run across the Maritza plain, some 15 miles north of Adrianople, and form the frontier of Bulgaria. So difficult, indeed,

was the ground in places that whole companies had
sometimes to be turned out to man-handle the vehicles and
guns. The Bulgarian cavalry, relieved of its protective
duties on the frontier, was sent southwards to scout
towards Adrianople, and, according to the Military
Correspondent of *The Times* with the Turkish army in
Thrace, was so exhausted by its arduous screening duties
that it was unable to pursue the enemy effectually after
their defeats at Lule Burgas and Bunar Hissar, at a
moment when an energetic pursuit might have proved
the ruin of Turkey. But would it have been wise for the
Bulgarian army, which compared with the Turks was so
weak in mounted troops, to advance without such a
screen ? They could not have foreseen that, though
according to the same writer the Turks were quite aware
of their concentration at Yamboli and that their objective
was Kirk Kilisse, the enemy would remain passive until
October 21. On that day Abdullah Pasha suddenly
ordered a general advance. It would have been, perhaps,
wiser for him to remain upon the defensive, as " with a
first-class fortress at Adrianople and an intrenched camp
at Kirk Kilisse, with a space of only 30 miles between
these two and with almost impassable country beyond
their outer flanks, the Bulgarian field armies could not
advance without first taking one or the other ; and which-
ever was attacked, the other must be masked." The
attack upon fortified positions would certainly entail great
loss of life upon them, and their forces would thus be
weakened before they met the Turkish main army.
But these considerations were thrown to the winds. On
October 21, as I have said, the Turks moved forward in
apparently two main columns, the Third Corps under
Mahmud Mukhtar Pasha from Kirk Kilisse towards
Petra and Erikler, the First from Yenidje towards
Tartarlar : the Second advanced towards Adrianople ;
the Fourth remained at Kavakli. Although the Army

Operation Orders were captured a few days later at Kirk Kilisse, the Bulgarian Staff was utterly unable to ascertain Abdullah Pasha's object in making these moves. At best, as a German-trained officer, he may have acted under the influence of Marshal von der Goltz's teaching, that the offensive is the one object in war—attack, attack, attack, whatever the odds against you. By acting in this spirit Abdullah Pasha became the author of the first Turkish disasters in Thrace. Meanwhile the picturesque side of warfare was to be seen at Sofia, and peace reigned unbroken at Starazagora.

Thousands of Macedonians had flocked to Sofia, and officered by their priests, were being trained by General Geneff for guerilla warfare.* They numbered some 36,000, and all that they needed to live upon was $2\frac{1}{2}$ lbs. of bread and a ration of cheese per day. Many of them were stationed at Shumla and at Varna within striking distance of the frontier of the Dobruja. In the review at Sofia, 5000 of them were mustered in companies of 180. " Each wears the traditional sandal or upuka, common to all Balkan inhabitants, rough brown coats of various patterns, but all short and thick. Many wear leggings made of white or brown woollen cloth, fastened with leather straps or thick whipcord. No other uniform is supplied them, as their national costumes make them sufficiently distinctive in appearance. Each company is ranged under the particular banner or sort of religious society to which they belong. The exiled chaplain comes to harangue them, and makes them promise on solemn oath to liberate their country and brethren from the Turkish yoke. The religious fervour and enthusiasm with which they respond, though the Macedonian is not usually a religious fanatic, shows the depth of patriotic sentiment which animates these rude volunteers, who, after spending the greater part of the day in drill, return

* *Daily Telegraph*, Saturday, October 19, 1912.

to their hovels in the town, or workshops, where they sleep with the priests."

Meanwhile the Bulgarians were steadily advancing into northern Thrace. The upper reaches of the rivers Struma, Bregalnitza, and Mesta were also in their hands, and it was reported that many Moslem Bulgarians, who had been armed by the Turks, were surrendering their rifles and welcoming their presence.

On the night of October 21–22, the First Bulgarian Army Corps was advancing southwards from its bases upon Tartarlar on a front Buyunli–Sari–Talisman–Omar Abbas–Terzi Dere, over a front some 30 miles long, whilst the Turkish forces were also advancing on Tartarlar from Erikler, Petra, Yenidje, and Haskeui, over a terrain consisting of open undulating downland. A Bulgarian cavalry division was pushing forward from Karamza towards the line Kaipa-Seliolo, south of Tartarlar, and on this line the two armies came into collision. These downs extend southwards to the Sea of Marmora, and, like Salisbury Plain, are covered with turf affording excellent ground for a cavalry advance, except where it has been ploughed up within recent years, when, after rain, the going is extremely heavy. Early on October 22 the Bulgarian cavalry reported large camps of Turkish troops of all arms about Kukiler, right across the line of advance of the First Army Corps, but, as that corps had detached the 3rd Division to help the Second Army to surround Adrianople, for the moment it was too weak to take the offensive. It was reinforced by a brigade of the 4th Division of the Third Army, which accordingly advanced from Karamza towards Seliolo some time during the 22nd.

During that afternoon the Turkish advanced troops became engaged with the leading advanced troops of the 1st Division of the First Army a few miles north and north-west of Seliolo. The three Bulgarian divisions seem to have been somewhat scattered, and only two brigades and six batteries took part in the actual fighting. The Turks deployed their right on the hills just east of Seliolo, which lies in a cup, but is commanded by a knoll to the east, on which a Turkish brigade was placed, and their left on hilly ground, mostly covered with scrub, which extends west to Gechkenlia. The Bulgarian divisional commander Tosheff attacked the Turkish centre with four battalions, and tried to envelop the Turkish left; whilst a brigade (two regiments) of the 4th Division attacked their right. On the western front the 1st (Sofia) Bulgarian Regiment happened to meet the 1st (Stambuli) Turkish Regiment, and a fierce struggle took place. The numerous trenches held first by one side and then by the other, the thousands of spent cartridges and shrapnel shell, the number of the graves, all bear mute witness, even now, to the severity of the conflict.

In the meantime a separate battle was going on to the eastward. The Third Army was advancing from Kaibilar on Kovchas, at the western extremity of the Istrandja Balkan range, and Karamza, when on the afternoon of the 22nd its advanced troops came into contact with the Turks of the III. Corps, just north of Eski Polos and Erikler, the former of which the Bulgarians seized during the night. Eski Polos is a fair-sized village situated at the foot of a comparatively isolated peak with an old fortress, which commands a view over the plains of Thrace extending from Lule Burgas to the heights near Adrianople, and is therefore of great value as an observation point.

The Turkish forces under Mahmud Mukhtar Pasha were deployed along some ridges extending from just south of Eski Polos southwards towards Petra, which were entrenched by the Turks during the night. They consisted of two divisions, a Turkish division, however, being only equivalent to a Bulgarian brigade; whilst two or three miles farther north, beyond the river Teke Dere, the 7th (Kirk Kilisse) Division was in touch with the 5th Bulgarian Division about Erikler.

On the morning of the 23rd, the Bulgarian 4th Division, under General Boyagieff, using Eski Polos as a pivot, attacked the Turkish left. The Turks made some stand upon a hill just west of Petra, but elsewhere their resistance quickly collapsed, and they fled towards Kirk Kilisse in a disorderly rout. Their artillery retreated early and so was saved for one day, but all their transport was taken, and their right was all but enveloped by a Bulgarian column working south from Kovchas.

On the night of the 23rd General Dimitrieff's headquarters were at Petra, and he slept in the room which had been occupied by Mahmud Mukhtar the night before. It was decided to attack the famous forts of Kirk Kilisse on the morrow, but when the Bulgarian advanced guard reached the town early on October 24, they entered it without resistance, for the Turks had stampeded during the night. The town was soon occupied by the Bulgarian 6th Division; whilst the 4th and 5th Divisions, passing respectively east and west of the town, became engaged with Turkish rearguards on the line Kavakli–Uskubdere on the 24th, and eventually halted there for three days.

Meanwhile Abdullah Pasha's army was in full retreat before the First Bulgarian Army Corps, pursued by the Bulgarian cavalry, which having been ordered to fill up the gap between the First and Third Armies, advanced from Karamza, halted near Seliolo on the 22nd, and on the 23rd occupied the village of Yenidje, on the road between Adrianople and Kirk Kilisse, thus threatening to cut the line of retreat of its garrison, and took numbers of fugitives, only halting when it approached Kavakli, where Abdullah Pasha had established his headquarters and lay with a considerable force. The Turkish cavalry never showed itself at any time during these operations.

Gossips at Vienna attributed the collapse of the Turks

to differences between Abdullah Pasha and the War
Minister, Nazim Pasha, who, thinking the theatre of war
in Macedonia more important than that in Thrace, had
sent the reinforcements from Asia Minor to Macedonia.
Others attributed the breakdown to the want of transport
and supplies, to the fact that there were few first-class
troops at the front, and even to the treachery of Christian
soldiers who had been enrolled by force in the Turkish
ranks.

Although the Bulgarians occupied Kirk Kilisse with
practically no opposition, it may be interesting to put on
record the version of the occupation of the place which
appears to have been circulated at Sofia on the morning
of its fall.*

" The series of attacks on the positions at Kirk Kilisse
began in brilliant moonlight after 10 o'clock, preceded
by a vigorous bombardment.   It appears that General
Savoff, the Commander-in-Chief, issued peremptory
instructions to General Dimitrieff that the fortress must
be taken yesterday morning.   The order recalls the Tsar's
famous command, ' Let Plevna be taken.'

" The troops, who appear to have suffered nothing in
moral from the unsuccessful issue of the previous attacks,
advanced to the assault with alacrity.   Throughout the
night successive positions were stormed at the point of
the bayonet, a weapon in the use of which the Bulgarians
excel, and before 10 o'clock yesterday morning the
situation of the defenders became desperate.   Mukhtar
Pasha, the Commandant, Prince Abdul Halim, and other
Turkish superior officers, with a portion of the garrison,
had already succeeded in escaping in the direction of
Bunar Hissar, some 15 miles south-east, and in saving a
considerable amount of war material.   An hour later the
remnant of the garrison hoisted the white flag and surrendered.

* *The Times,* Saturday, October 26, 1912.

" The Bulgarian losses are estimated in well-informed quarters at 5000 killed and wounded. All the Turkish dead and wounded were left on the field. The care of the wounded will prove a serious embarrassment to the already overtaxed Bulgarian hospital staff."

The Bulgarians had also by now advanced and were firmly planted round Adrianople, where they had strengthened their positions, whilst the Turks had lost twelve guns in a sally from the place. The Adrianople forces had advanced before the fall of Kirk Kilisse to co-operate with Abdullah Pasha, but had, as was ascertained after the surrender of Adrianople, lost their way and returned to the city without having fired a shot or seen an enemy.

In the meantime General Todorov* with the 7th Division had been instructed to advance down the Struma Valley towards the Constantinople–Salonika railway, which runs comparatively close to the coast of the Ægean, and after cutting it, thus destroying all land communications between Constantinople and the Turkish armies in Macedonia, Epirus, and Albania, to proceed to Salonika. His base was Dubnitza, near the head of the Struma Valley, and he had with him large irregular forces, who guarded the roads leading from Tatar Bazardjik and Philippopolis to the Mesta Valley. The Turkish forces opposed to him consisted mainly of Redifs, and were commanded by Ali Nadir Pasha, whose headquarters were at Seres.

The first week of the war saw Todorov in possession of the upper parts of the Mesta, Struma and Bregalnitza Valleys, whilst the Turkish garrisons at Djuma-i-lala and Mehomia, whose line of retreat across the Kresna and other passes had been intercepted by Bulgarian irregulars, soon surrendered. A force marching to their relief was

---

* *United Service Magazine*, June 1913, " The Balkan War of 1912–13," by Captain H. T. Russell, late R.A., pp. 316–317.

ambushed by the irregulars at Kresna on October 19, and sustained heavy losses. The Bulgarian advance was hampered by small Turkish forces on their flanks, so that Nevrokop was only reached on November 1. The same day the irregulars seized the railway station at Buk, thus isolating Macedonia from Thrace, but their advance across the mountains between the Mesta and the Struma Valleys was so slow that they did not reach Seres until November 9, and they occupied the place after scattering a large Turkish force in an engagement fought to the south of the town.

Thus, as the Greeks had entered Salonika on November 8, Todorov saw that the main object for which he had been detached into Macedonia had escaped his grasp. The race for Salonika was thus the origin of the disputes which have since so sharply divided the Balkan League. About the same time a Bulgarian detachment occupied the seaport of Kavala.

CHAPTER VIII

MONTENEGRO UP TO THE ARMISTICE OF DECEMBER 1912

THE first State to declare war against Turkey was Montenegro. On October 8, 1912, his own birthday, King Nicholas I., the father-in-law of the King of Italy, took up the sword which Victor Emmanuel III. was upon the point of laying down. Nor was it, perhaps, unfitting that the Balkan country, over whose rude crags the Crescent had never flown, should be the champion to throw down the glove of defiance in that death-struggle which was to free the Balkans from the Turk.

Pretexts for war were not wanting, for the normal state of life upon the frontier between Montenegro and Albania is one of disguised warfare. A Montenegrin post had been besieged by the Turks, and the apologies of the Turkish Minister at Cettigne were not accepted. Nothing further was needed to set alight the conflagration.

War against Turkey was declared, and at once every Montenegrin sprang to arms. They have been used to bear them. When Ivan the Black was in 1484 forced back by the Ottomans into the mountains of Czornahora, he caused the general assembly to pass a law somewhat as follows : " In times of war against the Turk no Montenegrin shall be able, without the order of his chief, to leave the field of battle ; he who takes to flight shall be dishonoured for ever, despised, and banished from the

midst of his family, who shall give him a woman's dress
and a spindle ; the women shall drive him out with blows
of the spindle, as a coward and traitor to his country."
Such were the conditions under which the Montenegrins
began that struggle against the Ottoman which has lasted
until our own day.

The object of that struggle can be best explained by a
few sentences on the history of the Montenegrins. The
country takes its name, the Black Mountain, from the
forests of black pines which once covered its mountains,
and which furnished timber to the ship-builders of Rome
and of Venice.   Under the Romans it formed part of
Illyricum ; later as the Principality of Dioclea it belonged
to the old Servian Empire, which had its headquarters
under a *Zhupan* at Novi-Bazar, but which in 900 held
Ragusa. From that Empire it passed to the Byzantines,
but was recovered by Servia under the Nemanya dynasty,
which descended from one of its princes (1180–1389).
After the death of Stephen Dushan (1336–1355) and the
murder of his son Stephen (Urosh) V. (1355–1367), a
noble Servian called Balsha or Basha founded a principality which included Montenegro.

From 1360 to 1421 Balsha's descendants are said to
have reigned as independent princes in Northern Albania,
and one of them proclaimed himself prince of Zeta in
1367, after seizing the fortress of Skodar (Skutari), and
is sometimes said to have extended his territories as far as
Cattaro, which, however, voluntarily accepted the suzerainty of Venice in 1420. His dominions included the
present Montenegro, Podgoritza, Spuzh and Jabliak,
the isles of Lake Skutari, and the territory of Antivari.
In 1484 one of his descendants, Ivan Czernowitz (Ivan
the Black), was driven from Jabliak by the Turks, and
forced to take refuge in the Black Mountain. He installed
a printing-press at Cettigne, and the splendid missals
printed at it are the oldest specimens of printing in any

Slavonic tongue. His successor, George V. Czernowitz, abdicated in 1516, and placed the government in the hands of its metropolitan (Vladika), who ruled the country as Prince-Bishops, aided by a civil governor, from 1516 to 1833. Until 1696 the dignity was an elective one, but in that year it became hereditary in the family of Petrovich, which had immigrated from Herzegovina in 1476. The first of the dynasty, Daniel I. (1696–1735), made a treaty with Peter the Great of Russia in 1715, since which time Montenegro has always been the spoilt child of the Russian Tsars. Nicholas I. ascended the throne in 1860. In 1876, in alliance with Milan of Servia, he waged a successful war against Turkey, and in 1878, by the Treaty of Berlin, Montenegro received Niksic, Spuzh, Podgoritza, Plava, Gusinie, and Antivari, thus more than doubling her territory. As the Moslem inhabitants of Plava and Gusinie objected to annexation, a conference of the Powers in 1880 decided to give those towns to Turkey, and Montenegro received Dulcigno in exchange. Two daughters of King Nicholas married two grand-dukes of Russia in 1889, one has become Queen of Italy, and a fourth Crown Princess of Servia. In 1905 a national assembly was established, which proved a failure. In 1910 Prince Nicholas took the title of King of Montenegro.

There is a tradition that at the creation the Lord passed above the earth distributing stones out of a bag, and that when He was passing above Montenegro the bag burst and all the remaining stones fell upon the Black Mountain. The Kingdom of Montenegro has an area of 3255 square miles, being less than that of the united counties of Kent, Surrey, and Sussex. The centre of the country is composed of Triassic and Cretaceous rocks, and forms a portion of that high arid tableland called the Karst which extends southward along the east coast of the Adriatic from the Triglav, the highest summit of the Julian Alps (in Gradisca and Carniola), to the Shar-Dagh

Range, near Prizrend, in Macedonia. The name is derived from a Celtic word akin to our " Cairn," and means the Land of Stones. This district has a rolling surface, with numerous oval-shaped depressions ("sinks") and deep fissures, with a severe climate subject to great extremes of heat and cold. It ranges in height from 2500 ft. to 5000 ft. The vegetation is sparse (grass, scrub-oak, and beech), and there are few streams. The east side of Montenegro is also a high tableland, but is intersected with the well-wooded valleys of the Tara and the Lim, which produce a good deal of fruit, including melons and grapes, tobacco, corn, maize, and potatoes. The coast-belt is fertile, mild, and well cultivated, and two harvests are generally reaped in a year, chiefly of fruits (grapes, olives, figs, pomegranates, mulberries, almonds) and corn. The wealth of the people consists in sheep, cattle, goats, swine, horses, and bees. A little wine is made. They number about 250,000, nearly all of whom are of Servian descent, and of the Greek Orthodox faith, but there are about 5000 Albanian Catholics. The Montenegrins are thus closely akin, not only to the Servians and to the inhabitants of the sanjak of Novi-Bazar and of the vilayet of Kossovo, but are separated only by religious differences from the Croats, who inhabit the Austro-Hungarian provinces of Croatia, Slavonia, Dalmatia, Bosnia, and Herzegovina. The trade of Montenegro is mainly in Austrian hands. The little kingdom, however, is unable to support its population, and many thousands of Montenegrins are to be found, chiefly as miners, in the Western States of America and on the Pacific Coast Belt of Canada. Curiously enough, many Italian masons and navvies have found employment on the public works of Montenegro.

The only really fertile territory adjacent to the frontiers of Montenegro is to be found in the plains round the lake and town of Skutari, which, as we have seen, from 1367 to 1484 formed a part of the Principality. Their population is, however, Catholic and Albanian, and is profoundly hostile to the Montenegrin rule. The high tableland of the sanjak, with its rigorous climate and bare grazing lands, although much of the pasturage, especially in the region extending between the rivers Lim and Ibas, is excellent, is claimed by Servia, and in any case would have but little attraction for Montenegrin immigrants.

Consequently the main object of Montenegrin policy has been for centuries to recover Skutari, although their efforts have been opposed not only by the Turks but also by the Catholic and Moslem Albanian clans who inhabit Skutari and the territories to the north and east of it, and whose road to the coast pastures near Alessio, where they winter their sheep, lies through that city. To the Montenegrins the capture of Skutari became the chief object of the war.

The Montenegrins began the war by an advance from Podgoritza upon Tusi, a position upon the eastern shore of the Lake of Skutari, which bars the road to that fortress. At Shiroka they had been ambushed by the Turks, who fired upon them from the heights and even from guns mounted upon the steamers which ply upon the lake. Two of these, the *Chioggia* and the *Liceni*, played an important part in the defence of Skutari.

From Shiroka the wounded had to be brought to Cettigne, over a distance of about forty miles, part of the way being in cabs and carriages over roads that must have jolted them agonisingly, then by steamer to Rjeka, where the motor-omnibuses brought them down the mountain passes to Cettigne. It was a journey of six hours across the rough mountain roads, and many of them had legs and arms broken by the Turkish shrapnel, bits of glass, zinc, and iron, tearing their bodies in the most hideous fashion, yet they bore it unflinchingly. They even smoked.

The Montenegrin preparations for war, so far as offensive operations were concerned, were very complete, but so far as her hospitals were concerned she was miserably prepared.

When war broke out the Montenegrins had at Cettigne just a thousand odd beds, but they had not enough drugs, instruments, or nurses, and they had only one doctor to a division. It is true that all the Red Cross Societies in Europe were sending them supplies, but in the meantime the mountain warriors had to lie suffering tortures, suffering silently and gladly for their country.

It is good for Englishmen to remember, and, as a Herefordshire man, I am proud to relate that the chief organiser of such hospitals as existed at the outset of the campaign was a brave Herefordshire lady.

" Miss Edith Mary Durham, who acted as lady war correspondent for the *Daily Chronicle* and the *Manchester Guardian* jointly, is a sister of Dr. Herbert E. Durham of Dunelm, Hampton Park, and for some time resided with her brother at Broomy Hill. Miss Durham, whose father was the late Mr. Arthur Durham, a famous Brook Street surgeon, is an artist of considerable reputation. She studied in the Royal Academy School, and has had her pictures hung in the Academy, but she abandoned art for travel, and for the last twelve years or more she has been frequently in the Balkans, where she has on many occasions had the distribution of the relief funds for the benefit of families who have suffered as a result of massacres by the Turks. Miss Durham is especially well known at the Court of the Royal House of Montenegro. The philanthropic and literary work which she has done in connection with the Balkan States has earned her the gratitude both of rulers and people. In consequence of this she has, of course, been the object of much suspicion on the part of the Austrian Government, who have regarded her as an emissary engaged in promoting the interests of some rival Government. It is needless to say that there is no justification for this suspicion, Miss Durham having spent her life with no other object than that of benefiting the oppressed peoples of that country. She has great courage, lively wit, remarkable powers of conversation, and a common sense which immediately impresses those who meet her. She has already taken the lead as the most successful correspondent in the field. Her telegrams were the first full ones to reach London." *

To these mountaineers it is heaven to die for Montenegro. Long ages of conflict with the Turks have made their country to them what Spain was to the Spaniard of the Middle Ages. It is only those peoples who have had such a training who nowadays understand what the word " country " means.

On October 14 there were not more than forty thousand Montenegrin troops in the field, and in the first week of the war the official list of killed and wounded was more than a thousand. Not one wounded man could be spared, and it was clear that such heavy casualties were not expected.

The same rain which was drenching the prisoners at Podgoritza was turning the roads round Antivari into a swamp, and rendered General Martinovitch's quarters round Tarabosh inaccessible, at least so he stated, to strangers. He graciously, however, conceded permission to the correspondents to view the operations from a high mountain, which they reached from Antivari over roads covered with wounded men, riding in creaking carriages, and mules laden with ammunition and stores struggling through the mud, whilst every small cottage flew the Red Cross flag—all outward and visible signs of the desperate struggle going on before Tarabosh beneath a pall of fog which hid the bombardment from the onlookers on their mountain top.

* *Hereford Journal*, Saturday, October 19, 1912.

Fugitives from Skutari brought flattering tales of the terrible plight to which the city was reduced. A Turk who had escaped said that famine threatened the inhabitants. A loaf of bread cost 10s.

On Sunday, October 27, at ten in the morning, the bombardment of the city began, and Skutari was subjected to a cross fire from the Montenegrin batteries on the north, west, and south, and from those on the island of Vranjina in the Lake of Skutari, whence King Nicholas watched the action.

After the first hour thick clouds of smoke were seen rising from the eastern quarter of the town, but the result of the bombardment, which was favoured by splendid weather, could not be ascertained.

Meanwhile how had General Martinovitch been faring at Tarabosh ?

Fortunately for the Montenegrins the heavy artillery had been brought up before the rains turned the roads into quagmires, although it was feared that the guns could not be brought back before the summer, but long trains of mules laden with ammunition continued to plough their way from the base at Antivari to Tarabosh, the chief point of the attack upon Skutari. A correspondent who attempted the journey on foot, which usually means an eight hours' ride, was forced to give up the attempt after being at times in mud up to his waist, and at others chest-deep in water.*

However, by Saturday, October 26, Mr. John Prioleau, the correspondent of the *Daily Mail*, had been able to reach Mourican, General Martinovitch's headquarters, about eight miles from Skutari, after a tramp during which he crossed rivers in flood. Tarabosh was being bombarded, and shells burst on the mountain above Mourican.

" General Martinovitch says that the spirit of his troops is excellent despite the terrible weather conditions, and

* *Daily Express*, Monday, October 28, 1912 (Albert Wyndham).

that they are eager to make an assault on the great fort.

" The hill of Sirokskagir, which commands Tarabosh, was taken yesterday by assault. Both General Martinovitch and his staff are suffering great privations. According to General Martinovitch the resistance of the Turks is magnificent, and they fight like madmen.

" I am writing this message on a hilltop above Mourican and opposite Tarabosh, watching the fine marksmanship of the Montenegrin artillery. Hour after hour the heavy bombardment continues, drawing but perfunctory replies from the great sullen stronghold I have come so far and waited so long to see. The huge fort-crowned hill stares grimly at me two miles away across the valley. Minute by minute the Montenegrin guns on my right thunder out, and shells go ringing over the deep ravine.

" Without glasses I can see a heavy plume of smoke jet out on the sides of the fort, marking the place where the sure aim of the Montenegrins spreads a ring of destruction. From time to time the crackle of rifles and the rattle of machine guns add themselves to the chorus of war which fills the rich valley. With glasses I can distinguish the Turkish soldiers working in the trenches on the hillside.

" I was interrupted by an officer, who requested me to move below the sky-line for fear of drawing the fire of the Turks. In the valley to the south of Tarabosh I could see the shelling of thirty Turkish food-stuff boats.

" In the distance the Adriatic gleams like molten silver. Over this exquisite panorama speeds the wailing of the messengers of death, the only other sound being that made by a solitary shepherd who is drawing a monotonous tune from a rude and ancient ' gouzla,' a native single-stringed fiddle. Between each crashing series of gun-shots the wild complaint of the clumsy instrument quavers out amongst the sun-baked rocks.

" The food and sleeping accommodation here are of the roughest nature. The supplies are very short, with only the barest necessaries for both officers and men, who fare equally. Yet we are welcomed most heartily and given everything obtainable.

" The friendliest sentiments are entertained towards us as Englishmen wherever we go. 'England is Montenegro's best friend,' I hear everywhere.

" The present position of the Montenegrins attacking Tarabosh is this. The fortress is being attacked from the south, the south-east, and the north-east; and the only way open to Skutari is to the east through Bascelek." *

By October 29 the prospective southern line of retreat of the Turks from Skutari to San Giovanni di Medua had been cut by a Montenegrin flying column.

Shiroka Mountain had been taken on the evening of October 24, after a desperate assault. The houses on the mountain showed the extent of the panic which seized upon the Turks. All the portable belongings were taken away, while empty cartridges scattered on the floor told of the last desperate firing before the flight to Skutari.

" One house was littered with dried tobacco leaves, onions, and maize. Here was an amulet in a feathered case, there a painted cradle with a child's clothes still lying on it.

" Throughout the journey through the conquered territory, I saw no burnt or pillaged houses.

" The Turks are fighting like madmen, but there is a general hope that we shall soon be in Skutari.

" On the morrow a spectator of the bombardment from Mount Mourican saw the whole theatre of war spread out before him. Tarabosh stretches sheer and bare, rising bleakly to the sky, grey and enormous. Behind lies Skutari, the key to Albania. Only this fortress lies between the town and General Martinovitch's army.

* *Daily Mail*, Tuesday, October 29, 1912.

" The mountain was booming with sound like the blows of a gigantic hammer. The air was torn apart with the passage of the swift messengers of death flying with hoarse screams growing ever fainter, till white columns of smoke drifting above Tarabosh showed the truth of the gunners' aim.

" On the top of the fortress one could distinguish the clusters of Turkish huts, while lower down, hidden under the shoulder of the smaller range of wooded hills, the sunlight gleams on the white roofs of a bivouac.

" Across the plain could be seen the shining waters of the Boyana River where thirty captured Turkish provision boats were being made into a pontoon bridge.

" Never was warfare waged in fairer setting with the sun beating down from a clear sky after days of pitiless rain.

" We slept on planks in a Turkish stable by a wood fire, two aged Montenegrins keeping guard by their own log fire. We slept in the clothes in which we had marched all day." *

On that same day, October 27, *The Times* correspondent was privileged to accompany King Nicholas, with the Austrian attachés and the Servian General Alexandrovitch, to a point of vantage on the shores of the Lake of Skutari, from which he obtained a distant view of the battle between General Lazarovitch and the Turks in the plain north of Skutari. On the 26th His Majesty had ventured on a launch beneath the heights of Tarabosh, but in view of the possible activity of the Turkish gunboats, had been persuaded by Prince Danilo, who was directing the operations, not to expose himself to such risks.

On the same day a Turkish force of 5000 or 6000 Nizams and a similar number of Bashi-bazouks, which was entrenched two or three miles to the northward of

* *Daily Express*, Tuesday, October 22, 1912.

Skutari under the command of Hassan Riza Pasha, engaged the Montenegrins under General Lazarovitch, with whom were Prince Danilo, the Generalissimo, and Prince Mirko. Their forces were about equal in number to those of the Turks, whose defeat would have implied annihilation or surrender, but they had the advantage in artillery, having with them four heavy guns. As, according to Montenegrin accounts, Skutari was completely surrounded, the only way open for the Turks to retreat would seem to have been across the Drin to the Mirdite country, where, however, no very friendly reception awaited them.

The Turks opened the attack, and the Montenegrins fell back. " The Montenegrins," it was explained in official quarters, " are so certain of eventual victory, that their tactics are rather to wear the enemy out by shell fire, than to advance at all costs and incur unnecessary loss of life." *

On Sunday, October 27, the Montenegrins were in the neighbourhood of Gruda. " About ten o'clock puffs of smoke from the bursting Turkish shells indicated that the engagement had recommenced. Although the weather was very fine, a slight haze and the refraction of the sun from the lake made it impossible to follow the course of the operations. Heavy firing, with which was mingled the sound of the guns at Tarabosh, continued until the return of the King to Rjeka in the afternoon. The ground on which the battle is taking place is described as flat and sandy."

It was the sixth day of the bombardment of Tarabosh, and a determined but unsuccessful attempt was made by the Turks to retake the Shiroka heights above the fortress to which their Montenegrin captors had imagined that they would prove the key. However, on Friday, October 25, the Montenegrins were asserted in official

* *The Times*, Tuesday, October 29, 1912.

quarters to have occupied Obleka, " a position south of Tarabosh, from which in the event of the refusal of Skutari to capitulate after the capture of the fortress it is stated that it will be possible to shell the town."

But a new foe was entering the field against Montenegro. " At Puleni, on the banks of the Boyana, the Montenegrin column marching from Mourican met a few Turks and some Malissoris. Here also a skirmish took place, both sides using their small bronze guns, and the brief artillery duel caused many losses, being carried on at a range of a little more than a thousand yards. It is calculated that the Montenegrins had three hundred wounded.

" Similar incidents are taking place every day around Skutari, in expectation of the final battle for the surrender, which seems to become more and more improbable. A state of panic prevails in Skutari, and many Christians have hoisted white flags over their houses. The Mussulmans immediately remove these, and owing to this there are frequent disturbances." *

A fresh factor was complicating the conflict. Albania was beginning to assert her claims to be a nation.

" Later on, attracted by a group of soldiers sitting in a circle smoking cigarettes, I strolled across to them. They broke apart as I came up and disclosed a shape under a canvas sheet, stiff and stark and very still. A priest came with a purple and silver cassock over his khaki coat, and a Bible and a bottle in his hands. A grizzle-faced soldier with eyes that were wet, but not crying, stood at the head of the bundle, and helped to lift it. This was the thing that gripped at the heart-strings, for this man was the father ; and since it is the glory of every Montenegrin to die in battle for his country, he did not weep for his son. ' Otche . . . Otche,' he said, as they laid the bundle carefully into the grave, that had been dug above

* *Daily Telegraph*, Friday, November 1, 1912.

another grave. 'That's it . . . That's it. . . . Now he's all right. Eh, father,' turning to the priest; ; 'he'll sleep well now, won't he? His soul's in heaven now, isn't it? What else can we do in these days than die ourselves or give our sons' lives for Montenegro?'

" The priest read the burial service. A shell dropped from Tarabosh with a clap of noise away in the woods on the hill above where the guns were hidden. The priest poured red wine from his bottle into the grave, and scattered earth on it. All the soldiers took up handfuls of earth and sprinkled it over the shrouded body of their comrade." *

The next afternoon the correspondents set out for Antivari, and passed the night at Katrikol, which is a sort of half-way house between Antivari and the front. " The warmth of the welcome and the food they gave us there had something of the quality of an Arabian Nights' entertainment. We squatted round the table, the commandant, the doctor, and Mehmet Pekovitch Mirkovitch, a Mussulman Serb who commands a thousand Albanians. Their courtesy and grace were splendid. The commandant picked from the bowl of mutton the finest pieces for us ; he broke the pomegranates into four ; he gave us rice and cheese and figs, with black coffee afterwards, and we stretched ourselves on the mattresses by the fire and smoked until they made up beds of canvas sheets on the floor for us."

The road was full of Montenegrin women carrying up stores to Mourican. " Burdened as they were with heavy packs they outdistanced us easily, for the hard way was familiar to them, and their soft-soled sandals were more suited to the rocks than our heavy boots. Most of the women were wrinkled and old ; they had carried provisions to their men before. Some of them had been on the road for three or four days, plodding along always with

* *Daily Express*, Monday, November 4, 1912.

bent backs, stopping now and then to rest their packs on a ledge of rock in the stone wall that edged the way in some parts. Meanwhile the Turkish women, veiled and white, worked in the maize fields, and every Albanian we passed knew Mehmet Mirkovitch and greeted him. All the way the soldiers we met wanted to know who we were. Many of them had been in American and spoke English with the twang which they had learnt in the Montana mines. It was odd to hear a Montenegrin soldier say, ' Wall, so long, Johnny. See you again sure '." *

All through the week infantry combats took place daily.

Meanwhile Tarabosh was undergoing a terrible bombardment. The Montenegrin artillery on Mourican poured a dense and continuous hail of shrapnel and shell upon the two summits of the mountain and upon the saddle which unites them. " But in spite of the fire which invested them, the Turks replied with much spirit and considerable accuracy.

" The smaller guns in the trenches half-way up the slope felt the effects of the quick-firing guns on Mourican, which poured into that intermediate position more than two hundred shrapnel in a very brief space of time. A portion of a wall near the embrasure was beaten down by the Montenegrins, and into the breach were successively fired more than a thousand shrapnel, which dismounted a gun, killing five artillerymen.

" As this was regarded as a general attack Turkish infantry were seen hurrying to occupy the trenches. But the combat was only an artillery engagement, and the troops, who in the meanwhile had suffered some losses, returned to their shelters.

" Towards three o'clock on the afternoon of October 31, dense columns of smoke were perceived rising from Tarabosh. It might have been caused by the bursting of

* *Daily Express*, Monday, November 4, 1912.

Montenegrin shells and shrapnel, but the smoke persisted until the evening, and it is believed that one of the
barracks built of wood had been set on fire."

Heavy rain towards evening suspended the operations,
but at night two Turkish battalions unsuccessfully
attempted to retake the Montenegrin positions at Sirotsi
Gora by surprise. Fighting also continued daily along
the Boyana, and at Apulaj lasted several hours, the
Turks attempting a turning movement which did not
succeed." *

In the eyes of good military judges the Montenegrin
operations against Tarabosh cannot be acccounted a
success. As a military critic writing in *The Times* on
October 19 had said, in speaking of the first attack upon
Tarabosh : " There is little doubt that the twenty battalions of Martinovitch's column which attacked Tarabosh
Hill, some 2000 feet high and immediately to the southwest of Skutari, were repulsed with heavy loss." It was
thought that the difficulties of the terrain would render
it difficult for Lazarovitch to bring up his eighteen
battalions from Tusi over thirty miles to support him,
whilst Vukotitch's column, which took Berane, was out
of court for operations round Skutari. But it was felt
that the ups and downs of the war in Montenegro, even
if a Servian force advanced to support the Montenegrins,
would not decide the fate of the main armies, and that
the contest must be fought out upon a wider theatre.

An attempt, in part successful, to blow up the Montenegrin arsenal at Antivari occurred on November 2,
when " two English Red Cross assistants named Beverstock and Williams entered the fortress whilst the shells
were exploding, and assisted the wounded lodged there
to escape at the peril of their own lives " ; † but this
event had little permanent effect upon the fortunes even

* *Daily Telegraph*, Saturday, November 2, 1912.
† *Daily Express*, Monday, November 4, 1912.

of Montenegro, and events were now moving fast to a climax in a wider field.

In defiance of the high hopes of the Montenegrins the siege of Skutari was destined to drag on for months.

To Montenegro, as we have said, the war came to mean purely the siege of Skutari, if we except the slight diversion which they made by occupying San Giovanni di Medua.

The lines before Skutari were reinforced by General Martinovitch, who withdrew his right wing, which had been advanced too far towards San Giovanni di Medua on to the Boyana, on November 7. The weather was terrible; sharp frosts at night and heavy snowstorms rendered the work of supplying the Montenegrin outposts in the mountains very difficult.

In the meantime Skutari had been vigorously bombarded, and shells fell in the town, killing women and children in the streets, and damaging the Catholic Cathedral. A protest was sent by the Consular Body to King Nicholas, but he refused to discontinue the bombardment on the ground that Skutari is a fortified town. Captain Habka, the Austro-Hungarian military attaché, who had accompanied the Montenegrin envoy, Major Matanovitch, to the city, was received by Hassan Riza Bey, the commandant of the fortress, who said :

" I have ammunition for several months, and I am well supplied with victuals. The *moral* of my troops is excellent. The word ' surrender ' will never pass my lips ; before that I should have seen my last battalion slaughtered, my last gun shattered. I believe that I can hold the city as long as the war lasts, and hold it I will. If, when peace is made, I am compelled to evacuate the city by orders from Constantinople, I will do so, but as long as the war goes on I will resist. If ever Constantinople ordered me to haul down my flag I would refuse, for as long as I live I will not permit any dishonour to the flag I have sworn to defend.   If one of my officers or soldiers came to me and spoke of surrender I would have him shot at once.   I have nothing to add, either to-day or to-morrow." *

The hardships suffered by the besiegers were terrible. Snow fell for thirty-two hours without intermission, a furious gale was raging, and the mountain paths were buried knee-deep in drifts.   The temperature was Siberian.   A battery of Montenegrin artillery and a company of infantry were posted at a height of nearly three thousand feet on Mount Kraja, from which Tarabosh was being bombarded.   The men had not even tents to protect them, and had to seek refuge from the cold and snow in improvised shelters in the crevices of the rocks. At night the temperature fell to eight degrees below zero. The men unhesitatingly sacrificed their big greatcoats for the protection of the guns and ammunition.   While the sentinels remained watching at their posts, the men spent the night huddled round their fires, striving to keep alive the feeble flame which the whirlwinds of snow continually threatened to extinguish.   From time to time a fierce shriek, followed by a report, rent the air.   A Turkish shell warned the Montenegrins to keep a sharp look-out, and the night was soon lit up with the flashes of contending batteries.

The weather made the work of furnishing the outposts with supplies desperately laborious.   The Montenegrin women, who had taken upon themselves the work of carrying up the supplies, made on foot journeys hours in length and never allowed themselves to be deterred by the raging of the storm.   They came and went daily, despite wind and snow, bent double under their loads of bread and flour; and the fate of some who had been killed by the Turkish fire did not intimidate the survivors, who did not shrink from going into the foremost trenches to seek out

* *Morning Post*, Saturday, November 9, 1912.

their relations, and bear away the bodies of the slain ; some of them, too, sank down on the mountain pathways worn out by cold and weariness. Noble acts were performed as simply and naturally as the common duties of the day.

Much as the Montenegrins had to suffer, the Turks suffered still more, since their ranks were filled with men but ill fitted to resist such hardships. Indeed the garrison of Tarabosh was already suffering intensely from the cold, and the Montenegrin shells had damaged the barracks and forced the soldiers to retire to underground casemates.

In the meantime General Martinovitch had removed his headquarters to Sukadajeit, south of the Boyana, where the Montenegrins were endeavouring to drive the Turks from the isolated hill of Brusati, which cut the road to San Giovanni di Medua, and thus to effect a junction with General Lazarovitch's force. The Turks still held Brditza Hill on their own right and had flooded the marshes of the Drin to their left, so that a close investment of Skutari was impossible.

The fort-crowned hills round Skutari, Tarabosh, and Mourican were wrapped in a white snow mantle, and not a sign of life was to be perceived. The town itself looked dead. The little shops in the bazaar remained open, but there were no buyers, and even in the week of Little Bairam, when every Mussulman purchases new finery for the festival, the tailors who, in other years, had worked day and night, were idle. Seated on the ground the workmen looked through the door and watched the people pass. In one day bread rose fourpence a pound, although there were between nine and ten thousand bags of flour in the town, but wood and coal were lacking to bake it. Fuel was confiscated everywhere, all the wooden lampposts and fences were pulled down, and the stores of builders' timber were guarded by sentinels. Gipsies flying from the hill villages before the Montenegrins sought refuge in the town, but were driven back by sentries, and wandered about between the armies exposed to the fire of both. To damp the ardour of the enemy, rumours were assiduously spread that the Moslems would massacre the Christians before the Montenegrins could occupy Skutari. A similar ruse was tried at Constantinople, and undoubtedly produced some effect upon the Great Powers. A violent bombardment took place in the middle of November, and the Mussulman quarter suffered severely. At the first shot the Turks fled for the Christian quarter, leaving everything behind them. Most of the crowd were women dragging children behind them. Those who had time to think took away what bread they had. The women did not cry or scream. They ran lightly and silently along the road almost like phantoms. If they stopped it was to tell each other hurriedly what they had seen. One of them had left six dead in her house. Another had seen nine, but the dead were everywhere. Shells continued to fall in the streets, many passers-by were killed, many wounded, but it was impossible to help them. Soon fires broke out, and the red glow served as a target for the Montenegrin guns. Two rich Turks were unwilling to abandon their houses full of valuable property, and offered a large reward to a few Mussulmans to remain in their company. Everybody fled. Terrified as they were, the Turks decided to remain to protect their goods. During the night a shell struck their house, killing one of them. The other, unable to remain, at last quitted his dwelling, almost crushed by the heavy load he carried off with him. To husband his ammunition Riza Bey would not allow his batteries to reply to the Montenegrins.

During this time General Martinovitch occupied San Giovanni di Medua, from which he marched with four battalions in the direction of Alessio, fighting two engage-

ments on his way with the retreating Turks. The Austro-
Hungarian Minister at Cettigne pointed out to King
Nicholas that neither Montenegro nor Servia could be
allowed to hold any portion of the Albanian coast permanently. The King's reply, " that it was inconceivable
that Alessio and San Giovanni di Medua should not be
annexed to Servia, and that since Turkey no longer
exists, Albania has ceased to be autonomous," created an
unpleasant impression at Vienna.

A very severe engagement between the Montenegrins
and the Turks took place in the marshes of the valley of
the River Boyana on November 12, when the Turks
endeavoured to surprise the Montenegrin position at
Kodaic on its eastern bank.

" During the night two Turkish battalions, supported
by several field-guns, pushed quietly forward with the
object of surprising the enemy. They succeeded in crossing the marshy ground unobserved, and reached the
bottom of the declivity. Then they opened a galling rifle
fire and rushed shouting up the slope. The Montenegrins
quickly recovered from the first surprise caused by the
unexpected attack, and used their favourable position on
the brow of the hill to harass the advancing Turkish
column with a vigorous fire, which strewed the slope with
the bodies of fallen Turks as the attacking force made its
way up the steep ascent.

" The Turks, seeing their hope of taking the enemy by
surprise shattered, hesitated for a moment; then they
brought the field-guns into action. These rained a deadly
hail of shells on the Montenegrin position. The commandant of the Dulcigno battalion, seeing his men hesitate
for a moment under the Turkish fire, sprang forward,
snatched a rifle from the hand of a dead man, and began
to fire like a common soldier. The example of their
leader put fresh courage into the Montenegrins, who
dashed forward and put to flight the head of the Turkish

column, which had just reached the brow of the hill. The gallant commandant, however, paid for his heroism with his life. A piece of a bursting shell struck him in the chest, and he was carried by his men to the rear and laid on the ground close to the colours of the battalion. The chaplain gave the dying man the benediction. Then he snatched up a rifle, dashed forward, and cried to the soldiers, waving above his head the cross which hung at his breast, ' Forward, sons of the Chornahora ! In defence of the Cross and for the glory of King Nicholas ! '

" The priest, brandishing his cross like a banner, had reached the firing-line, when a fresh and more furious volley came from the Turkish column. He stood alone among the recumbent soldiers, who continued their fire without interruption, stretched on their chests. Then he began to chant the sacred hymn ' God against the infidels.' Beneath his calm and even tones could be distinguished the fierce note of battle. He had reached the lines which, translated into English, run : ' Tribulations shall not avail to bend the army of the Lord ! ' when his voice suddenly died away ; he waved his arms above his head and fell on his face, a bullet through his heart.

" The rifle fire had given the alarm to the second line of the Montenegrin force. A battery was hurried, helped by the strong arms of the soldiers, over the wellnigh impassable swamp to the hill, and succeeded in repelling the Turkish advance. The Turks endeavoured by a series of furious attacks to obtain possession of the guns, but were every time driven back, although the officer in command fell shot through the head. Eventually the whole Turkish force was compelled to beat a retreat. The Montenegrins, having repelled the Turkish attack, withdrew to the Boyana." *

On November 14 simultaneous proposals with a view

* *Morning Post*, Saturday, November 16, 1912.

to mediation were made to the Balkan States by the representatives of the Great Powers. At Sofia, Belgrade, and Athens the governments agreed to take the matter into consideration. At Cettigne the King's representative declared that Montenegro could not now consent to an armistice except subject to the unconditional surrender of Skutari.

On November 18 the Turks made a sortie from Skutari and endeavoured to seize the bridge over the Kiri River so as to cut the Montenegrin line of communication, but were repulsed. At San Giovanni di Medua the garrison repulsed an attack by a party of 500 Turkish soldiers, who came up disguised as Malissori tribesmen, cheering for the King of Montenegro, and lowering their rifles in token of surrender.

Operations before Skutari were greatly delayed by the floods caused by the overflow of the Boyana which had been dammed by the Turks, who had diverted the waters of the Drin into its channel. The besieging army barely outnumbered the besieged, who might have worn them out by constant sorties, but the Turkish commander remained passive. Possibly he knew that he had no hope of relief from outside, and preferred to prolong his resistance by husbanding his men and ammunition.

Writing from Mourican on November 19, a correspondent of the *Daily Telegraph* says:

"Living as I have now done for a week with the Montenegrin army in the field, I realise what a peculiar mixture of tribal and military systems prevails. I see a commandant of a battalion order a private to do something or other, and I observe that the man argues with much vigour as to the advisability of his doing it; the commandant, equally vigorous, entering by no means unwillingly into the wordy combat. Perhaps the soldier agrees to do what he was told, perhaps he does not. In the latter event he walks off, apparently unconvinced as to its desirability or necessity. The officer turns aside with a gesture, and either leaves the thing undone or asks another man to get on with it." *

On Wednesday, November 20, the Montenegrins received a very welcome reinforcement.

" General Vukotitch, at the head of the three victorious brigades which in the space of a month succeeded in conquering almost the whole of the Sanjak of Novi-Bazar and half Old Servia, arrived outside Skutari after a remarkable march over the mountains under the most severe climatic conditions imaginable. Old Servia is separated from Montenegro by a high mountain chain, the journey over which is at all times painful and wearisome ; a détour for the purpose of securing an easier route would have cost the army fifteen days of valuable time. Accordingly it was decided to undertake the difficult march over the snow-covered mountains. The long columns of men, with guns and baggage-wagons, set out to make its way up the snow-sprinkled slopes, cut by raging torrents swollen by the heavy rains. The weather, which it had been hoped would improve, became worse ; the men were obliged to plough through snow-drifts in which they sank above the knees. Nevertheless the column succeeded in arriving practically intact at Alto Vallico, a position situated at a height of 2190 metres (over 6000 feet), although its path was dotted with the bodies of dead and dying baggage animals. A few men, too, sank down by the way, and were lost in the snow-drifts, but the column pursued its march without faltering. The crossing of Mount Boroditza will fill a worthy place in the history of mountain marches."

General Vukotitch's troops were allotted to the positions to the south of the town.

The task of the Montenegrins was made all the harder because the country surrounding Skutari is divided into

* *Daily Telegraph*, Tuesday, November 26, 1912.

four segments by the Rivers Kiri, Drin, and Boyana together with Lake Skutari.

The army of Prince Danilo occupied the two to the east of the Drin, and General Martinovitch, whose army was thus astride the Boyana, the remainder. To his lot it fell to besiege Tarabosh. A long razor-backed ridge rises abruptly from the southern shore of the Lake of Skutari to a height of 2000 feet. At the end of this ridge are the two peaks of Tarabosh, a mile apart, of which the smaller looks down directly upon Skutari.

In order to take Skutari more speedily, General Martinovitch surveyed the ground between Gruda and Vraka, a Serb village lying to the east of the city. Vraka, although exposed to the Turkish projectiles, was not deserted by its inhabitants, who said they would live and die with the Montenegrins. Between Vraka and Skutari the ground is open, and very favourable to an assault. Here the advanced Montenegrin batteries were posted. The guns were either covered by undulations of the ground or hidden by screens of earth.

In the task of constructing their works the Montenegrins received great aid from the Italian navvies, numbers of whom are employed in Montenegro. It was these men who transported the heavy artillery to Zogai and Rioli. Italians organised the flotilla of three steamers and one benzine launch on Lake Skutari which brought the stores and provisions to the advanced dépôts, from which long files of women carried them to the fighting line, and which brought back the wounded to the base despite the fire of the Turkish batteries, against which the Geneva Cross afforded them no protection.

Politically, however, Italy was supporting Austria at Cettigne in her demands for the evacuation of San Giovanni di Medua and Alessio, as forming parts of an autonomous Albania.

It was true that the Government papers supported

Austria, and pointed out that the independence of Albania was the keystone of Italian policy in the Balkans, but the opposition papers not only disapproved of the action of Italy in putting pressure upon the Serb states but pointed out that a Servian port upon the Adriatic would be of advantage to Italy, because meat, which was cheap in Servia, could then be imported to supply the Italian markets. As the *Messaggiero*, the *Daily Mail* of Rome, put the matter : " There is in the Italian people a sense of strong sympathy with the Serbs and their allies, who are entitled to the gratitude of all Europe for liberating it from the Ottoman Government, and from the incubus of war perpetually hovering over the Balkans. We are, therefore, ready to follow Austria diplomatically, but with reason, and without relinquishing the intention of circumscribing the area of the war. Beyond that the Italian people will not move. Austria, which has never had any sense of liberty because it has never been a nation—Austria, which in Europe expressed and expresses the principle of absolutism, as many Italian provinces can remember, suddenly shows concern for the poor Albanians and plays with Irredentism. What a comedy ! We all desire an Albanian principality, but not that it may become an Austrian fief. Are we to act as Austria thinks convenient ? The Government knows well that the people would not follow it in that policy. Italy, with all respect to our ally, wants peace."

Meanwhile the Albanians themselves were proclaiming the principle, " Albania for the Albanians ! " Only the Hoti and Grudi tribes held to Montenegro.

The Albanian problem was a complicated one. During General Pavlovitch's march from Prizrend and Djakova to Alessio, his forces had, it is true, suffered no opposition from the Mirdites, but these are a Malissori Roman Catholic clan, and might also have been influenced by the presence of Turkish troops in their country whom they might have wished to see expelled. The Albanians of the Skumbi Valley who cluster round Durazzo are Moslems, and therefore more friendly to the Turks.

The great object of both Austria and Italy in desiring an autonomous Albania is to prevent either Power from acquiring possession of the Gulf of Vallona, situated behind the long tongue of Cape Linguetta, the ancient Acroceraunian Mountains, at the entrance to the Adriatic. But such a country will not be an easy one to govern. The Malissori tribes in the north are predatory clansmen, and will prove as inconvenient associates for the more civilised Tosks south of the Skumbi River, many of whom are traders, as are the Calabrians for the Piedmontese in Italy itself. They are not fanatical Moslems, but are on the whole in favour of Turkish rule, and assisted the Turks during the operations in the Kossovo vilayet. Moreover, it was supposed that they could rely upon the help of the Turkish fugitives from Monastir and Florina, who had reached the hills west of Kastoria and Lake Ochrida, and might stir up the tribesmen to resist the Servian and Greek advance. Even, leaving the strictly Albanian territory out of extent, Western Macedonia is eminently favourable for guerilla warfare, and such bands might easily be found.

Thus, in the end, the attitude both of the Turkish fugitives and of the Albanians themselves proved a very negligible factor so far as the operations around Skutari, and even at Durazzo, were concerned.

At Skutari the artillery duel between the opponents was resumed on November 28. The Montenegrins brought up several battalions to strengthen the positions they held to the east of Skutari, and held a line running from Dristi on the north through Muselimi and Rogami to Gajtani on the south-east of the town. From their batteries at Gajtani they bombarded the Turkish positions to the south of the city, especially the detached hill, 445 feet high, near Bardanjolt, which was looked upon as

the key to the defences, which were weakest on that side.
On November 29 hostilities were suspended by orders
from Cettigne, on account of the negotiations for an
armistice, which were in progress in Thrace.

The preparations for this bombardment had been very
complete. The heavy guns from Mourican were brought
up to the advanced position of Oblok, and every available mountain, including that of Siroka, which directly
commands Tarabosh, was occupied by Montenegrin
artillerymen. Between Mourican and Oblok twenty-four
battalions were concentrated, whilst other troops were
stationed between Zogai on the lake and Mount Siroka.
Hand grenades were provided for the stormers.

The stormers were preceded by a voluntary corps,
called the " death volunteers." It was their duty to
discover and to destroy or damage the mines which had
been laid by the Turkish troops, and though their task
was almost certain death, they never hesitated for a
moment. Amongst them were some Italians, one of
whom, a man named Albini from Brescia, was arrested by
some Montenegrins when on his way from San Giovanni
di Medua to Oblok carrying a Mauser rifle. He was
brought before General Lekotitch and sentenced to death
as a spy, but was saved by the arrival of the Head of the
Italian ambulance, Dr. Cappellari, who explained
matters.

On their side the Turks armed two lake steamers, the
Chioggia and the *Liceni*, with quick-firing guns, and these
played a part in an attack on the Montenegrin lines, which
the *Liceni* tried to enfilade, supported by the guns of the
fortress and by searchlights. She was, however, driven
off by shrapnel fire and forced to take refuge behind the
point of Siroka, whilst an attempt of the Turks to dis-
lodge the Montenegrins from the positions threatening
Bardanjolt failed.

Such was the last fighting which took place before the

conclusion of the armistice, at least with the sanction of the Montenegrin commanders.

On December 8, however, Riza Bey refused to receive a Montenegrin *parlementaire* bearing a letter from the German Minister announcing the conclusion of the armistice, and the garrison of the town took the offensive. Fighting occurred on Tarabosh, and the Turks were repulsed with loss, but, with this exception, things remained quiet until Christmas night (old style, January 6, 1913) when the Turks attacked the centre of the Montenegrin position, but were repulsed with loss. This event led political circles at Cettigne to urge their Government to break off the peace negotiations in London, but this was not done. Within Skutari itself there were several mutinies amongst the Redifs and Bashi-bazouks, who found the iron discipline imposed by Hassan Bey very irksome. Two mitrailleuses, indeed, had in one instance to be brought into play against the mutineers.

King Nicholas definitely declared that Skutari was to remain Montenegrin in an Order issued to his troops on January 7, 1913.

" In conveying his good wishes on the occasion of the Greek Christmas to his army, ' King Nicholas expresses his admiration of the endurance and sacrifice of the soldiers, whose iron wills, he says, have never for a moment faltered throughout the continuous fighting in which they have been engaged, and the hardships occasioned by the weather. He is proud of his army, and is persuaded that it will distinguish itself even more should anybody dispute the rights of Montenegro to incorporate its old capital within its boundaries.'

" This is apparently in reference to Skutari, and the reports that Austria-Hungary might oppose its possession by Montenegro. The King's Order continues : ' It is our duty and right to annex the homes of our ancestors, and to assemble round their graves. For that it would be a joy for us to die.'

"Finally the King informs the army that his good wishes and blessing are to be conveyed to it personally by his three sons, and expresses a hope that this bloody war may come to an early end." *

The commander of the garrison at Skutari, Hassan Riza Bey, continued hostilities notwithstanding the armistice.

"The Servian troops at Alessio, after having repulsed a Turkish attack, sent *parlementaires* to Riza Bey to inquire whether he knew that an armistice had been concluded, and if he were willing to observe it. The Servian envoys, having reached Gorbelusha, met Ibrahim Talad Bey, who stated that the garrison at Skutari had no official knowledge of the armistice, and therefore intended to continue hostilities. The behaviour of Riza Bey has produced indignation, as the Servians, on account of their observance of the armistice, cannot take proper measures to reduce the garrison of Skutari to a strict defensive under the protection of the forts, but are constantly exposed to sudden attacks on the part of the garrison." †

* *Daily Telegraph*, Thursday, January 9, 1913.
† *Ibid.*, Friday, January 10, 1913.

CHAPTER IX

MONTENEGRO AFTER THE ARMISTICE TILL THE FALL OF SKUTARI

THE most important question which arose out of the war, so far as Europe was concerned, was that of the delimitation of Albania, and it was owing to the division of opinion upon this subject that the peace of the world for some weeks trembled in the balance.

To explain the question we must go back to the beginning of the war.

As already shown, the efforts of the Montenegrins were throughout its course chiefly, though not wholly, directed to the occupation of Skutari, which they consider to be all-important to their economic development. But whatever their rights to Skutari may be upon historic grounds, in the present it is inhabited by Albanians and of its population of 36,000, 27,000 are Moslems and 8000 are Christians. But the Christians in Northern Albania are nearly all Roman Catholics, and their great clans, the Mirdits, Khthela, Shkreli, Shala, and Nikaj, have, as Mr. D. G. Hogarth shows, held aloof altogether from either side. The Moslem Albanians have held by the Turks; only the Malissori have supported the Montenegrins to a certain extent. The Turks from the first took advantage of the situation to detach the Malissori from the Montenegrins, but effected little.

On the other hand, national feeling has long been strong amongst the Albanians of Central Albania, who constituted a provisional government under Ismail Kemal Bey with its own flag at Durazzo at an early period of the war : in Southern Albania the population were divided in their opinions, some joining the Greeks, others assisting the Turkish stragglers who had escaped being shut up in Yanina.

Thus Albania was divided against itself, and at the outset looked as if it would fall an easy prey to the Montenegrins, the Servians, and the Greeks.

But it was not to the interest of two of the Great Powers that the coast-line of Albania should pass under the control of either the Slavs or the Greeks. If Italy had good reason to fear the Greeks in Epirus, Austria had even more reason to fear that if Montenegro and Servia succeeded in attaining their ends she would see the great Albanian harbours in their possession. Moreover Austria, as Protector of the Albanian Roman Catholics, could not be deaf to their appeals to her to save them from being crushed down under the heel of the Orthodox Montenegrins. Thus the question of Skutari became of menacing importance, for if Austria was the Protector of the Catholic Albanians, Russia was the natural protector of the Orthodox Slavs. Both Austria and Russia mobilised forces on the Galician Polish frontier, whilst Austria kept a strong force on her southern border.

Undeterred by military or diplomatic threats, the Montenegrins pressed forward the siege of Skutari. If Austria accepted their challenge, Russia, they believed, would fly to their help. But behind Austria are Germany and Italy, behind Russia stand France and England. Thus all Europe might have been involved in war for the sake of a few wretched and decayed ports on the coast of the Adriatic.

It is to Sir Edward Grey and to the Tsar of Russia that

we owe it that this awful calamity has been averted from the world.

King Nicholas, when addressing his troops before Skutari on Old Christmas Day, which in Montenegro falls at the beginning of January, said plainly that he meant to retain Skutari for Montenegro.

The question formed one of the principal subjects which were discussed by Prince Gottfried Hohenlohe during his mission to St. Petersburg, but, on his return to Vienna on February 10, it soon became plain that no settlement had been reached.

The *Neue Freie Presse* was informed that the Austro-Hungarian and Russian standpoints in regard to the Albanian question were still antagonistic. Russia supported the Montenegrin demand for the possession of Skutari, and while disposed eventually to accept a compromise that would leave the town of Skutari to Albania and give the plain and the lake to Montenegro, had hitherto found no disposition on the part of Austria-Hungary to accept the compromises. Differences also existed with regard to the future of Ipek, Djakova, and Prizrend.

An official article in the *Fremdenblatt* insisted that the conquest of Skutari by the Serbo-Montenegrin forces would not decide the fate of the city, which would be determined by the Great Powers.

" The standpoint," continued the article, " of Austria-Hungary and Italy is well known to the Montenegrin Government. In this, as in other cases, a military *fait accompli* would not possess decisive significance. It would be desirable that the allied Serbo-Montenegrin troops, taking these warnings into account, should avoid further sacrifice of life."

Prince Gottfried Hohenlohe was confined to his room for some days by a chill, so could not have a personal interview with the Emperor Francis Joseph. Thus his reply to the Tsar's letter was delayed.

But while these warnings were appearing in Vienna the Montenegrins were sustaining a serious disaster before Skutari. It was some time before the details were allowed to transpire, and they did not reach England before February 24.

The Servians, whose strength was generally stated to have been 15,000, succeeded on February 6, under Colonel Popovitch, in capturing the outlying position of Bushati, about seven miles to the south of Skutari. Next day, in order to support the Servian advance upon Brditza, the Montenegrins opened a heavy bombardment against this position and against Tarabosh. Simultaneously, General Vukotitch, who had at his disposal about 30,000 men, almost all of whom had been massed on the east side of the River Kiri, launched an attack from the north against the Turkish positions on Bardanjolt. The remainder of his force was left in the plain north of the town in order to guard the Montenegrin lines, and to occupy the Turkish troops on this side of Skutari. In the course of the day these troops made a counter-attack on the Montenegrin trenches which, according to independent eye-witnesses, looked at one time as if it might be successful. Meanwhile General Vukotitch's force, supported by the fire of covering batteries, attempted to advance from Musselimi and Nerfusha up the slopes of Bardanjolt. On this side the fighting continued practically without intermission until three o'clock on Sunday afternoon, February 9, when the Turks were finally dislodged from their position.

The same afternoon a gallant and successful attempt was made to destroy the wire entanglements on the southern slope of Tarabosh, in order to prepare the way for the attack which was planned for the next day. General Martinovitch having called for volunteers to undertake the dangerous task, a hundred men came forward to whom were entrusted twenty bombs. These consisted of metal tubes, 9 ft. long and a couple of inches in diameter, which are filled with explosives and fitted with a time-fuse. The volunteer party having advanced with the greatest coolness to the wire entanglement, were able to place the bombs in position, and successfully destroyed a considerable length of the barricade, losing, however, about one-fifth of their number.

All night long the bombardment continued, and it was hoped next day that the Servians would take Brditza. But those who expected this were reckoning without knowing the strength of Brditza's armament, and were in ignorance of the state of the plain which the Servians had to cross. The transverse canals, made either expressly by the Turks as a means of fortification, or possibly by the peasants for carrying off superfluous water, effectually prevented anything in the shape of a night surprise, while the long range of the Turkish guns, in regard to which the Servians assert they had no information, kept the attacking force, who were armed only with mountain guns, at a safe distance during the daytime.

Meanwhile, doubtless believing that all was going well with the Servians and elsewhere, General Martinovitch, on Saturday afternoon, prepared to complete his operations by attacking Tarabosh. Troops were pushed forward from Zogaj along the shore of the lake on the one side and up the slopes of the hill on the other. At five o'clock the principal advance along the knife-edge ridge leading from Shiroka Gora to Tarabosh began. The Turks having been shelled off the absolutely bare ground surrounding the summit of Tarabosh, one Montenegrin battalion, supported by two others, advanced with perfect coolness to take their place. But for the same reason that the Turks were unable to remain there it was impossible for the Montenegrins to maintain their position. With splendid endurance they lay out all Saturday night, and the greater part of Sunday practically without cover under a hail of shrapnel, apparently from the Turkish guns on the far shore of the lake close to the town of Skutari, and were only withdrawn on Sunday evening after heavy losses.   It was a magnificent exhibition of courage, but in the circumstances a useless one.

Earlier in the day (Sunday) General Vukotitch's troops had been proving that when it comes to the point the Montenegrin is still as good a fighting man as ever. Gradually they had succeeded in pushing their way up the slopes of Bardanjolt until they were close enough to the enemy's position to deliver an assault.   The Turks were well protected by trenches and behind breastworks and sandbags.   Further, there was a triple row of wire entanglements to be crossed.   The final encounter at close quarters seems to have been of the fiercest description.   According to accounts of some who took part in the fighting, it was not until they had been repulsed once that the Montenegrins finally drove the Turks out.   Both sides seem to have fought with the greatest bravery, but by three o'clock the position had been captured, and the Turks were retreating to the lower ground on the western side of the hill, where they entrenched themselves, it was supposed, along the Kiri, which must be crossed before the Montenegrins could enter the town.

It was officially stated that the whole summit of the hill was in Montenegrin hands, but from other information it appeared that the Turks were still in possession of part of it.   No attempt apparently was made to drive in the Turks from the trenches to the north of the town. The Montenegrin losses on this side were something approaching 4000, while the action round Tarabosh cost General Martinovitch nearly 1000 men.   The Servians lost over 1000.

A fortnight later there were 1700 or 1800 wounded in Cettigne, a town whose normal population is under 5000.   Considerable difficulties arose as to the food supplies. But in spite of the fact that there could hardly be a family in Montenegro which had not suffered loss, since the number of killed and wounded must have amounted to nine or ten per cent. of the whole army,— or in other words, of the whole adult male population,— there appeared to be no question in the minds of the people that, when all was ready, the attack on Skutari would be resumed.

Could Montenegro now give way? In diplomacy there is no sentiment where small states are concerned. On February 25 the Austrian Premier, Count Stürgkh, made a statement that the tension would soon slacken. This the *Reichspost* explained by saying that since February 22, when an exchange of views on the Balkan question took place between the Austrian and Russian ambassadors in London, the improvement in the international situation had made great and notable progress. An important agreement had been arrived at on the Albanian question at least as regards general principles. Skutari was to remain Albanian. Russia thus evacuated an advanced position which had hitherto impeded the settlement of Balkan affairs. Thus the greatest difficulty was removed though others remained behind. Austria had reason to thank German diplomacy for her labours to remove the distrust of Austria which had been felt in Russia since 1909. The defeat of Russian policy about Bosnia-Herzegovina had lain at the root of all subsequent difficulties.

These hopes were premature.

The King of Montenegro appealed for the last time to the Tsar of Russia from the decision of the Powers which gave Skutari to Albania, and M. Popovitch, the Montenegrin delegate in London, on February 27, made public the following Declaration on behalf of his Government:

"My Government has no reason to alter its views on the subject of the capture and the possession, already decided upon, of Skutari and its environs. Skutari is a vital question for Montenegro. The Treaty of Berlin itself recognised the fact when it stipulated by a theoretical and ill-contrived provision that Turkey should give Montenegro access to the sea through her territory. The sacrifices we have made to attain this object are enormous. The diplomatists of the Great Powers, with Russia at their head, may come to any agreement they like among themselves, and on paper, but we shall see if their peoples allow us to be stifled. . . . Our cause is just. All our Allies are with us, as is also the whole public opinion of civilised Europe. Heroism gave Montenegro its birth and so far has dowered it with life. If such be her destiny heroism will teach her to die. This is my last word."

Montenegro was appealing from diplomacy to democracy, but, fortunately, ill-informed democracy is not all-powerful with the real statesmen of Europe. Such was the situation at the beginning of March.

The Montenegrins reckoned that the Pan-Slavist agitation would force Russia to support them against Austria, and her allies Germany and Italy. Russia is in alliance with France, upon whom, in these circumstances, she could call for support, and, like France, is united with England by the closest understanding. But an understanding is not an alliance, and no written treaty exists by which England is bound to send military forces to the Continent to support France and still less Russia.

Two facts dominated the situation. Although England had in 1905, 1908, and 1911, when France and Germany were on the verge of war about Morocco, assured France that she would fight in her defence to her last man and her last shilling, yet she was under no treaty obligation to do so, and thus was left free to use her own discretion as to the occasions on which she might think it fit to take military action to support France. Secondly, the Tsar was

determined to keep in his own hands the entire control of
Russia's foreign policy. The statesmen of France and
Russia were well aware that they had no legal right to
claim the support of England unconditionally, and thus
were naturally disinclined to support the Southern Slavs,
if such a policy should bring them into collision with the
Triple Alliance.

Further, from the English point of view, as will be
seen, the Montenegrins possessed absolutely no title
whatsoever to claim either Skutari or a single acre of
Albanian soil, for, like the other Balkan states, they
professed to be waging war in defence of Mr. Gladstone's
policy of the Balkans for the Balkan peoples. This the
Great Powers had authorised when, at the commencement of the war, they had substituted in their Identic
Note the words " Localisation of the War " for " maintenance of the *status quo*," which were used in the French
Draft. But as the claims of Albania to be a nationality
could not be contested, England held that Montenegro
had put herself in the wrong by attacking Albania, a view
Russia, in the end, came to share.

But time was required to show that Mr. Asquith was
right in standing by Mr. Gladstone's policy, and that by
standing by Mr. Gladstone's policy he might preserve the
peace of the world. Few outside the French, English,
and Russian Foreign Offices, and a few newspaper men,
knew the exact nature of the Triple understanding. That
understanding has always been opposed by a certain
section of French opinion, represented by the *Temps*, and
that section might well be reinforced by those Radicals
who still felt sore that M. Poincaré should have been elected
President by the votes of the Right. The leading newspaper of the Var, the department which M. Clemenceau
represents in the Senate, assumed an anti-English tone.
In Russia the organisers of the Pan-Slavist banquets
openly spoke of the back-sliding of England. In England,

many of those Labour and Socialist members who keep
Mr. Asquith in power have long leaned towards Germany,
partly out of sympathy with the German Socialists,
partly out of sheer ignorance of the means by which her
friendship can be kept, whilst all Europe knew that
General v. Bartholdi had, in his famous pamphlet, openly
said that France and Russia would be hopelessly weakened
if England were lured away from her understanding with
them. Who could tell what effect an offer on the part of
Germany to limit her naval armaments might produce
amongst English Liberals, who wanted to divert their
naval and military expenditure to social reform ? Hence
causes which might create suspicion and mistrust between
the French and English democracies were not wanting.
It is to the lasting credit of the English Opposition that
they stood firmly by Mr. Asquith when he entered upon a
policy which could only be carried out by methods
susceptible of the gravest misunderstanding. To support
Germany and Austria, at a moment when France and
Russia were straining at the leash, seemed absolutely
repugnant to the everyday Englishman and to the everyday Frenchman. Not a murmur had been heard amongst
the English working men when the Agadir crisis was at
its height, and when they knew that any moment might
bring them the call to fight Germany in support of France.
Treachery to our allies is a rare incident in English
history. To ourselves and to the French Mr. Asquith's
policy might well have seemed treachery. Yet he was in
the right and was fully justified by the results.

At Vienna the outlook in the first week of March was a
black one. The slow progress of the Russian negotiations, the danger of complications if Skutari fell, the
refusal of Servia to evacuate Durazzo, and the discussions
amongst the Balkan Allies which might impede unanimity in regard to the conditions of peace, were the causes
of the depression. The Allies were at loggerheads. The

entry of the Greeks into Yanina had taken place on March 7 ; but whereas the Servian troops in garrison at Salonika heartily associated themselves with their Greek comrades in their rejoicings, the local Bulgarian journal, *Pravo*, failed even to mention the event. The harbour of Salonika was crowded with transports destined to convey 20,000 Servian troops, amongst whose armaments were numerous Krupp guns, to San Giovanni di Medua, that Albanian harbour from which they were to march to the assistance of the besiegers of Skutari. Finally, Austrian observers noted with disquietude the instability of the Mahmud Shevket Cabinet, which the instinct of self-preservation prevented from working for peace with the unanimity which its head desired.

Amongst these disquieting questions the question of Skutari evidently stood foremost. There was reason to believe that Austro-Hungarian diplomacy was negotiating earnestly with Servia in regard to the delimitation of Albania, and, though nothing was positively known, it was shrewdly suspected that Servia would be able to purchase Austro-Hungarian consent to the incorporation of Djakova, with its neighbouring monastery so sacrosanct in Serb eyes, by agreeing formally to recognise Skutari as an integral part of Albania. The action of the Servian military authorities, who were sending considerable quantities of ammunition and war material to Durazzo, and who, as has been said, were reinforcing the forces besieging Skutari, did not, however, augur well for their tractability.

An Austrian military journal which knew every gaiter-button on the list of the stores sent by Servia to the Adriatic coast, claimed that if Servia and Greece intended to confront Europe with a *fait accompli* at Skutari they would not only be opposed by one group of the Great Powers, but would have to reckon with a general insurrection in Albania supported on this occasion by artillery.

To Austria, Skutari in Montenegrin, Durazzo in Servian hands were, indeed, questions of gravest import. The readers of the journal in question might, however, well have asked what effect the spectacle of an Albanian insurrection, supported by the House of Hapsburg, might have had amongst those populations of Austria-Hungary which are neither German nor Magyar. Such an argument, therefore, was one more proof of the gravity of the situation.

It was plain that until Skutari fell it could not be clearly seen what attitude any Power, or group of Powers, would adopt in regard to it. Italy had, for the moment, evidently decided to swallow with rare good grace the capture of Yanina by Greece, for it was stated on Italian official authority in the *Neue Freie Presse* that Italy would do nothing to prevent the incorporation of Southern Epirus with Yanina in the Greek kingdom, and, so it was argued, would not take any active share in a dispute about Northern Albania, in which she was far less directly concerned. It was suspected, moreover, that the military party in Russia wished to drag out the negotiations with Austria-Hungary until the military fate of Skutari was decided.

Had the Allies been cordially united amongst themselves the fall of Yanina, which took place upon March 4, might have greatly increased the gravity of the situation. Servia, it is true, congratulated the Greeks warmly upon an event which filled every Greek heart with rejoicing, but the Bulgarian official congratulations were chilly.

But whilst the Greek churches were resounding with Te Deums for the success of their army, events of even greater importance were transpiring in the Parliaments of Europe.

The German Emperor had been seriously disquieted by the lessons of the war. He had seen the Turkish Army, the creation of a German officer, Marshal von der Goltz, crumbling to pieces under the blows of the

Bulgarians. Those Bulgarians had been trained, in the
main armed, by French officers and manufacturers. He
had noted the rising spirit of France ; he saw that Austria
had failed to coerce Russia and the Southern Slavs. His
allies had become mere auxiliaries, and Germany saw
herself forced to face the possibility of being attacked on
two sides at once. A Bill raising the annual levy of recruits
to 700,000 men, and authorising an expenditure of
£60,000,000 on fortifications chiefly in Silesia, was
introduced into the Reichstag. France replied by increasing the length of her obligatory military service to three
years at a cost of £20,000,000 additional expenditure.
Italy, Austria, Russia, and Great Britain increased their
military and naval preparations. Chauvinism blazed up
in France, and shouts of " To Berlin ! " were heard in the
boulevards. Fortunately the provinces kept their heads,
and an article in *The Times*, blaming these manifestations,
was quoted with approval in provincial journals.

In the middle of March the Powers informed the Allies
that they would act as mediators and requested them to
formulate the terms of peace.

On Saturday, March 15, the Conference discussed their
reply, which they considered to be merely an acceptance
of the offer of mediation, for the proposal would, doubtless, be withdrawn or modified under pressure from the
Powers. The prestige of Europe, it is true, did not stand
high amongst the Balkan States, partly on account of the
fiasco of their original declaration as to the *status quo*,
partly owing to the prolonged wrangle between Russia
and Austria-Hungary about the Albanian question, which
would, however, it was hoped, be settled within a few
days.

Turkey remained calm. The Government were prepared to cede Thrace up to the Enos-Midia line, and to
leave the question of the Islands to the Powers. They
would even consent to allow certain concessions as to the

share of the Public Debt which was to be assumed by the Allies, and as to the claims made by them for the maintenance of prisoners and commandeering of war vessels, which would be equivalent to a war indemnity.

The official German Press remained surprisingly composed, even optimistic. The *North-German Gazette*, the Government organ, wrote :

" The demands of the Balkan League are in part very far-reaching.   Moreover, on more than one point they trespass on questions which are bound up with European interests, and which, therefore, cannot be solved without the co-operation of Europe—for example, the decision with regard to the future of Skutari and of the Ægean Islands, and the demand for a war indemnity.   In these circumstances the proposals of the Allies must be submitted to an exhaustive examination by the Powers. That means, unfortunately, exposing the universally cherished desire for peace to a new trial of patience. Nevertheless, we hold firm to the hope that the difficult work of European mediation can be happily carried through despite the obstacles which still stand in the way. . . .   Skutari, whatever its fate may be in this campaign, is to be united with the future Albania in accordance with the unanimous wish of Europe."

Would that wish have remained unanimous but for the policy of Mr. Asquith and of Tsar Nicholas II. ?

It is true that Turkey and the German financiers were on the best of terms, and that the Berlin correspondent of the *Frankfurter Zeitung* could discuss the possibility of cutting off the financial supplies of the proud victors by an understanding between the Powers which control the international money market.

But the soreness between Austria and Russia still continued, despite the fact that the Austrian demobilisation had begun, and quarrels of a grave nature were taking place amongst the Balkan Allies themselves.

Fighting took place between the Greek and Bulgarian forces of Nigrita, a village of 2750 inhabitants, one-third of whom are Servians, in the Macedonian vilayet of Seres, arising out of the refusal of the Greek garrison to allow the Bulgarian forces to enter. Thus, within 33 miles of Salonika, a Bulgarian force of two squadrons, four Krupp guns, and 600 bayonets lay facing a Greek force to which large reinforcements were being sent. The incident was bitterly commented on in the Bulgarian Sobranye, in which the Opposition, debating a statement made by M. Gueshoff in reply to interpellations, vigorously condemned the attitude of the Greeks and Servians, who, they said, were pursuing a policy of conquest to the detriment of the Bulgarians in the occupied territories, and attempting to demoralise them by methods of intimidation and violence. In speaking of the terms of peace offered to Turkey, and of the relations between the Allies, M. Gueshoff said :

" However desirous we may be of arriving at peace, this peace must fully recompense us for our enormous sacrifices before the armistice, and for our considerable losses after the renewal of hostilities, which were provoked by the refusal of the new Young Turk Government to accept the unanimous advice of the Great Powers, and the decisions not less unanimous of the Great Divan convoked by Kiamil Pasha. The elementary principles of justice demand that we shall be given more than we should have been content with before. Only people of superficial judgment can assert that after the renewal of the war we should gain no appreciable advantage. The failure of the Turkish landing in the Sea of Marmora, so long and carefully prepared, the destruction of a warship in the absence of any warships on our side, the memorable defeat at Bulair, when the Turks, according to their own statement, had more than 14,000 killed and wounded, the inability of the enemy to show themselves outside the fortified positions—these are facts that, together with the brilliant capture of Yanina by our Allies, the Greeks, prove irrefutably that our enemies have now no right to demand conditions more favourable than those which were offered to them by the Allies' delegates during the negotiations in London, and which they then refused so light-heartedly. It was therefore perfectly legitimate, in our opinion, for the Allies to recall these conditions in the reply which they sent to the Great Powers to-day, and to express their views concerning what should be given to the Allies after the new and heavy sacrifices which they have borne, not by any fault of their own. We hope that the judgment will be such as by its wisdom and justice will commend itself to both parties."

On the following day, March 15, M. Venezelos, speaking in the Chamber at Athens as to the relations between the Allies, said that difficulties in the question of the assignment of the various districts must arise, for the feelings of national exclusiveness were always strong. He hoped that in spite of everything the difficulties would be surmounted, and he was confident that the partition of the conquered territory would be traced, not by the local military authorities who regarded things from the somewhat restricted outlook of the soldier, or by chauvinistic elements, but by the responsible Governments, and that the Governments would have enough patriotism to be inspired with equity and justice, having in view the future and the importance to the Balkan peoples of continuing a line of policy which would have results very different from those of their former antagonism.

About the same time the Greeks occupied the Island principality of Samos amidst the enthusiasm of its inhabitants, and in Epirus were pushing north towards Argyro-Kastro, the northern limit of the Greek-speaking population, 47 miles north-west of Yanina.

The echoes of M. Venezelos' words had scarcely died

away in the hall of the Boulé when, for a few moments, the hand of Death came to bid the wrangles of Balkan diplomacy cease, and the nations stood in spellbound silence before the bier of the murdered King of Greece. On March 18, King George, whose last words had been of the Greek successes, was struck down at Salonika, which he had won for Greece, by an assassin's hand.

But whilst the heirs to the Bulgarian and Servian thrones were kneeling in homage to a monarch of whom even the Turkish Press spoke with the courtesy due to a chivalrous foe, and whilst the funeral chants were sounding through the flower-decked Cathedral at Athens, the wranglings of the Great Powers continued till, suddenly, Europe started back appalled when an article in *The Times* and a speech by Sir Edward Grey raised the curtain which had concealed from her the fact that she had, all unconsciously, been standing on the very brink of war.

The obstinacy of Montenegro and of Servia in regard to the delimitations of the northern and north-eastern frontiers of Albania, that is to say, the question as to whether Skutari and Djakova were to be Albanian or respectively Montenegrin and Servian, had all but brought the difficulties between Russia and Austria to a head. Yet Skutari is but a town in a marsh, always liable to inundations, with a population of 36,000, three-fourths of whom are Moslem, whilst Djakova is described as a burgh of 2000 houses, with a population of 25,000, of whom four-fifths are Albanianised Mohammedans. The dispute about these delectable possessions, with their joint population of 61,000 inhabitants, scarcely exceeding that of Bath, might well have brought into collision six great Empires, with a population amounting in all to at least a third of the total population of the globe. It may well be asked if diplomatic folly and *amour-propre* could go further.

On dynastic grounds Montenegro could not give way about Skutari; whilst Servia was not only pledged to support her ally until the end of the war, but, on religious grounds, was eager to retain Djakova and the sacred monastery near it.   They were backed by all the Pan-Slavist feeling in Russia, where agitation was rising to fever heat.   Austria, in her desire to play off the Albanians against her dangerous neighbours the Serbs, was equally firm in defence of Albania, whilst Germany supported her both as an ally and, indirectly, in defence of her own economic and financial interests both in Turkey in Europe and in Turkey in Asia.   But for the difficulties occasioned by the Agrarian party in Austria, the whole question might probably have been settled by the Balkan Allies agreeing to maintain the existing Turkish Customs tariff, which is far more favourable to Austrian manufactured goods than their own, and to guarantee Austrian trade favourable freight rates over the Balkan railways, in which Austria has large interests, for a long term of years. The Austrian agriculturists, however, refused to grant the Allies, in return for Customs, concessions for their agricultural produce.

It was left to Mr. Asquith to speak the word which in all probability prevented a European war.   The British Parliament reassembled, after a brief recess, on Monday, March 10, for the session of 1913.   In the course of the debate on the Address in reply to the King's Speech, the question of the Balkan War naturally came under discussion.   In the course of Mr. Asquith's speech, Lord H. Cecil interrupted the Prime Minister with a question as to whether we had any agreement with France and Russia which bound us to send troops overseas to support France in case of her being engaged in war with a Continental Power.   Mr. Asquith at once replied that we had no understanding or engagements with France other than those which were known to the House, and that under these agreements no engagement existed which bound us in any way to render military aid to France in any contingency whatsoever.

Pulveris exiguo iactu. " It was but a pinch of dust," yet that pinch of dust may, under Divine Providence, have saved Europe and the world from a war of wolves.

Mr. Asquith opened the eyes of the man in the street, by whom, in this age of democracy, the Foreign Policy of the great nations, with the possible exception of Germany, is in the last resort determined. Yet, in making public this truth, he ran a very serious risk of making the Entente with France and Russia impossible in the future, without acquiring the friendship of Germany, Austria, or Italy. Once more England might find herself in a position of splendid isolation. The Radicals in France were fretting under the stigma of their defeat in the Presidential Election in January, and might well have raised an anti-English agitation as the means of putting M. Poincaré's power under an even stricter control than now exists. The reactionary elements in Russia also might have made common cause with the Pan-Slavists in order to put an end to the Tsar's plans of Reform, and have sacrificed the understanding with England without regret. On the other hand, Germany has not shown the slightest intention of limiting the naval construction programmes of either herself or her allies in order to meet the wishes of England. Mr. Asquith, however, relied upon the support of the statesmen of France and Russia, who were, of course, fully aware of the footing on which their understanding with England really stood, and the incident passed off without awakening any serious ill-feeling in either country. Yet Mr. Asquith by his quiet words knocked the arms out of the hands of the French and Russian Chauvinists, and checked the war fever in Europe, although, as Sir Edward Grey said, we were for some days on the very verge of war.

But if the Tsar had bowed before the Pan-Slavist storm, Mr. Asquith's effort for peace would probably have failed, and might have cost us the friendship of both France and Russia.

The men who conduct the Foreign business of the Russian Empire are M. Sazonoff and M. Kokoffsteff, men as versed in diplomacy and as well acquainted with European affairs as are Lord Lansdowne, Sir Edward Grey, or M. Delcassé. They work entirely with the Tsar, and do and say nothing which has not his approval. His Imperial Majesty, though devoted to the Slav cause, was determined that the Balkan question should be settled pacifically by the European Powers, and with that end in view, from the very outset of the crisis, agreed to the transfer of Skutari to Albania, even if pressure had to be applied to Montenegro by the Powers. This matter has been emphasised by his representatives in the Balkan capitals without reserve, and His Imperial Majesty's conduct towards them has been as frank and loyal as that of England. Had the Tsar deviated but a hair's-breadth from this policy, war must have been the result. The Montenegrins would have forced the hands of Europe; for, as it was, a serious misunderstanding very nearly arose between France and England when the negotiations for applying naval coercion to the recalcitrant State were in progress.

On Saturday, March 22, a leading article in *The Times* had warned the British public that Europe stood on the very brink of war. On that day, however, the Conference of Ambassadors in London arrived at a settlement respecting the northern and north-eastern frontiers of the Albanian State, which on Monday, March 24, was known to have been accepted by the Powers. The danger had, indeed, been great. In defiance of the warnings of Austria-Hungary the Montenegrins had concentrated their bombardment on the Christian quarters of Skutari, and the efforts of the Consuls to check it had been useless. The Italian and Russian representatives at Cettigne were, however, supporting the Austrian representations on the subject. Several other occurrences in Albania had also roused Austro-Hungarian feeling to fever heat. A Franciscan monk, Father Palitch, had been shot at Djakova by the Montenegrin police, and Catholic Albanians in that neighbourhood had been forcibly baptized into the Orthodox Church by the Montenegrin authorities. The captain of the steamship *Skodra* of the Hungaro-Croatian Line had also been arrested by the military authorities at San Giovanni di Medua, on grounds said to be wholly frivolous, and was severely maltreated. In the first two cases, although the persons concerned were not, like the captain of the *Skodra*, Austro-Hungarian subjects, the Monarchy claimed the right to intervene in view of the protectorate which she has, since 1617, exercised over the Catholic population of Albania. Fortunately the Austrians had to call upon Mgr. Miedia, Archbishop of Uskub, for a report throwing light upon the circumstances of Father Palitch's death. That prelate, although drawing a stipend from Austria, is a very sturdy Albanian Catholic, and well knows how carefully the question of the Austro-Hungarian Proctectorate over his co-religionists requires to be handled if it is not to cause serious friction between Austria, Italy, and Servia. Austrian zeal for undenominational humanity was regarded with suspicion in some diplomatic quarters at Vienna, where men laughed at the fervour with which that great Viennese Jewish organ the *Neue Freie Presse* described the Christian fortitude of the martyred Palitch. It would have been in better keeping to have selected the *Reichspost* for the publication of his acts.

The Montenegrin version of the affair was that Father Palitch had publicly stirred up the population against the Montenegrins, and was being taken, under escort, from Ipek to Djakova for trial along with other guilty persons. On the way he tried to escape. The gendarmes summoned him three times to stop, but he did not heed the warning, and the escort fired, killing him and two of his companions. The Catholic Archbishop of Prizrend was informed of the unfortunate occurrence and undertook an investigation. However, information reached Cettigne from an outside source which threw some doubt upon certain of the details, and therefore on March 24 a Montenegrin official was sent to Djakova to hold an independent inquiry. The Montenegrin Government did not attempt to deny that Father Palitch was shot, but said that if it was proved that any person was guilty of having acted in excess of his powers he would be punished accordingly.

As regarded the alleged forcible conversion to the Orthodox Faith of Catholic Albanians at Djakova and its neighbourhood to the number of about 800, Montenegro absolutely denied that force was used. The Montenegrin Government stated that in the newly conquered territory many Moslems and Catholics announced their desire to become members of the Orthodox Church. The Montenegrin clerical authorities tried to dissuade them, pointing out that it was better to postpone their entry into the new faith until conditions became more settled. In order to make this advice more effective the Archbishop of Prizrend was permitted to come to Djakova, so that by the exercise of his influence the Catholics might be dissuaded from changing their religion. Finally they denied that the town of Skutari had been definitely bombarded, although it was admitted that shells might have fallen elsewhere than on the fortifications.

The strongly worded communications made on March 21 and March 23 by the Austro-Hungarian representative at Cettigne on these subjects, as to the last of which he was supported by the Italian Minister, highly incensed public opinion in Montenegro.

On Monday, March 24, two weekly organs of the Press Bureau of the Vienna Foreign Office sounded a threatening and a bellicose note. One of them claimed that the Austro-Hungarian rejoinder to Montenegro as to the case of Father Palitch was in reality an ultimatum, as it would prove to be unless Montenegro quickly yielded. The other argued that since a European war over Skutari in Albania was out of the question, Austria-Hungary should act as she thought best and " requite every insult with a kick."

This action had not found the Russian Government unprepared. Pretexts for intervention had been accumulating during the previous days somewhat too rapidly. It was admitted that Montenegro was by no means blameless. At the same time it was felt that if the Dual Monarchy had chosen that moment to raise a point of honour as to grievances which had been just as acute in some instances throughout the whole campaign, it was because she thought it would be easier for her to secure compensation for the change in the balance of power in the Balkans, and for the expenses which her mobilisation had entailed upon her, before than after the fall of Skutari.

King Nicholas's expectations that Russia would desert the concert of the European Powers on his account had so far been disappointed. Any attempt, however, on the part of Austria-Hungary to obtain redress from Montenegro single-handed would have raised an outcry in Russia with which the Tsar's Government would have had to reckon.

Fortunately the Montenegrin answers to the Austrian representations were not regarded as unsatisfactory.

The question at issue as to the rights of Protectorate over the Albanian Catholics was no simple one. Italy stated that if Austria held a Consular inquiry into the circumstances of Father Palitch's death and the alleged forcible conversions, she would do the same so as to prevent the creation of a precedent in favour of Austria. The Pope, too, who never forgets that in his youth he was an Austrian subject, and owes it to Victor Emmanuel II. that he is an Italian, showed that, not for the first time in the history of the Papacy, the Pope was less Papist than the Hapsburgs. He gave a useful hint to their Catholic zealots.

His organ, the *Osservatore Romano*, after saying that the alleged horrors appeared equally incredible whether they were attributed to Servia or Montenegro, added:

" If, indeed, it does not seem probable that such acts of violence and atrocities against ministers of religion and Catholics could be perpetrated by officials and soldiers of a country (Montenegro) that has a concordat with the Holy See, it would seem equally unlikely that they should have been perpetrated by Servians, inasmuch as they would stand in too glaring and monstrous a contrast to the reports recently divulged by their Government concerning its intention to initiate negotiations with Rome."

Italian opinion was unequally divided. The *Tribuna* admitted that the Austrian Note did allude to coercive measures in the event of a Montenegrin refusal, but thought the threat was justified. It suggested that Servia might hand over Djakova to Montenegro by way of compensation for Skutari. The *Giornale d'Italia*, on the other hand, asserted that Italy had an equal right with Austria to exercise a Protectorate over the Catholics of Northern Albania, and reminded the Government that the bonds of the Triple Alliance should not signify passive adherence to anything that Austria-Hungary pleased to undertake.

At St. Petersburg the decision of the Montenegrins, " adopted from considerations of humanity," to allow non-combatants to leave Skutari was applauded, and was regarded as an earnest of success for the collective representations to be undertaken with regard to the bombardment. This action was taken on the strength of the definition of the northern and north-eastern boundaries of Albania agreed to in London on Saturday, March 22. The Austro-Russian agreement as to the future of Skutari and Djakova, which was the direct outcome of the recent St. Petersburg negotiations (that is, of those carried on subsequently by Prince G. v. Hohenlohe's mission), formed an essential link in the completion of the task of the Powers. It was not clearly understood, therefore, why, on March 21, Austria-Hungary should have forestalled single-handed a step which was so manifestly imminent, and have reiterated her demand on March 23. That Note was regarded as an ultimatum, and it was felt that an ultimatum at that juncture would be incompatible with the spirit of the St. Petersburg Agreement. The basis of the Skutari and Djakova settlement was Austria-Hungary's assurance that she did not cherish aggressive designs towards her southern neighbours. The Russian Government was inquiring at Vienna as to the Austro-Hungarian intentions, which, it assumed, remained unchanged. The possibility that Austria might succumb to a sudden temptation to reassert her claim to ancient rights in the Balkans or recoup herself for her military expenditure was always present in the Russian mind. The attitude of Russia was made clear by the decision taken as to the Albanian frontiers on March 22 in London. By rendering such a settlement possible Russia had shown that she possessed a high conception of her mission for peace in Europe. This settlement was regarded as the first step towards the pacification of the Balkans, for it was thought that the Allies concerned would immediately be invited by the Powers to withdraw their troops from Albania, which was now no longer an Ottoman province, but the newly defined territory of a friendly state.

Such were the circumstances under which, on March 25, Sir Edward Grey unexpectedly delivered in the House of Commons a speech which did much to preserve peace.

It made a great impression, and was heard with strained attention. It was supplementary to the statement made by the Prime Minister on the first day of the new session.

The Secretary of State for Foreign Affairs first called attention to the efforts of the Great Powers to secure that the war should be localised and should not involve any of these Powers in disagreement. When members recalled the great apprehension with which the prospect of a catastrophe in the Balkans was viewed, they would realise that it was creditable to the diplomacy of the Powers that they had weathered the storm up to the present moment, and that a point had been reached when there was every prospect that it would be weathered to the end. In the opinion of the Powers the greatest point of danger had been the question of Albania and its delimitation, but now, though no agreement had been reached in regard to the southern frontier, it was not thought that there was any likelihood of such discord as to cause danger. As to the frontier on the north and north-east, an agreement was come to upon the one outstanding point at the end of the previous week. There were still, of course, points of detail awaiting discussion. For instance, it was essential that there should be some guarantees for the protection of Albanian, Mussulman, and Catholic minorities in the territory ceded to Servia and Montenegro; but none of these points ought to give rise to the same anxiety as existed before an agreement had been come to regarding the littoral of Albania and the northern and north-east frontier. Once the announcement had been made to Servia and Montenegro that the Powers had come to an agreement, there ought to be a cessation of attacks upon Skutari itself. " If the siege of Skutari is persisted in when the Powers have decided to take its destiny into their own hands, if the bloodshed which accompanies that siege should go on, and if the place is taken greater bloodshed will follow—this will involve a useless, purposeless, and criminal amount of suffering, which I am sure would alienate all sympathy in this country." If the decision of the Powers should not be respected, he trusted that those disputing it would be confronted with the united pressure of all the Powers. Their first step would be to take collective diplomatic action at Belgrade and Cettigne and to announce their decision.

It was true that the question of the southern and south-eastern frontiers of Albania had yet to be settled ; but, although the possession of Koritza and of the Kutso-Vlach districts on the slopes of Pindus might involve considerable discussion with Greece, the Powers had a basis to work upon in the Agreement of July 1, 1880, by which the *thalweg* of the Kalamas, a river flowing into the channel of Corfu, had been unsuccessfully recommended to the Porte as a suitable frontier for Greece in Epirus. As it was, the north-eastern frontier was so drawn as to include very large Albanian populations in Servian territory.

Turning to the general question of the war between Turkey and the Allies, Sir Edward Grey called attention to the conditions which the Powers had put forward as affording a reasonable basis for peace. He did not say that the Powers had made up their minds to enforce compulsory arbitration or to impose terms ; but they had suggested a frontier line in Thrace, and he would point out that if a demand were made for another frontier raising questions concerning Constantinople and the Straits, or if the war were prolonged until questions were raised concerning Asia Minor, it would be certain that in the settlement of the terms of peace one or more of the Powers would be concerned not as disinterested mediators but as interested parties. In the interests, therefore, of the belligerents themselves, the terms suggested by the Powers ought to be accepted. He hoped that after peace had been concluded Turkey would be left in a position to consolidate and strengthen her possessions in Asia Minor and to develop the country. But if she was to do this the terms of peace ought not to impose upon her financial burdens which would make her task after the war a struggle against bankruptcy. As to the Allies, they would need the goodwill and financial support of Europe if they were to develop the territories which they would have acquired when the war ended. After thanking the House for the confidence which it had reposed in the Government during the Balkan crisis, he expressed warm appreciation of the moderation, forbearance, and patience which the Governments of the Powers more directly interested than ourselves had displayed. To them the chief credit would be due if a final settlement were come to.

Mr. Asquith followed, and after cordially acknowledging the patriotic support which the Government had received from the Opposition during the past anxious months, emphasised two points made by Sir Edward Grey. To the Great Powers the gratitude of Europe was due for the assured prospect that no serious difficulty was now likely to arise. The other point upon which he laid stress was that the further continuance of the war would be absolutely purposeless. Turkey on the one side and the Allies on the other ought to see—and he did not believe that they did not see—that they had nothing whatever to gain from a prolongation of the struggle. The useless expenditure of blood and money ought to cease. " I hope," said the Prime Minister amid cheers, " that it may go forth as the considered judgment of the House of Commons, speaking with full authority as the representatives of a united British people, that this terrible war, with all its devastation and waste, should come to an end."

Opinion at Vienna was upon the whole but ill pleased at the Albanian arrangements. The *Reichspost*, which had led the opposition to Montenegro, asked what it had cost Austria to be able to say " Skutari belongs to Albania." " What is Skutari to us and what is Albania ? " The value of an Albanian Skutari to Austria is, doubtless, debatable, and at best is merely a satisfaction to Austrian self-love which had, possibly, become indispensable when Montenegro declined to cede Lovchen, the mountain commanding Cattaro, to Austria in exchange for Skutari, and was indirectly supported by Italy in her refusal to do so.   As clear-sighted Austrians said, " We have insisted upon keeping Servia from the Adriatic and upon preventing Montenegro from getting Skutari.   If Montenegro now makes common cause with Servia and gives Servia access to Antivari and Dulcigno, what advantage shall we have, except having earned the bitter hatred of the Southern Slavs ? "

On March 26 Sir Edward Grey and the ambassadors formally accepted, on behalf of all the Powers, the delimitation of the northern and north-eastern frontiers of Albania which had been adopted on March 22, as a compromise between the lines proposed in the first place by Russia and Austria-Hungary respectively, and those suggested in their respective Memoranda by the Balkan Allies and the Albanian Provisional Government.   This frontier was so drawn as to leave the Tarabosh ridge to Albania, a great grievance to Montenegro for sentimental reasons, but restored to them a great part of the provinces of Gusinje and Plava, which had been given to Montenegro by the Treaty of Berlin, but which the opposition of the Albanian League had forced them to surrender in 1880. On the whole, Montenegro gained but a small increase of territory, whilst Servia obtained not only the important

Albanian towns of Ipek, Djakova, and Prizrend, but also a large territory in Old Servia inhabited by Albanians, although they are, it is true, but recent immigrants into Serb territory. The Rjeka valley and Dibra, with a large Bulgarian population, were also taken from Albania, which thus lost the Gruda and Hoti clans, the people of Plava, of Djakova, and the Rjeka valley, whilst it only included one Serb village, Vraka, on the Lake of Skutari. If it is the essence of a compromise that it should be distasteful to both parties, then the new frontier of Albania is an unqualified success. The Gruda and the Hoti clans indeed have already informed the Admiral at Skutari that they will not become Montenegrin subjects. Montenegro, which gained nothing, did not abandon the siege of Skutari.

At Paris Sir Edward Grey's speech was hailed with enthusiasm, though it was thought that Servia would have to cede a large portion of her own spoils to Montenegro as compensation for the loss of Skutari, and that the two Balkan States might refuse to accept the delimitation unless it were brought home to them that it was the result of an arrangement between Austria and Russia. At Berlin high tributes were paid to British diplomacy and to the success of Sir Edward Grey's co-operation with Germany.

A telegram to the *Cologne Gazette* said :

" Sir Edward Grey during the Balkan War served important interests of his own country, but that makes no difference to the fact that Europe has to thank him to-day for the service which he has rendered at the same time to the cause of European peace. The ideas which Sir Edward Grey developed in his speech yesterday have been already advocated in the diplomatic negotiations, and are therefore familiar to diplomatic circles. The value of yesterday's proceedings in the House of Commons is that Sir Edward Grey gave in public a lucid summary of these ideas, and that he secured for them the unanimous approbation of the House of Commons. As regards the details of the speech, we should like to call special attention to the fact that Sir Edward Grey's declarations as to the Albanian question and the future of Turkey accord completely with the aims and efforts of German policy."

The Italian official paper, the *Tribuna*, wrote : " The words of Sir Edward Grey cannot fail to have produced a sense of relief in all European political and diplomatic circles. Apart from the pacific, benevolent, and serene intention of his words, the insistence with which he counsels moderation to both Servia and Montenegro equally is worthy of note."

Great faith was placed, especially at Paris, in the effect of immediate collective action at Belgrade and Cettigne, for Austria would thus be prevented from acting on her own initiative, and by so doing putting a perilous strain on the Austro-Russian understanding. From the beginning of the war, France had, indeed, been chiefly preoccupied with the policy of Austria-Hungary.

But on that same March 26, the news of the fall of Adrianople was announced, and these tidings might well have neutralised the effects of Sir Edward Grey's speech. Although by inspired German and Italian writers the event was said to have removed the last obstacle to peace, Pan-Slav feeling in Russia burst into a flame, and, but for the firmness of the Tsar and his Ministers, might have precipitated a European war.

Fortunately the efforts of diplomacy were aided by the second Bulgarian failure to pierce the lines of Tchataldja, which had ended a week of fierce fighting between March 25 and March 31, and undoubtedly made both Bulgaria and Turkey more inclined to peace. Turkey, as we have already said, unreservedly accepted the proposals of the Powers on March 31, and placed herself in their hands for the negotiation of peace.

But the question of Skutari still remained.   In King Nicholas's eyes the boldest policy was the best.   He defied the Great Powers ; and on Monday, April 21, the fortress fell into his hands, with, as will be seen, very unexpected results.

What, indeed, had Montenegro to fear ?   The Great Powers might bluster and threaten.   Their ships might make a naval demonstration off the coasts, but, as Lord Salisbury once said when asked to intervene on behalf of Armenia, " ironclads cannot sail over mountains."   Montenegro has no navy, and only a few coasting vessels fly her flag, though to a certain extent her supplies of provisions reach her by sea.   Hence a blockade of her ports could do her no serious economic injury, although the operations round Skutari might be impeded if her Servian allies could only reach her by a toilsome march over the north Albanian mountains, instead of arriving by sea at Durazzo or at San Giovanni di Medua in Greek transports from Salonika.

At home for King Nicholas and his dynasty there were far greater dangers to be feared if he raised the siege of Skutari than could ever threaten him from foreign coercion.   Assassination is a by no means unknown political weapon in the history of the Balkan States.   The Montenegrins who have returned from the American mines are saturated with anarchical and socialist teaching ; the fierce clans of Southern Montenegro openly threatened to disobey their King's injunctions if he ordered them to desist from their military operations.   It was almost certain that the Powers would not unite to give a mandate to Austria to carry any ban they might issue against Montenegro into execution by invading her by land, for France would not act without Russia, where, in such a case, a wave of Pan-Slavist feeling might well sweep away all diplomatic considerations, whilst yet other Parliaments might hesitate if they were asked to sanction a joint expedition into the fastnesses of the Black Mountain. Hence the exhortation and the threats of the representatives of the Great Powers at Cettigne fell upon deaf ears.

Collective representations were made to Montenegro on March 28, to Servia on March 29, to the effect that the Powers, having reached an understanding concerning the northern and north-eastern frontiers of Albania, summoned Servia and Bulgaria to abandon the siege of Skutari, to cease hostilities in Albanian territory, to withdraw as soon as possible their troops from Albanian territory, and to give guarantees for assuring the real religious liberty of the Catholic and Mohammedan Albanians.

In Servia these claims were not taken too seriously, for experience has taught the Servian statesmen that Austria is particularly skiful in finding pretexts for a quarrel with them whenever it happens to suit her interests. Hence those who best knew the situation believed that Montenegro would be supported by Servia if she refused to comply with the wishes of the Powers, and pointed to the fact that General Voynovitch had arrived before Skutari on the very day the Collective Note was handed to the Montenegrin Minister of Foreign Affairs.

A naval demonstration became inevitable, but, at first, it was uncertain if it would be confined to Austria and Italy, or whether France and England would also send ships. Russia had joined in this resolution, which was adopted upon March 29, but had no vessel at hand which she could send to the Upper Adriatic. The one small gunboat she had at Salonika was escorting the corpse of the murdered King of Greece across the Ægean.

But whilst Russian diplomatists were assenting in London to schemes for the coercion of the Southern Slavs, in the Russian Parliament enthusiasm for those Slavs was at its height.

Whilst the Duma was in session on the afternoon of

Wednesday, March 26, a telegram was handed to its President. The Deputy who was speaking interrupted his speech; the President, M. Krupensky, stepped into the tribune and called out " Adrianople has fallen. Hurrah ! "

Dr. Daneff, the President of the Bulgarian Senate, and M. Bobtcheff, Bulgarian Minister at St. Petersburg, were present at the sitting. Shoulder-high they were carried by the Deputies to greet the President and Vice-President of the Duma. Again and again the Russian and Bulgarian anthems echoed through the Catherine Hall, until the hoarse and weary members joined in the Te Deum which was celebrated by the Chaplains of the Parliament.

In Vienna the conduct of King Nicholas caused very uneasy feelings. If he continued defiant, Austria might be forced to adopt very drastic proceedings to bring him to reason, yet, at the same time, she felt that she might incur the displeasure of the Southern Slavs through her conduct about Montenegro, whom she was at the same time forcing into a closer union with Servia. Such a greater Servia cannot but be a constant menace to Austria in the south, unless she should become a member of an Eastern Empire, and thus be kept in check by Bulgarian, Greek, Kutso-Vlach, and Albanian elements. Hence the Viennese journals began to flatter Montenegro by reminding her of the benefits which Austria had conferred upon her in former days.

The tension continued unabated all through the first fortnight of April, but whilst the Powers were arranging a naval demonstration against Montenegro, which was destined to prove as effective as if it had been directed against Geneva, the Montenegrins, aided by 15,000 Servians brought from Salonika to San Giovanni di Medua in Greek transports, carefully convoyed, to guard them against a raid from the Turkish cruiser *Hamidieh*, were pressing on towards Skutari.

The Austrian statesmen, encouraged by the friendly

action of the British Government, and by the support of
the other Powers, had agreed that the naval demonstration should be carried out by the ships of Austria-Hungary,
Germany, England, and Italy. Russia had no ship in the
Mediterranean which she could send, but the attitude of
her Government might be judged by the fact that mounted
police charged the processions which had gone to offer
their congratulations on the great victory of Slavdom at
Adrianople to the Bulgarian and Servian Legations at
St. Petersburg. The Cossacks used their whips with a
vigour which proved they had not forgotten their old
traditions. The Duma seethed with righteous, if ineffec-
tive, indignation. Undeterred by fears of the *nagaika*,
crowds went to see General Radko Dimitrieff, the
Bulgarian Napoleon, set off from St. Petersburg station
on his way to Adrianople to visit Tsar Ferdinand before
resuming his command before Tchataldja. The French
also hung back from sending vessels, on the ground that
they could not do so before they had learnt the wishes of
Russia. Matters were not improved by a Press polemic
between Italy and Greece, caused by the refusal of Italy
to agree to a frontier proposed by Greece for Epirus which
would leave Vallona in the hands of the Hellenic kingdom.
Germany, through the mouth of her Foreign Secretary,
Herr von Jagow, expressed her hearty approval of
Austrian policy, but at first was disinclined to send a vessel
to the Adriatic.

Meanwhile the attack upon Skutari was resumed and
the place was violently bombarded on March 31. In this
attack the Montenegrins were aided by the Servians.
A demonstration was made on the River Kiri, but the
real attack was upon the Turkish positions on the great
Tarabosh. On April 2 it was announced that the troops
of the southern column, under General Martinovitch, had
stormed the Turkish position, capturing tier after tier of
entrenchments after a desperate struggle. The assault

was led by 200 bomb-throwers, all picked men, chosen from several battalions. These men, clambering up the mountain under a murderous fire, cut the wire entanglements, and getting to close quarters, threw their bombs among the Turks, thus opening the way for the rush of the storming party. Every man of the bomb-throwing detachment fell under the Turkish fire, but they had accomplished their task. The Montenegrin infantry followed close after them, and charged the trenches. The Turks held their ground, and a bloody hand-to-hand fight ensued, lasting for an hour and ending in the victory of the Montenegrins, who lost 300 killed and wounded.

French feeling was at first completely against the naval demonstration. Popular opinion revolted against the coercion of the Montenegrins in the interests of Austria, and was not well pleased that the Triple Entente, which did not heartily approve of such a policy, should support the Triple Alliance in promoting it. At best, outsiders thought that the demonstration might build a golden bridge for King Nicholas by enabling him to give way about Skutari without endangering the interests of the Petrovich dynasty. France was, however, at last convinced of the necessity for taking part in it, both by assurances given by the Russian representatives in Paris and by a semi-official *communiqué* published at St. Petersburg on April 2, which made it plain that Russia, while herself not taking part in the naval demonstration in the Adriatic, had expressed a desire that it should be international in character, and that England and France should join in it. The Conference in London had decided that a demonstration was inevitable. If it was made a collective one, it would alleviate the danger of isolated action by Austria-Hungary, it would keep the Concert in being, and give the Powers time to discuss and to decide what further measures might be necessary as the situation developed.

Public opinion in Montenegro was not greatly stirred

by the news that warships flying the flags of five Great Powers were to lie in Antivari roads, or that the coast-line of Montenegro was to be blockaded. The awful tidings did not silence a single gun in the batteries before Skutari, and the effect of the demonstration may be best summed up by a photograph which appeared in a London illustrated paper. This photograph, taken from the life, showed King Nicholas lying on a rock by the sea and gazing through his glasses at the Allied Fleet in the offing.

Prave words. It would be needless to go into detail as to the events of the naval demonstration. The King's yacht was captured, and the prices of provisions rose in Montenegro when the coasting trade to its ports was suspended, but upon the whole the " solemn affirmation of the will of Europe " proved singularly like the action of a boy who hopes to scare away a policemen with a white sheet, turnip, and lighted candle. The Concert of the Powers seemed to have reached its dotage. Six giants saw themselves flouted by a dwarf.

The chief sufferer was not Montenegro, but Austria-Hungary. As the Burgomaster of Vienna, Dr. Weiskirchner, formerly Minister of Commerce, said at a public meeting, the mood of Vienna was a mood of disapproval. Viennese industry could no longer bear the mismanagement of Austrian diplomacy. Unless a change soon came they would be on the eve of an economic catastrophe. Men who had grown old in business were all but ruined. Unemployment was spreading fearfully. " Therefore," continued Dr. Weiskirchner, " I feel bound to call aloud to the Ballplatz [the Austrian Foreign Office], either we have an interest in the Balkans or we have none. If we have a rightful interest it must be safeguarded. If we have none then let things be. We cannot stand this finicking about."

The international blockading fleet was commanded by the British Admiral, Cecil Burney, who notified the

Montenegrin Prime Minister of its presence, and requested his Excellency to inform him immediately that his Government was ready to carry out the wishes of the Great Powers. The reply was a flat refusal, the Montenegrin Government stating that it regarded the action of the Powers as " a gross breach of neutrality " and was prepared to continue its operations against Skutari at all costs. Fresh Servian troops were thrown ashore at Bushatir on the Albanian coast on April 3, and at once hurried forward to Skutari. King Nicholas dictated a message for the correspondent of the *Temps* at St. Petersburg expressing regret that France had taken part in the blockade, and adding, " Montenegro will only yield to violence. Europe has only to add to her injustice the ridiculousness of violence." M. Sazonoff in vain said that even if Skutari were taken the Allies would be compelled to evacuate it. They declared that they would keep it.

An assault of the joint Montenegrin and Servian forces upon Skutari on April 4 was repulsed with heavy losses to the besiegers, and Servia, which was becoming entangled in territorial disputes with Bulgaria, dreaded the loss of the goodwill of Great Britain and began to slacken in her efforts. The Pan-Slavists, too, were becoming weakened in Russia, since for party purposes the Constitutional Democrats were beginning to oppose an active propaganda which they believed would involve Russia in war. Yet grand street demonstrations were still going on at St. Petersburg : solemn Masses were held not only for the Slavs killed in the Balkan War but for the Slavonic victims of Austrian cruelty, and a banner was paraded through the streets bearing the inscription, " The Cross on Santa Sophia." Italy, too, witnessed some half-hearted demonstrations in favour of Montenegro, which, however, only served to stiffen Italian opinion in favour of Albania, an attitude in which it was confirmed by

M. Sazonoff's consent to the naval demonstration, whilst German opinion found consolation in the thought that Europe remained united.

On April 7 Sir Edward Grey made a second very important statement as to British policy in the House of Commons. In explaining the objects of the naval demonstration he said, " We were a party to it, because we were parties with the other Great Powers to an agreement which the naval demonstration was intended to uphold—the agreement that there should be an autonomous Albania, the Albanians being separate in race, language, and, to a great extent, religion. The war was no longer a war of liberation. The operations of Montenegro against Skutari were part of a war of conquest, and the same sympathy felt at first for Montenegro might now be extended to the Albanian population of Skutari and its district. The agreement of the Powers as to the frontiers of Albania was the result of long and laborious diplomatic effort. It was essential to the peace of Europe, and had been reached, in his opinion, only just in time to preserve the peace between the Great Powers. It was essential for the continuance of peace to uphold it by international action. We had no direct interest in the details of the agreement; but, believing it to be in its main lines in accord with humanity, liberty, and justice, and knowing that the peace of Europe depended on the maintenance of concord between the Powers most directly interested, the Government had thought it right to take part in the international action now proceeding."

Such was the language in which the man who has done, perhaps, more than any one man to preserve the peace of Europe, justified the policy of England, and arraigned Montenegro at the bar of a public opinion which until then had taken the assassin for the victim. Servia hesitated, influenced more, perhaps, by her disputes with Bulgaria than by any other sentiment. She now attached greater weight to the interests of herself and of Greece than to those of Montenegro. Montenegro, who was supposed to be rapidly getting exhausted, was left to carry on the siege of Skutari by herself, and, it was thought, would accept pecuniary and territorial compensation for her claims, unfounded as they were, to Albanian lands. Bulgaria was said to be willing to accept as her Thracian frontier the direct line Enos—Midia, which was the latest suggestion of the Powers. She had more pressing questions on hand than those connected with her Thracian frontier. For the moment the partition of Macedonia, the fate of Salonika, interested her more than the future of Constantinople. Both Greece and Servia were concentrating their troops in Macedonia.

In view of these facts Servia became more pliant as regards Skutari. At the request of the Russian Minister at Belgrade, she on April 11 engaged that her troops should take no further part in any attempts to storm the place, and although she resolved not to demobilise her army until the territorial claims of the Allies had been adjusted after the peace with Turkey, she arranged to begin to withdraw her troops from Skutari on April 16. On that same day, as has been said, Bulgaria signed an armistice with Turkey until April 23, the term being subsequently extended until May 5. It was said to have been entered into by Bulgaria at the request of Russia, which had come to an agreement with Austria as to the northern and north-eastern frontiers of Albania, completely excluding the possibility of any territorial compensation being accorded to Montenegro. In point of fact, as that shrewd observer, Dr. E. J. Dillon, pointed out in the *Daily Telegraph*, it was thought that the whole of the Pan-Slavist demonstrations in favour of the Southern Slavs were the work of a few citizens in the Balkans who had come to an understanding with some pushing Russian politicians before the outbreak of the

war and had used them as their tools during its whole
course.   The bulk of the Russian population outside
St. Petersburg, Moscow, and Kieff cared nothing for
their southern brethren, and willingly supported MM.
Sazonoff and Kokofftseff in their policy of compromise for
the sake of peace.   The moujiks have not forgotten the
disgust with which their fathers, in the war of 1877,
looked upon the smiling fields and prosperous villages of
those Bulgarians whom they were come to save from
Turkish slavery and whom they found to be far happier
and wealthier than themselves.

Consequently, a long *communiqué* explaining the attitude
of the Russian Government as regards Montenegro which
was issued by the Foreign Office at St. Petersburg on
April 10 provoked little hostile comment.   In it Russia
explained that to localise the Balkan War the Powers had
been forced to renounce their individual and territorial
advantages, and their right to take any individual action,
unless with a mandate to show that they were carrying
out the unanimous decision of Europe.   Under these
circumstances the Conference of Ambassadors in London
was convoked, and had just completed the task of laying
down the northern and north-eastern frontiers of Albania,
although, in doing so, they naturally opposed the expansion of Montenegro and Servia.   However, they had to
consider the interests of the Albanians, who were protected by Austria and Italy, the Powers mainly interested
in the maintenance of the *status quo* in the Adriatic.   This
could be best effected by the constitution of an autonomous
Albania, with a homogeneous population of Albanian
origin.   For the sake of effecting a compromise Austria
agreed that Prizrend, Ipek, Djakova, and Dibra (places
now inhabited by Albanians, but formerly Slav) should be
left to the Slavs, whilst Russia, in return, agreed that
Skutari should go to Albania.   Her grounds for this
decision were that Skutari is a purely Albanian town and

the seat of a Catholic Archbishop. The reports of the Russian Vice-Consul at Skutari clearly showed that Montenegro has proved herself incapable of assimilating several thousand Catholic and Mussulman Albanians who had been her subjects for thirty-five years.

If a portion of the Sanjak of Skutari were annexed to Montenegro with her scanty population of 250,000, she would be incapable of assimilating an influx of 100,000 men—foreigners to them in religion, blood, and language —and she would thus be threatened with internal discord and, through the new Roman Catholic element, with the penetration of foreign influences. " King Nicholas broke the understanding into which he had entered to warn Russia in the event of war, and to obtain her consent. Nevertheless the Tsar magnanimously came to the aid of Montenegro by supplementing the resources of her population.

" When the question of Skutari was settled, a friendly notification was sent to King Nicholas, and he was at the same time warned of the grave responsibility which he would assume if he continued his resistance. He was subsequently advised to desist from all recrimination and the pursuit of his personal aims which would condemn his people to useless massacre. These representations to King Nicholas have proved to be without effect. It has become clear that he bases his calculations on embroiling Russia and the Great Powers in a European war."

Russia hoped, however, that Montenegro would bow to the will of Europe " supported by an imposing display of naval force," in which case some way would be found " of alleviating the lot of the Montenegrin people who have been overwhelmed by the excessive sacrifices demanded by the siege of Skutari."

The manifesto produced an excellent impression at Vienna. The effect was not the same at Cettigne. The bombardment of Skutari was vigorously resumed, and

King Nicholas, who according to cynical financiers was only haggling until he could get a compensation from the Powers of £4,000,000 in cash in place of a guarantee for a loan of £1,500,000 at 5 per cent., issued a *communiqué* that although she was abandoned by all, " Montenegro would persist in her struggle, conscious of her glorious past and her ideals.

" It is not impossible that Montenegro will yield to *force majeure*, though never in the dishonourable manner suggested to her by the European Powers. She will only do so in streams of blood. In the 500 years of darkness in the Balkans, Montenegro did not exist by the goodwill of European diplomacy. She was rather diplomacy's stepchild, and has lived by the blood of her sons. Montenegro dies without Skutari, but she dies with honour."

Such was the attitude of King Nicholas on April 14.

Skutari, meanwhile, was said to be suffering all the horrors of famine. It was reported that there was no more meal for making bread and that many of the Catholic population had died of hunger. Still there was no thought of surrender, and the town would only be taken by storm, which King Nicholas still considered possible.

Turkey tried to obtain at least a Protectorate over an autonomous Albania. Austria and Italy joined in putting forward schemes for its internal organisation. The Montenegrin and Albanian coast blockade was extended. Beef rose in price as smoked mutton fell at Antivari, and, crowning triumph of the diplomacy of the Six Great Powers of Europe, the motor-bus service was suspended between Cettigne (population 3000) and Cattaro (population 4000). Montenegro was, indeed, cut off from the world when its people were once more driven to ride upon asses !

Bulgaria, Greece, and Servia notified the Powers that they regarded their last proposals as affording an acceptable basis for peace. Montenegro returned no answer but made hurried preparations for assaulting Brditza and Bardanjolt, the chief positions in front of Skutari.

Late on the night of April 22 a rumour was current at Cettigne that the surrender of Skutari was impending, but it was not until two o'clock on the morning of April 23 that the news was definitely made known by the firing of cannon and ringing of bells. On Monday, April 21, Essad Pasha sent a message to the Montenegrin officer commanding the siege operations and informed him of his intention to surrender Skutari, since its supply of provisions had run out. On receiving the news the King convened the Privy Council, who sent General Vukotitch and M. Plamenatz, formerly Montenegrin Minister at Constantinople, to treat with the Turkish general, who had only been brought to negotiate by the events of the previous day.

" Last night," says an official report of April 22, " the Montenegrin troops took the offensive along the whole front, and an engagement took place which lasted the whole night, even bayonet-fighting being resorted to. On the west and east fronts the Turks lost two lines of posts, over which the Montenegrin flag was hoisted. Early this morning the Turks attempted a counter-attack, but they were repulsed. Confusion prevails everywhere in the town of Skutari and in the Turkish positions. The Montenegrin losses in the fighting were considerable, but their number has not yet been ascertained. The fall of Skutari is imminent."

The chief difficulty in the negotiations was the fate of the Albanian refugees from the villages west of the lake but in districts occupied by Montenegrin troops ; eventually they were allowed to return to their homes.

The protocol of the capitulation of Skutari was signed about midnight. Subsequently Essad Pasha and the troops of the garrison marched out of the town with the honours of war. The Turks stipulated that they should be allowed to take away some of their light guns.

Skutari was short of foodstuffs, especially flour, but there was a certain amount of mutton left. The Ottoman ammunition had been nearly all spent when the town surrendered. When the protocol had been signed the Turks gradually fell back from the outposts, the places which had not yet been taken by the Montenegrins being the first to be evacuated. Little by little every position was denuded of its defenders, and the Montenegrin flag was hoisted over the citadel. The victorious troops then entered the town, and the firing of salutes announced to the world that Skutari had been occupied. Great was the demonstration at Cettigne when the news arrived; crowds rushed out into the streets firing revolvers and singing patriotic songs. The King, accompanied by the Princesses, appeared on the balcony of the Palace and made a speech amid thunders of applause.

Sofia and Belgrade went mad with joy. In Bulgaria it was thought that the event would accelerate peace, since now Montenegro, having satisfied her military honour, would be able to accept the compensation offered by the European Concert if she conformed to their desires. It was felt that much depended on the attitude of Russia, who might be forced by Pan-Slavist enthusiasm to cease to work together with the Powers. Organs pealed, incense smoked, and the deep bass chants of the Russian liturgy resounded in triumph through every church from the Arctic to the Danube. Vienna was wild with anger, but that anger was felt by the Germans and Magyars alone. The *Fremdenblatt* might utter hopes that " this brutal attack upon the authority of the Great Powers will have the effect of raising Europe from her lethargy and bringing home to her a sense of the errors hitherto committed. . . . In view of the tidings of victory from Cettigne, which are at the same time tidings of a European defeat, we cherish the certain expectation that Europe will now at last resolve to employ sharper methods in order to restore her damaged prestige and to break the resistance of Montenegro."

But the *Narodni Novosti* of Agram, the organ of the Absolutist Croatian Government, of those Croats whose grandfathers under Jellachich saved Austrian unity in 1848, said plainly :

" We rejoice with our whole heart at this success, which proves again that our Montenegrin brethren still possess the heroic qualities of their glorious ancestors. The courage and self-sacrifice of the Montenegrin soldiers assure them the recognition of Europe, and add a fresh leaf of laurel to their crown of fame."

Popular feeling in France was, doubtless, in favour of Montenegro, but it was recognised that she could not hope to retain Skutari after the sacrifices which Austria had made to prevent her from taking it. It might be true that Russia and France would rightly object to the task of coercing her being entrusted to Austria-Hungary alone, but their objections would be less were another Power called in to aid in the work. Public opinion in Germany remained optimistic as to the prospects of European peace. To England the news came as an unexpected shock. The tidings were discussed at the Conference of Ambassadors sitting on April 23, but they came to no conclusion, although Mr. Asquith, speaking at a banquet the same evening, said that he had there that night, " as fellow-guests of your Association " (that of the Foreign Journalists in London), " the Ambassadors of the Great Powers of Europe," who, the Prime Minister continued, had been engaged that day in the prosecution of the great task of conciliation. The Great Powers, more than one of whom were acutely and directly interested in the upheaval of the old *régime* in the Near East, had worked, and worked so far successfully, for an honourable peace amongst themselves, and he thought, without an excess of optimism, that sooner or later, and sooner rather than later, they would reach the goal which had been so long and so laboriously sought.

At that moment, however, he had not received the despatch in which Austria-Hungary intimated that if the Powers were unable to arrive at a speedy decision she might herself be obliged to take action to vindicate the authority of Europe and to preserve Skutari for Albania. It was rumoured that she thought an expedition of 40,000 men would be sufficient to coerce the Montenegrins.

King Nicholas had reserved a dramatic surprise for Europe. Scarcely had the pious monarch entered Skutari, where he proposed to celebrate the Easter festival undisturbed by diplomats, when Europe learned that the surrender of the city had been effected by an agreement with its commander, Essad Bey, which left the latter free to march into the interior of Albania with forty thousand fine Turkish troops and all his guns. Essad Bey is a great Moslem Albanian landlord, whose history as a land-grabber and adventurer much resembles that of many a Highland chief of old. With the connivance of King Nicholas he marched with his forces to Tirana near Durazzo, and was there reported to have been proclaimed King or Prince of an autonomous Albania under the protection of the Sultan. Austria, which had just agreed to accept the aid of Italy in coercing Montenegro, saw herself flouted. The Concert of Europe was defied. Pan-Slav sentiment once more rose high in Russia. Never had the Great Powers seen themselves in such a position since the day when Belgium became, in 1830, an independent state.

CHAPTER X

AFTER SKUTARI

DIPLOMACY was for the moment baffled by the apparition, or rather, the rumoured apparition of Essad Pasha as King of Albania. King Nicholas was reported to have given his cordial assent to Essad's assumption of the regal dignity, and to have received his reward in the shape of a treaty by which the new sovereign ceded to him the whole of Albania north of the river Drin. Thus Montenegro became by a stroke of the pen the legitimate possessor of Skutari, by virtue of a treaty concluded with the man who, if the Powers were really sincere or consistent in their policy, had alone the right to dispose of Albanian territory. Such was the transformation scene of the long-drawn-out drama.

The Ambassadors met; they decided nothing, nor could they recommend any measure calculated to meet the difficulty save that the blockade should be rendered even more stringent. Their own admirals told them that not a cock-boat could run the blockade already in existence.

The Great Powers, fortunately for the peace of Europe, were not in a hurry. Italy, indeed, might profess herself willing to join Austria in the task of coercing Montenegro, but though the Consulta might act in accordance with the dictates of a consummate diplomacy, the Queen of Italy had not forgotten that she was a daughter of the King of Montenegro. The Italian Minister might utter grave warnings at Cettigne ; the telegraph flashed burning words of congratulation and rejoicing from the Quirinal to the Konak at Skutari. The Greek Easter in 1913 fell a month later than the Western one, and never were the precepts of the Church with regard to its observance kept more rigidly. They formed a welcome pretext for delay, although it was scarcely to be hoped that the time thus afforded them for meditation would enable those who controlled the foreign affairs of Europe to recognise the triviality of the object which threatened to plunge them into war.

Austria threatened separate intervention, and the Emperor held prolonged conferences with Count Berchtold and Baron Konrad von Hötzendorff, the Chief of the General Staff. Austria, indeed, saw that the decision arrived at unanimously by the Conference of Ambassadors in London on April 26, officially to notify King Nicholas that he had to give up Skutari, could only be put into force by military coercion. A sovereign who had entered Skutari in state on the very morrow of that decision, thus carrying out his assurance to the Powers that he would keep Easter within its walls, was hardly likely to yield to mere verbal persuasion. Nor could Austrian pride entertain any proposal to compensate Montenegro. In the eyes of the Ballplatz King Nicholas was simply a robber. But Russian opinion had to be considered, for it was certain that Austrian intervention, even though favoured by the Tsar's Ministers, would lead to a violent outburst of Pan-Slavist feeling, which would be strengthened by the popular belief that Austria was not really prepared to take action. Moreover, were war to break out between Austria and Montenegro the latter would undoubtedly be supported by the other Slav States in the Balkans, if not by Greece, and whilst the Serb army was concentrating nearer its base, the Bulgarians were making use of the armistice to withdraw troops from the lines of

Tchataldja. Russia would be supported by France, if not by England, in her refusal to undertake a collective intervention of the Powers, and, for a moment, it looked as if the Dual Monarchy would have to swallow the affront.

But if one maxim more than another holds good in diplomacy it is that when in doubt you should present a Note. This at least the Powers could do, so a Collective Note was prepared, and, after a short delay, due to the fact that the Russian Minister at Cettigne had not received his instructions, it was presented to the Montenegrin Government. The reply was deferred until after the Easter holidays.

Skutari, at that time, was, perhaps, not a very pleasant residence. The Montenegrins on entering had found the inhabitants all but exhausted. Many of the lower classes had died of starvation ; the hospital was in a harrowing condition ; a temporary hospital in the zone of bombardment was choked with unburied corpses ; Essad Pasha had not dared for days to appear in the streets, as he was followed by hungry crowds crying for bread or a capitulation. General Vukotitch took active measures to relieve the distress, and the soldiers gave away their own bread to the sufferers. They might derive some consolation from King Nicholas's proclamation on taking possession of the city, for he guaranteed them all the benefits of a civilised Christian State.

Meanwhile Ismail Kemal Bey, who was the Chief of the Provisional Albanian Government which had been installed at Vallona on November 15, and who, during the Hamidian period, had held high office in Syria and Tripoli, and had subsequently sat for his native town of Berat in the Turkish Parliament, had arrived in London to interview Sir Edward Grey in the cause of Albanian independence. He had, until the defeats in Thrace, been in favour of developing Albania on its own lines under Turkish suzerainty, but seeing that it was now completely cut off from Turkey, he had become an advocate for its complete independence. The intrigues of Essad Pasha led him to desire the appointment of a Prince of Albania by the Powers as speedily as possible in order to bar the way to foreign intrigue. In Ismail Kemal Bey's eyes the possession of Skutari and the Maltsor tribes to the north of it was indispensable to the independent existence of Albania, although the Hoti and Gruda tribes, and possibly even the Klementi, might be left to King Nicholas. The proper capital of Albania should, he thought, be Elbasan, the ancient Albanopolis, a town of 15,000 inhabitants equidistant between Durazzo and Vallona, and with a dialect sharing the characteristics of both the Tosk and the Gheg. The population of the new state would be about one and a quarter millions, and its revenue 40,000,000 francs. He was quite willing to accept Austrian aid to oust the Montenegrins from Skutari, but would not subject Albania to international control, either by allowing Servia to have access to the Adriatic through Albanian ports, or by the institution of an international gendarmerie. The oldest race in Europe desired permission to govern itself. Such was the message Ismail Kemal Bey brought to London from the National Council of Albania.

At last the devotions of the Greek Easter were over, the last *Christos voskress* had been duly said, and the Montenegrin Foreign Minister was free to return his answer to the Collective Note. His dilatoriness was taken to mean that Montenegro would maintain her bitter obstinacy to the end.

Russia was straining every nerve to preserve the peace; in a verbal communication subsequent to the Austrian Emperor's conferences with Count Berchtold and Baron von Hötzendorf, her Ambassador at Vienna had informed the Austrian Government that Russia, thinking that all means of putting pressure upon King Nicholas had not been exhausted, begged Austria-Hungary to refrain from taking any precipitate action, lest grave consequences should ensue, though Russia's position as to Skutari remained unchanged, and she felt herself bound to work for the removal of the Montenegrin troops. Germany, on the other hand, could not see that the problem involved any vital German interests, but out of devotion to the Triple Alliance contented herself with urging Austria-Hungary not to intervene unless jointly with Italy. At the same time *The Times* correspondent in the Balkan Peninsula suggested that Skutari might either be occupied by detachments from the international fleet, or that Essad Pasha and his troops, who, in the meantime, had arrived at Alessio, might be recalled to preserve order after the Montenegrins had withdrawn. But difficult as the position was, there were elements of hope. Italian opinion was turning against Montenegro, owing to the discovery of King Nicholas's intrigues with Essad Pasha ; in Russia the excitement was largely on the surface ; the Powers were straining every nerve to keep together through the Ambassadorial Conference in London ; Essad Pasha's conduct was regarded as mere bluff, his object being rather to be the first subject in Albania than its Prince. Austria, however, recognised that the military coercion of Montenegro would be a hard task, and, consequently, was disposed to wait for the decisions to be adopted in London.

The Montenegrin reply was handed to the Powers on May 1. In it they claimed that the delimitation of Albania should have been undertaken after the Allies, by whose arms the country had been delivered from Turkey, had consulted on the subject after the conclusion of peace with the Porte, and that any demand by the Powers for the evacuation of Albanian territory before such a Peace had been signed was a violation of neutrality.

Moreover, Montenegro had occupied Skutari as the legitimate consequence of warlike operations, and her troops had been warmly welcomed by its inhabitants. They therefore reserved the right of deciding as to the evacuation of the town until the question of the definite delimitation of Albania came to be discussed between the Allies and the Great Powers in the course of the peace negotiations with the Ottoman Empire.

That same evening the Russian Minister at Cettigne again urged the Montenegrins to evacuate Skutari immediately, and said they ran a risk of meeting their ruin, a remark which was taken to mean that Austria-Hungary would intervene alone. It was thought that in such a case Italy would intervene by herself in the south of Albania, and that the excellent relations between the two Powers would not long survive the rivalry and friction which would ensue. In view of the agitation on the Vienna Stock Exchange, the Austrian Foreign Office on May 2 issued a notification that the situation remained unchanged, but that Austria-Hungary maintained the standpoint that the decisions of Europe must be carried out as soon as possible. In Russia it was clearly seen that, in the interests of the new Albanian State, Albania should be jointly occupied by the Powers, the country being divided into sections on the Cretan model, and that the occupation should continue until the new Government was in a position to assert authority. If Russia herself refrained from participating in the intervention of the Powers, whilst allowing France to do so, the Concert would be dissolved. Men felt that the peace of Europe lay in Russian hands. Bulgaria, too, sent grave warnings to Cettigne, yet Montenegrin troops continued to gather upon the Austrian frontier towards Cattaro. In the south of Albania Djavid Pasha was rumoured to have seized Vallona, to have expelled the Provisional Government, and to have rehoisted the Ottoman flag. Italian warships were ordered to Brindisi, which faces Vallona Bay.

But the influence of Russia prevailed in the Montenegrin Councils. On May 1 it was rumoured that King Nicholas was sounding the Powers as to whether they would allow him some small territorial compensation if he surrendered Skutari to the commanders of the International fleet. It was said that this suggestion had been laid before the Ambassadorial Conference on the afternoon of that day, and that the Conference had thereupon adjourned its decision as to the adoption of coercive measures until May 5, thus deferring Austrian action till May 6.

Notwithstanding this report, and an optimistic speech by Lord Morley at the banquet of the Royal Academy in London, in which he stated his belief that peace would be maintained, the outlook on the first Sunday in May was very black. The *North German Gazette* published a semi-official communication which, after describing the steps taken by the Powers to persuade King Nicholas to give way, declared in so many words that they had failed, and that action by Austria-Hungary and Italy was imminent. Austria-Hungary was known to maintain her unyielding attitude. She would not discuss even pecuniary compensation to Montenegro until Skutari had been evacuated, and would not, in any circumstances, agree to her receiving territorial compensation. M. Barthou, the French Prime Minister, speaking on May 4, emphasised the " instability " of the European situation. Martial law was proclaimed in Bosnia-Herzegovina, and it was clear that an Austro-Hungarian advance upon Skutari would be accompanied by an Italian landing in the south, probably at Vallona. Yet the more Austria-Hungary looked at the task before her, the less she liked it. The Press and the public called for prudence and circumspection; they saw that 150,000 of the best Austrian troops might be tied up in an attempt to subdue Northern and North-Eastern Albania, and that Austria might have to pay for the privilege of doing so by handing over the harbour of Vallona to Italy. A prominent Foreign Office organ wrote that the monarchy had a free hand, but was also free to choose its own time. Action had been decided upon, but the right moment for action had yet to be fixed. This Fabian policy saved the peace of Europe.

On the evening of May 4, the day before that on which the Ambassadorial Conference in London was to decide on the question of intervention in Albania, the *Neues Wiener Tagblatt* published a telegram from Cattaro that a Montenegrin Crown Council held on May 3 had decided to recommend to the Skrupshtina the evacuation of Skutari, and the resignation of the Cabinet which took place on the following afternoon was taken to show that the peace party had prevailed.

The report was true. At the last moment King Nicholas had yielded to the pressure of Europe. In a telegram to Sir Edward Grey sent through Count de Salis, the British Minister at Cettigne, he placed the future of Skutari in the hands of the Powers. After recapitulating the arguments for the retention of the city by Montenegro which he had formerly advanced, the King concluded with the words : " I once more affirm with my people our rights which are consecrated by history and by conquest. As my own dignity and my people's does not allow me to submit to isolated summonses, I leave the fate of the town of Skutari in the hands of the Powers."

Montenegro had given way. The telegram was read by Sir Edward Grey to the Conference, which decided that a contingent from the international blockading fleet should take over the place from the Montenegrin authorities, pending the creation of an Albanian Government. It was thought that the Austro-Hungarian and Italian Ambassadors would be able to lay a scheme for the organisation of an autonomous Albania before the Conference on May 8. On May 5 the decision of King Nicholas to leave the question of Skutari to the Powers was announced in the House of Commons by the Prime Minister and in the House of Lords by Lord Morley.

The news was everywhere hailed with joy. The war party in Vienna foamed with rage at the thought that their prey had been snatched from them almost at the last moment; the general public, though relieved, after the many deceptions which the interminable crisis had brought, could not believe that it was out of the wood, but Dr. de Lukacs, the Hungarian Premier, when announcing the news to the Hungarian Parliament, attributed the " joyful result " to the determined steps taken by the Dual Monarchy, and a pronounced rise in the chief speculative sercurities on the Vienna Bourse greeted the announcement of the evacuation.

Many, indeed, rejoiced that no pretext any longer existed for the joint intervention of Austria and Italy in Albania, and that an expedition which would have involved handing over Vallona to Italy, without adequate compensation, could now be indefinitely postponed. Even if the two Powers had to intervene to save Albania from Essad Pasha, Vallona could now, it was thought, be neutralised. The Ballplatz, however, had already learnt that during the visit of the Austro-Hungarian and Italian Consuls to Tirana, Essad Pasha had himself assured them that he had never dreamt of proclaiming himself Prince or King of Albania, but was, on the contrary, disposed to recognise and support the Provisional Albanian Government. News arrived shortly afterwards that the rumour that Vallona had been taken by Djavid Pasha was totally false. Thus the " dangerous anarchy " which, according to the Austrian and Italian Press, prevailed in Albania proved to be the baseless fabric of a vision.

At Rome the *Tribuna* considered that all danger of

an intervention by Austria-Hungary at Skutari was at an end, that the importance of the Austro-Italian expedition was much diminished, and that it might even be avoided altogether, now that Essad and Djavid Pashas had received orders to disband and to retire from Albania. The Ministerial organ reminded its readers that a Provisional Government had already been established in Albania to which the constitution and administration of the new State might be entrusted, and added that no country would be better pleased than Italy to learn that quiet had been restored there. The Opposition papers still filled their columns with denunciations of Essad and Djavid Pashas and with demands that the decision of Europe should be enforced.

In Russia it was hoped that the step taken by King Nicholas would lead Austria and Italy to abstain from drastic action against him, and give time for the Ambassadorial Conference either to come to a satisfactory agreement or to postpone irremediable action, but the anxiety as to the decisions of the Conference was still very great. In France it was thought that a settlement might now be reached on the basis of the decisions of the Powers, that Albania should form an independent State, and that its pacification and the delimitation of its frontiers should not be carried out by giving a mandate to any Power or Powers, but that it should be the work of the Concert of Europe. This Concert should be emphasised by the occupation of Skutari by detachments from the international squadron after it had been evacuated by the Montenegrins. At Sofia the news was received with relief, at Constantinople with unconcern. The civil population in Bulgaria longed for the conclusion of peace, in order that the soldiers might return to their homes before reaping commenced in July; the military were anxious to employ the troops still facing the Turks to meet the Greek forces massed on the western frontier of

Bulgaria. The Turks hailed with ill-concealed joy the possibility of a division of Albania between Austria-Hungary and Italy.

King Nicholas is accustomed to decide important questions of home and foreign policy himself, so was not likely to be much troubled by the resignation of his Cabinet, and the meeting of the Skrupshtina on May 8, to decide the fate of Skutari was a mere formality. The King assembled the Montenegrin Parliament in the courtyard of the palace and informed them that in the interests of general peace, and in order to save Montenegro and the entire Serb nation, he had been forced to give in to the Powers. Russia, Servia, and Greece, he said, had counselled submission. Russia, however, would continue to protect Montenegro in the future, and Montenegro would go forward increased and strengthened, fitting herself for further deeds of national valour. As His Majesty said to a correspondent of the *Neues Wiener Tagblatt*, " I did it in order to yield to the will of the Powers, and from love of my people who longed for peace after the severe crisis. The fields must now be cultivated. The Montenegrins have fought with rare self-sacrifice and bravery, and this war will form an imperishable page of glory in their history. It must not, however, be forgotten that thousands and thousands of Montenegro's best sons have died in battle, and in leaving Skutari we leave also with the deepest grief in our hearts the graves of our fallen heroes. May Europe recognise with equal magnanimity the heroism of Montenegro, who now, by her renunciation of Skutari, has rendered an inestimable service to European peace."

King Nicholas had overcome the opposition of the military no-surrender party, headed by General Martinovitch and M. Plamenatz, who would have plunged Montenegro into ruin rather than give up Skutari, and found no difficulty in gaining the assent of the Skrupshtina. General

Martinovitch, to whom it was chiefly owing that Montenegro had, in October 1912, declared war without waiting
for her Allies, had already resigned the Premiership, in
which he was replaced by General Vukotitch, whilst
M. Plamenatz, who had formerly been Montenegrin
Envoy at Constantinople, took the portfolio of Foreign
Affairs and went down to San Giovanni di Medua to
negotiate with Admiral Cecil Burney, the British officer
who was senior admiral of the international blockading
fleet, as to the details of the evacuation and re-occupation
of Skutari. Yet one more interesting episode was to be
added to the history of the British Navy in the Mediterranean, and the British ensign was to float over yet one
more inland capital, as it had floated over Rome when
Troubridge's boats brought British sailors up the Tiber
to garrison the Castle of St. Angelo when it had been
evacuated by the French in 1799.

Skutari was duly handed over by General Becir, the
Montenegrin commander, to Vice-Admiral Burney, the
commander of the international force, on May 14, but
the population of the town maintained an attitude of quiet
indifference. The Montenegrins had behaved fairly
well during their occupation, although a fire which
destroyed half the bazaar quarter was said by the
Albanians to have been purposely occasioned by Montenegrin patriots, an assertion for which no warrant could
be found. A regular administration was organised by the
International Commission, to conduct the affairs of the
place, where there was still much suffering and distress
amongst the poor ; courts of justice were formed under
the presidency of naval officers ; vaccination stations were
provided ; the town was administered by an International
Commission under the presidency of Vice-Admiral
Burney.

"Skutari wears all the signs of its international
character. Early this morning, May 15, the Montenegrin

flag was hauled down from the citadel, and from above the weatherbeaten battlements which dominate the town now float the flags of the five Powers. Down in the city itself there are bright spots of colour where the Union Jack, the Tricolour, the Black Eagle, or whatever flag may be flying from the red-roofed houses show where the commanders of the international forces are quartered; while to the bright colours of the picturesquely-dressed crowd of Montenegrins that throng the streets are added the white drill or the dark blue uniforms of the pickets of the various naval detachments. With the arrival to-day of a further 250 men from San Giovanni di Medua the detachments are now brought up to the full strength of 1000, of which Italy, Austria, and France each contribute 200, Germany —in consequence of the ship by which she is represented in the international fleet being only a small cruiser—100, and Great Britain, in order to make up the full quota, 300. Each detachment is provided with one Maxim gun. The duty of this force, which is quartered in barracks in the middle of the town, is to police the city, which for this purpose has been divided into five sections. The guard for the citadel, which is included in the bazaar quarter, has been provided by Great Britain.

" The status of the town has been made known to the inhabitants in the following proclamation, printed in English and Albanian side by side :

" In the name of the international fleet representing the Great Powers of Europe.

A Proclamation

" On the withdrawal of the forces of His Majesty King Nicholas of Montenegro, the town of Skutari will be taken over and administered by a commission of officers of the international fleet representing the Great Powers of Europe until such time as autonomous government has been established in Albania.

" All persons are hereby warned that they must obey the orders of the officers of the Commission under penalty of military law.

" With regard to the Customs administration, it has been arranged that it shall be given into the charge of an official to be nominated by the Consular Body and appointed by the Commission, and that the proceeds of the dues, which will remain at 11 per cent. as under the Turkish Government, shall be handed over to the municipality. This body, which consists of some half-dozen Moslem Albanians and a similar number of Christians, was called together this morning and was requested to resume its duties, which were interrupted in consequence of the occupation. The Commission having been informed that there are a large number of cases of disease in the town, a sanitary commission, consisting of Albanian, Austrian, and Italian doctors, has been formed to report on the best course of action to be taken." *

Skutari for the first time in history settled down as a quiet country town, abandoned even by the Montenegrin sight-seers, in their red and blue national costumes, who had thronged its streets during the first days of the occupation. One interesting event, however, was a visit paid on May 26 to Admiral Burney by 130 of the principal men of the five Malissori tribes—the Hoti, Gruda, Klementi, Shkrelli, and Kastrati. Their object was to petition him to use his influence to prevent the Hoti and Gruda tribes from being severed from the " Five-Banner Group " and incorporated in Montenegro.

" In this petition, to which twenty-two of the principal men of the Five Tribes set their mark, it is pointed out that by blood, language, and customs the Tribes in question form a whole, and that in religion they differ from Montenegro. Their interests, further, are closely bound up with the province of Skutari, since they own lands in

* *The Times*, Monday, May 19, 1913.

the district stretching from Skutari to Kavaja. Instead of any diminution there has been an increase of hostility between the Slavs and Albanians as a result of the war, at the beginning of which they fought with the Montenegrins until it was evident that the latter desired not the liberation but the conquest of Albania. Finally it is predicted that unless the Five Tribes are allowed to remain entirely Albanian, blood will continue to flow." *

Vice-Admiral Burney in reply promised that the petition should be laid before the Ambassadorial Conference in London. The details of the tribesmen's reception by a British Admiral are well worthy of record.

" The tribesmen, who had come down from the mountains on the eastern side of the lake earlier in the day, leaving their arms at the outposts on the edge of the town, were received by the British Admiral, with whom were the other members of the International Commission, in the garden of his residence. Here the men, dressed in their picturesque costumes of rough white cloth braided with black and wearing white fezes, stood round in a large circle, while the following speech was read to them in Albanian by the British Vice-Consul on behalf of Admiral Burney :—

" ' Chiefs of the Malissori Tribes,—I, on behalf of the International Commission, am very glad to welcome you, especially as I know that your presence here to-day is a token of your loyalty and goodwill to us who were sent by the Great Powers to inaugurate the first steps in the formation of an autonomous Albania. We sincerely hope that you will preserve absolute order and quietude among your tribesmen, for by so doing you will materially assist us in our task.' "

" After expressing a hope that, for the future, the quarrels of Christians and Moslems would be entirely forgotten, and exhorting them to live as brothers for the

* *The Times,* Thursday, May 29, 1913.

benefit of the whole country, the speech concluded with an announcement that Admiral Burney hoped himself shortly to visit the tribes of the Hoti, Kastrati, and Klementi.

" On the conclusion of the speeches, the Malissori, accompanied by the Admiral and members of the Commission, went to the barracks, where, to the strains of a ship's band, they sat down to dinner. The proceedings were brought to a close by the playing of the National Anthems of the five Powers, and shouts of ' Long live the Powers ! Long live the Mountains ! ' It was easy to see throughout the importance which the tribesmen attached to the visit and the pleasure which they felt at the friendly and hospitable way in which they were received. So anxious, indeed, were as many as possible to take part in the visit and to manifest their feelings of respect for the representatives of the Powers that the number of the deputation was more than double that originally arranged. As one of the men expressed it to-day, it was ' the greatest day for the Mountains since the day when Christ was born.' " *

From the festivities at Skutari we must, however, return to the Ambassadorial Conference in London, in order to see how the Powers were dealing with the wider problems connected with Albania.

Sir Edward Grey had thanked King Nicholas for his telegram announcing that Montenegro would give way as to Skutari, and the decision was duly taken note of at the meeting of the Conference on May 8. That meeting failed, however, to discuss a draft for the Constitution of Albania which had been prepared by the representatives of Austria and Italy. The project was couched in the most general terms. Nothing was said as to either railways or loans, or as to the powers to be given to the head of the State. It was proposed that an international body of

* *The Times,* Thursday, May 29, 1913.

gendarmes, officered by the minor States of Europe, and organised on the system followed in Persia, should be placed at the disposal of the Albanian Government. The capitulations were to be abolished, and foreigners placed under the jurisdiction of mixed tribunals similar to those of Egypt. Albania was to be neutralised and a Prince named on the proposal of the Powers. At first the State was to remain under the suzerainty of Turkey, but, after a term of years, the Statute was to be revised and full independence granted. Russia, on the other hand, wished to build upon the old foundations and to see the country governed by a Vali, and Turkish soldiers placed at the disposal of the new Government. But it was soon seen that even a nominal connection between Turkey and Albania would be disadvantageous to both countries, and opinion came to be in favour of the recognition of Albanian independence. Two questions, however, of the first importance remained unsettled, namely, the choice of a Prince, and the delimitation of the southern frontier of Albania, a matter which intimately concerned the negotiations for the general peace. These questions still remained unsettled at the beginning of September 1913.

As to the choice of a ruler various candidates were suggested by the free-lances of journalism, including Prince Albert Ghika, himself an Albanian, but married to an Irish lady, a French Prince, or a descendant of one of the old Albanised French families who have been rulers in Albania since the thirteenth century, Prince Mirko, or Prince Peter of Montenegro. To Servians a British Prince appeared to be the best possible King of Albania, but the Duke of Teck had in January refused the Crown. Amongst diplomatists a candidate much spoken of was Prince William of Wied, a Prussian officer and a relation of the Queen of Rumania, who was finally chosen.

During the month of May the Turkish troops remaining in Albania were gradually removed by sea, whilst the

Montenegrin and Servian troops evacuated the coast towns. The Provisional Government at Vallona would not contrive to collect the taxes, and Southern Albania was being busily canvassed by the supporters of its annexation to Greece, who, according to Albanian patriots, were filling the deserted villages with Greek immigrants from Epirus. The European Foreign Offices were besieged with picturesque deputations in the rival interests.

By the definite Treaty of Peace all questions connected with Albania, which was declared to be an autonomous State independent of the Sultan, were left for settlement by the Great Powers, although it was rumoured that, in return for concessions as to the Ægean Islands, Greece was prepared to meet the wishes of Italy as to the delimitation of the southern frontier of Albania. Thus one of the greatest dangers to the peace of Europe has for the time been removed.

CHAPTER XI

SERVIA

MONTENEGRO had fired the first shot in the War of Liberation, but it was not long before the forces of the other Balkan States followed her into the field, even though Greece seemed for a moment to linger.

Servia, like Montenegro, had her own wrongs to avenge. At the moment when the Empire of Stephen Dushan, who at his death in 1355 was the lord of nearly all the western provinces of the Byzantine Empire save Salonika, Chalcidice, and the Morea, and dreamed of Constantinople as the capital of a Servian Empire, was broken up by Sultan Murad I. on the battlefield of Kossovo, June 15, 1389, the Servians had become the vassals of the Osmanlis. Within a century, after the power of Hungary to free the Balkan Peninsula had ceased with the defeat of Varna (1444), the Servians, won over by the religious tolerance of the Turks, which strongly contrasted with the intolerance of the Roman Catholics of Hungary, acknowledged the immediate sovereignty of the Sultans, and their country was broken up into a multitude of fiefs. The Servian Church, however, retained an independence of which it was only wholly deprived late in the eighteenth century.

But as the prosperity of Turkey decayed, the Turkish rule grew harder. Kara George rose in insurrection in 1806, and though he failed, owing to the treachery of Russia, who, to save her own freedom from the French invaders, delivered over the Servians to the tender mercies of the Porte, an insurrection broke out once more on Palm Sunday 1815, under the leadership of Milosh Obrenovitch. His rebellion proved successful, and on November 6, 1817, he was recognised by the Sultan as hereditary Ban of Servia. In 1830, by the Treaty of Adrianople, Servia became all but in name an independent state.

In 1868, after various revolutions, Milan, a great-nephew of Milosh Obrenovitch, was crowned as Prince in the Cathedral at Belgrade. In 1876 he joined Monte-negro in declaring war against Turkey, but was utterly defeated and only saved from territorial losses by the intervention of the European Powers. Later in the same year Milan took part in the Russo-Turkish War, and as a reward for his exertions received, at the Treaty of San Stefano, the territories of Nish, and what is known as Old Servia in Macdeonia. These latter districts were taken from him by the Treaty of Berlin, and Servia, so far as power and territory were concerned, was left inferior to Bulgaria, a circumstance which led to a war between the States when Bulgaria occupied Eastern Rumelia in 1885. For the time the change of dynasty in 1903, when the House of Karageorgevitch was replaced on the throne, on the murder of King Alexander, did little to improve their relations. Servians, however, as well as Bulgarians had to suffer under Turkish persecutions in Macedonia, and Servia, like Bulgaria, had to bear her share in main-taining hordes of refugees of her own blood. Taught by her sufferings, she forgot her jealousy of Bulgaria, and, when the Balkan League was formed, Servian swords were ready to leap from their scabbards to win the freedom of their brethren who groaned under the Turkish yoke in Macedonia. Whatever King Peter's faults may have been in the past, his dread of Austrian ill-will did not keep him back from lending a willing ear to their cry.

The risk of provoking the intervention of Austria was no slight one. There is a large Serb population in Croatia

and in Southern Hungary under the Austrian flag ; the
Croats themselves are only separated from the Serbs by
differences of religion ; Croatia, like Bohemia, has been
crying out for recognition as a kingdom united to the
Crown of the Hapsburgs by a purely personal tie, and
including Slavonia, Dalmatia, Bosnia, and Herzegovina ;
to co-operate with Montenegro the Servian generals
would have to occupy the vilayet of Novi-Bazar, which
barred Austria's road to the Ægean, and of which the
military occupation had been guaranteed to her by the
Treaty of Berlin ; the formation of a great Servian
kingdom would not only endanger her sovereignty over
the whole of the Southern Slavs, but would put a final end
to her hopes of winning Salonika.   It was true that
Servia was supported by Russia, but long leagues part
the Servian from the Russian frontiers, and the strong and
valiant army of Rumania lay in the path of Russia's legions.
On the other hand, the fortress of Belgrade lies under the
guns of Semlin, and Austrian gunboats make the Hapsburgs the lords of the middle Danube.   Yet King Peter
held on his way unperturbed, even though Austria was
beginning to mobilise on her southern frontier.   He knew
that he could rely upon the Russia Tsar, and Russian forces
were quickly gathering upon Austria's Galician frontiers.

The natural field for the operations of Servia was in the
basin of the Vardar, where lie the Old Servian vilayets,
and where intruding Albanians have occupied the once
Servian towns of Ipek and Prizrend.   Unless she occupied
the vilayet of Novi-Bazar it was only through Ipek and
Prizrend that Servia could stretch out a helping hand to
Montenegro and force her way to that port on the
Adriatic which, were it under the Servian flag, would at
once free her from her economic vassalage to Austria.

The Servians were strategically in a strong position.   As
the military correspondent of *The Times* pointed out on
October 19 : " The headquarters of King Peter moved to
Nish on October 18, and this is the best point from which

to observe and regulate the Servian movements referred to in previous articles. A Turkish offensive on this side is less easy for Turkey than for Servia, because, while the roads open for a Servian advance converge upon Kumanovo and Uskub, the same roads lead Turkish columns in divergent directions, and the further such columns march the wider is their separation. For these reasons it might be best for the Second Turkish Army to be massed between Uskub and Kumanovo, with strong advanced guards well entrenched upon the main lines of approach, and only to attack when the enemy is committed and his intentions are fully known. What with spies, light troops, and aeroplanes, the Turkish command should be well informed, and it will be particularly instructive to learn how in this daedalian theatre the aircraft are able to obtain information, and how this information will influence events." A weak spot might be found in the co-operation of the Servian and Bulgarian armies, both in the eastern region of Macedonia and Thrace, as allied armies rarely work cordially together, but, " in view of the diverse interests of these two allies in the ultimate settlement," this co-operation might have a political object in view. No great good could be expected from Servian guerilla operations either in the Sanjak of Novi-Bazar or in the regions south of the Rhodope, for the theatre of war was a most difficult one, the lateness of the season was against them, and the Moslem villagers were well armed to resist them. There were, too, large Turkish regular forces in those districts.

Despite these predictions the Servians took the offensive, and the first collision with the Turks took place on the evening of Wednesday, October 23, near Kumanovo. Desperate fighting lasted all day on the Thursday, and ended at sundown in a complete Servian victory and the capture of the town.

" The Turks, who had forty thousand men in the field when the battle began, only yielded their ground foot by foot.

"Their losses were very heavy, most of the casualties being due to the fire of the Servian artillery, which was splendidly served.

"The Servians lost fewer men than might have been expected from the stubborn resistance which they encountered. Both sides fought with the greatest gallantry."

The secret of the Servian successes may be summed up in a few words—perfect organisation and the marvellous spirit of the men. The advance to and taking of Uskub had been expected to be the work of eight weeks; it took eight days.

"It should be remembered that the Servian Army of to-day is a machine which has practically been created in about five years. It owes but little to foreign instructors, though the bulk of its officers have received courses of training in France and Russia. The French military influence is fairly strong, but it is not too much to say that the Servian army is entirely a Servian product, reared and trained specially for the task it has now achieved. Its genius is General Putnik, who has had the satisfaction of seeing, while still in active service, the triumphant result of his genius unremittingly applied. He is the organiser of and the leader to victory.

"Opposed to the Servians was an army armed with German weapons, led by officers trained in German ideals of strategy and tactics. The Servians were armed with French rifles, and used French artillery and French powder. The numbers of men and guns on both sides are given at so many different totals that it is dangerous to set forth any figures as being reliable, but the Turkish artillery was, at the battle of Kumanovo, superior in numbers to the Servian. The result, therefore, is certain to cause searchings of heart and surprise in Germany. The Turkish artillery was hopelessly outclassed from the start, and the superiority of the Creusot weapons and powder conclusively demonstrated.

"True, the Turks did not manage their guns at all as

they should have done, but even making allowance for bad working, the decisive victory is quite sufficient to make Germans ponder and Frenchmen rejoice. In fact, a number of Germans here are extremely uneasy at the failure, from one end of the Turkish position to the other, of an army ' made in Germany,' and made by such a brilliant soldier as Marshal von der Goltz.

" The Servian artillery alone might have won the battle of Kumanovo, but it was the cavalry which turned defeat into stupendous rout. The cavalry was led by Prince Arsène, a capable officer who has seen twenty-seven years' service in the Russian army. He handled his force with brilliant precision and deadly effect, sustaining particularly trivial losses. He had a magnificent chance, and he took advantage of it to the full. Had he not pressed home the advantage, it is undoubted that the Turkish forces would have been able to offer serious battle on the easily defendable heights of Ovce Poli, where, indeed, the Servians expected to have to fight a tremendous battle. As it was, Prince Arsène not only turned defeat into rout, but made a further stand by the enemy out of the question. With His Royal Highness the supreme laurels of the battle rest."

Encouraged by their successes the Servians now openly boasted that they would not only secure an outlet on the Adriatic, but that they would, in the long run, annex Bosnia and Herzegovina to their Empire.

After the evacuation of Uskub, the Turkish troops were driven by the Servians from Kuprili towards Tetovo and Gostivar. At these points they for a time made a determined stand with a force of about twenty battalions with artillery. Their defence of Dibra, to the north-west of Gostivar, was especially vigorous, but on November 8 it was taken by the Servians after severe fighting, and the Turks fled to Monastir leaving their guns behind them. At Prilep the Servians had an encounter with the Turks, in which they lost 1500 killed and wounded, the Turkish loss being 6000. The ground was difficult, the railway communications were inadequate, and the wounded suffered severely. Meanwhile the Third Servian Army was making its way slowly towards Durazzo over extremely bad roads. This movement, which was bringing the Servians to the coast of the Adriatic, was watched in Austria with the greatest jealousy.

The claim of Servia to an outlet on the seaboard was founded on her historical rights.

These go back to the twelfth century when, on the death of the Emperor Manuel Comnenus (1143–1180), the Southern Slavs became emancipated from the Byzantine Empire, and formed two kingdoms, that of Servia under Stephen Nemanya, a descendant of the Princes of Montenegro, and that of Bosnia under the Ban Kulin, which was dependent on Servia. Stephen's possessions included Nish, Dalmatia as far as the Bocche di Cattaro, Herzegovina, Montenegro, and Danubian Servia. He founded the monasteries of Kilandjar on Mount Athos, and the Tsarska-Lavra at Studenitza, where he and his successors were buried. He became a monk in that monastery, and died there in 1200. The Servians honour him under the name of St. Simeon. His successor Milutin (1281–1321) extended the Servian Empire over Macedonia, reached the Ægean at Kavala, and conquered Northern Albania. Under his son Stephen III. (Urosh) Dushan (1321–1355), Servia became an Empire and the mistress of nearly all the western provinces of the Byzantine Empire save Thessalonica, Chalcidice, and the Morea. Dushan even aimed at the conquest of Constantinople, in order to make Servia a naval power, but he was foiled by the Venetians and the Turks, who within a few months after his death seized Gallipoli (1356), closed the Dardanelles, and blocked the maritime route to Constantinople to the Slavs. The fall of Servia was as rapid as had been its rise. Murad I. (1360–1389) carried the Turkish arms through Thrace. Mace-

donia broke away from the Servian Empire under
Vukashin, and Southern Servia, powerless to resist the
Sultan, was struck down in the battle of the Maritza
(1371). Northern Servia shared the same fate within
eighteen years. For a moment its ruler Lazarus, who had
allied himself with the King of Bosnia, dreamed of recon-
stituting a strong central power, but Murad I. was
determined to terminate the conquest of the Balkan
Peninsula, and on June 15, 1389, his victory at Kossovo
laid the Servian Empire in the dust. We have seen how
the Servian chief Balsha, a man of Frankish origin, seized
Skutari and extended his Empire as far as Cattaro in
1367. His dominions, which included the present
Montenegro, Podgoritza, Spuzh, Jabliak, the Isles of
Lake Skutari, and the territory of Bari (Antivari), are the
origin of Montenegro.

During the rule of the Nemanya dynasty (1189–1371)
the coast towns of the Adriatic were the richest part of
Servia. Cattaro was an autonomous republic, which,
according to some authorities, was under Servian protection, though this is denied by others, until in 1371 it
placed itself under Hungarian protection, and in 1420,
from fear of the Turks, transferred its allegiance to
Venice, becoming Austrian in 1797, French in 1805,
and Austrian once more in 1814. Travellers who visited
the country in the early part of the nineteenth century
found the only stone houses at Cattaro, Antivari, and
Dulcigno. Stephen Urosh II. and Stephen III. Dushan
called themselves " Kings of the Maritime Region," and
the latter, who occupied Vallona and for a moment held
Durazzo, the ancient Dyrrachium, which since Norman
days had belonged to the kingdom of Sicily, could rightly
style himself King of Albania, though the Albanians seem
to have detested his rule. Ragusa, save for a moment in
900, never passed under Servian rule. Antivari was an
autonomous republic under Servian protection until,
with the coast towns north of it, Spizza and Budua, it

became Venetian in 1444. Thus Servia controlled for two centuries the western extremities of the great road which traversed the Balkan Peninsula from the Adriatic to Constantinople, and became a rich state owing to her trade with the Black Sea and the regions lying to its eastward and to her silver mines, from which the wealth was drawn which under Queen Elena of Servia and her son Stephen Urosh II. filled the coast lands with splendid churches.

Such are the historical grounds on which Servia bases her claims to an outlet on the sea. A century of economic disputes and customs wars with Austria have taught Modern Servia that without such an outlet she can become neither rich nor really independent. To obtain one on the Ægean she must become involved in ruinous disputes with Bulgaria and Greece. To reach the Adriatic she must either form a close union with Montenegro or trample on the national aspirations of Albania, at the same time as she throws down the glove to Austria and Italy, neither of whom wishes to see a third maritime Power rise up on the seaboard of the Adriatic. M. Pashitch, the Servian Prime Minister, announced on November 24 that Servia would claim a strip of coast-line measuring thirty-one miles long between Alessio and Durazzo, which she would reach by annexing a portion of Central Albania extending eastwards to Djakova and Lake Ochrida. Such being the views of Servia it is not to be wondered at that great excitement prevailed in Austria, which soon found a pretext for a very serious dispute with her southern neighbour, whose troops, as we have seen, were hastening to the sea across the snows of the Albanian mountains.

The Servians reached Alessio on November 17. Guided by friendly Albanians, the column managed to push its way through extremely difficult and mountainous country, where no troops had up till then been seen, without meeting with any resistance. Guns and gun-carriages had to be pushed through the snow, which at some points was thirty-nine inches deep. The cold was bitter, the temperature being from 10.4° to 5° Fahrenheit. In the inhabited districts the people were friendly and supplied the troops with food, but for several days the Servians passed through regions where there was not a single village and food was very scarce. During the whole march, which was over a distance of ninety-four miles as the crow flies from Prizrend, only one soldier reported himself sick.

On November 16 San Giovanni di Medua was occupied by the Montenegrins with three battalions of infantry, two batteries of artillery, and one battalion of volunteers. The muddy ground had occasioned them great difficulties.

From Alessio the Servians hastened to advance on Durazzo, about forty miles to the south, where, at that moment, the Albanian Provisional Government, under Ismail Kemal Bey, was installed. Durazzo is, as has been said, the ancient Dyrrachium, which played so great a part in the civil wars between Cæsar and Pompey. It was the usual port of transit from Brindisi, by which Italian travellers reached the Via Egnatia, their road to Thessalonica and Byzantium.

Its Mussulman population was greatly disturbed, and Austrian steamers were kept ready in the port to remove the Christian population in case of need. On one of these the Sisters of Charity, working in the town, took refuge. The population detested the Servians. Some amongst the Christians would have welcomed the declaration of an Austrian protectorate, but others, together with the whole of the Moslems, were ardent Albanian nationalists, and these, on November 27, hoisted the Albanian flag, consisting of a single black eagle on a red field, on the Government buildings. The Turkish flags were lowered; such Turkish functionaries as would not recognise the new government were expelled.

On the previous day the Servians had reached the village of Milot, only a few hours distant from Durazzo, accompanied by some hundreds of Malissori irregulars. A Commission, consisting of the Orthodox Bishop and three or four notables, accompanied by the Austrian Consul, was appointed to go over and meet them and to offer to surrender the town without firing a shot.

The Servians accepted the proposal, but did not actually occupy the town, though they encamped close to it, possibly on the site of that Asparagium which Pompey made his headquarters. Reinforcements of seven infantry battalions and one cavalry regiment, numbering about 7000 men in all, were hurried up from Prizrend, covering the distance of 106 miles in seven days, with no tents, and indifferent food, in awful weather. Yet a month later hardly a man was to be seen who looked pinched as the result of hardship, recruited as they had been by resting in a sunny valley with plenty of good food.

The coast-line which Servia claims as her seaboard on the Adriatic is thus described by my friend Mr. Henry W. Nevinson, one of the first European authorities on Montenegro and Albania.

" From Skutari," he says, " I drove by road—a Turkish road !—for about six hours to Oboti. It is Skutari's other so-called port upon the wild river Boyana, the long estuary of the lake combined with the old course that still takes about half the water of the Drin, the other half running out past Alessio.

" A Hungarian ' tramp ' took me down the winding and violent stream, and out to sea. As far as I discovered, she had no cargo but bugs ; yet she bumped upon the sandbanks, and was almost wrecked in the turmoil of breaking waves and furious currents at the bar. A few ramshackle huts and a ruinous Turkish office marked the port. Far to the south—some 35 miles away—I could just make out the long promontory of Durazzo, where Cæsar was. It is about as bad as any other Turkish harbour now.

" I did not think that those wretched ports and that

strip of fevered coast were so soon to be the danger-point of Europe. Are all the most intellectual peoples of the world to fly at each other's throats because a semi-civilised little country like Servia asserts a claim to this miserable gateway on the Adriatic, chiefly for the exportation of her hogs ? It seems incredible ; yet that very piece of coast which I saw from my ' tramp '—worthless harbours, fever swamps, and all—is just the thing that M. Pashitch, the Servian Premier, publicly claims as the ' minimum ' of his country's demand, And it is just that ' minimum ' which Austria resolutely refuses." *

Whilst the Fourth Army was pressing on to the Adriatic, the rest of the Servian forces were busily engaged in driving the Turks from Macedonia. On November 23 the Servian Morava division occupied Ochrida without resistance. Patrols sent out in every direction discovered no Turkish troops except remnants of those defeated at Florina and Resna, where Fethy Pasha was shot by one of his officers,who afterwards committed suicide. The Pasha had donned the uniform of a private soldier to facilitate his escape. The Turkish troops who escaped from Monastir were rapidly accounted for by the Servians and the Greeks. Dibra was taken at noon on November 26, after a desperate struggle with the Turks, who had rallied there after their flight from Monastir, and had been joined by reinforcements of Malissori and Arnauts. With the capture of Dibra the whole of Macedonia had been subdued. King Peter returned from Uskub to Belgrade on November 23, and was received with the wildest enthusiasm. His Majesty's return was taken to show that he considered the war in the western part of Turkey as finished, since before leaving Belgrade he had declared that he would remain with the army till it was completely victorious. The welcome offered to him proved that he had done much to inspire loyalty and devotion to the Karageorgevitch dynasty amongst the Servian nation.

* *Daily Chronicle*, Wednesday, November 27, 1912.

But, for a time, it looked as if Servia would be summoned to face a war with Austria.

Whilst hymns of victory were sounding at Belgrade, at Vienna animosity against the Servians was rising to fever-heat.

As early as November 8 the Austro-Hungarian Minister at Belgrade had been instructed to inform the Servian Government that Austria was prepared to resume Count Andrassy's friendly policy towards Servia, if she resumed a friendly attitude and gave guarantees, and the German and Italian Ministers received instructions to inform them of the solidarity of the Triple Alliance, and to declare that the Triple Alliance would consider the arrival of Servians on the Adriatic coast as contrary to its interest.

Servia, however, thanks to the attitude assumed by the Pan-Slavists at St. Petersburg, defied all the Austrian threats, in reliance upon the eventual support of Russia.

Herr Prochaska, the Austrian Consul at Prizrend, was suspected by the Servians of stirring up the Northern Albanians to oppose their advance. Consequently when the Servians occupied the town they intercepted the Consul's correspondence with the Austrian Foreign Office, and placed him under close arrest in his house. This proved the last straw.

Servia had for years been irritating Austria by a policy of pin-pricks. If Servian pigs had been excluded from the Dual Monarchy, Austro-Hungarian manufactured goods had been all but excluded by heavy customs dues from the Servian markets. Servian intriguers had kept up a constant ferment in Croatia and Bosnia, and were the foremost to encourage the Southern Slavs in their dreams of a South Slav Empire. Thus the news from Prizrend fell upon very hostile ears at Vienna, and troops were hurriedly mobilised both on the Galician and the Dalmatian frontiers. On the other hand, unofficial Russia openly supported the Servians in their policy of resistance, even though a peaceful solution of the dispute was not despaired of. All through November feeling was at fever-heat. An Austrian official who had been sent to Prizrend was not, it was alleged, allowed to communicate with Herr Prochaska; the report spread, indeed, that the Consul had been murdered by Servian soldiers, and the receipt by his wife of a picture post-card addressed in her husband's handwriting was not accepted by the Austrian authorities as a sufficient substitute for the missing official despatches. Rioting took place at Vienna, where a crowd of Servians who had assembled before the Servian and Bulgarian Legations, hooting Austria, were charged by the police. Rumours circulated that the Servians were massacring the Albanians and even their Turkish prisoners, whilst holding the Austrian Consuls prisoners in the Consulates in the districts they had occupied. An ultimatum might, it was thought, be presented any day at Belgrade. Russia hurriedly mobilised large forces in her Polish provinces, where a formidable agitation, aimed alike against Russia and Austria, was in progress, with a view to preparing the ground for a Polish revolt were war to break out between the two Powers. Still the Foreign Offices did not lose hope of peace.

Agitation was increasing in Dalmatia, where the Croat population at Spalato and Sebenico made extravagant demonstrations in favour of the Balkan States. Government dissolved the municipalities. In vain all the Great Powers used their influence to induce Servia to exercise moderation; it almost looked as if she was speculating on the unwillingness of Austria to make war. At Buda the Emperor Francis Joseph was holding conferences with the Ministers and Chiefs of the General Staff of the Army, whilst the German and Italian Ambassadors were daily closeted with Count Berchtold. It was said that the Emperor had remarked, "We are in favour of peace; but not peace at any price. We cannot stand everything." Owing to King

Peter's absence at the front the Servian answer to the
Austrian Note was delayed.   Military reasons were
the excuse given for their refusal to allow Consul
Prochaska to communicate with the Ballplatz.   The
Reichspost, as usual, did its best to stir up ill-feeling,
and published reports that Servia was entrenching
positions near Semendria so as to threaten Austria.

Germany, however, was doing her best to hold back
Austria from a policy of violence.   On November 25
the *North German Gazette* published an article to the
effect that the rumour that M. Sazonoff (the Russian
Foreign Minister) had altered his views as to the
harbour question was incorrect.   This was for the simple
reason that the Powers were unanimous in declining
to take up a position beforehand with regard to any
single problem relating to the Balkans.   The rumour
that Austria-Hungary had mobilised five army corps
was contradicted, and it was stated that she did not
intend to present an ultimatum at Belgrade.

Germany was using her influence to induce Austria
to adopt a proposal to hold a European Conference
to solve all pending questions in the Balkans, and
on November 27 articles appeared in the Berlin papers
to the effect that the Austro-Hungarian Ambassador at
St. Petersburg had had a very satisfactory audience
of the Tsar, who was thoroughly convinced of Austria's
peaceful intentions, and who now, therefore, endorsed
M. Sazonoff's peaceful policy.   News also arrived that
Herr Prochaska was safe and well, and was on his way
from Prizrend to Uskub, where he arrived on November
26 and conferred with Herr Edl, who had been sent
there from the Austrian Foreign Office.

Opinion in Europe was now coming round to the idea
that a European Conference should be held after peace had
been concluded between the Balkan belligerents, to revise
its terms in accordance with the interests of the Great
Powers.   Other conferences of competent authorities would

also be held to discuss any proposals relating to financial interests, railways, and other similar questions. Proposals for an International Congress were made by England.

Austria-Hungary, however, was greatly inclined to dissent from any proposal to invest an international tribunal with power to adjudicate on matters deemed vital to the Dual Monarchy, such as the autonomy of Albania and the annexation of Durazzo by Servia. Russian military opinion was indignant at the refusal of the Tsar to go to war, and demonstrations in favour of the Balkan States had to be stopped by the police. Finally Russia allowed it to be understood that her military preparations were in view of certain internal disturbances, the outbreak of which there was ground for apprehending. Possibly the attitude of England contributed to induce a more peaceful feeling in Russia, for Berlin rumour stated that " when the decision was on the razor's edge, and a rupture of relationships between Vienna and St. Petersburg was to be feared, since, in spite of the disinclination of the Tsar and his Ministers, the war party seemed to have got the upper hand, the English Cabinet let it be known in Paris and St. Petersburg that England was not disposed to take part in a war which she regarded, under the circumstances, as purposeless and contrary to her interests. Germany, it was hinted, had been informed of this, and such a proof of confidence had given great pleasure at Berlin.

In an important debate in the Reichstag on December 2 the Imperial Chancellor, Dr. von Bethmann-Hollweg, very clearly defined the attitude of the Powers as to the Balkan question, but his remarks were not heeded at Belgrade, where Russia, likewise, was making every effort to preserve peace.

The Chancellor said:

" Germany is not immediately concerned, and has no direct influences in the Balkans beyond economic interests. Should, contrary to my expectation, Germany's ally be attacked or threatened in her existence Germany will then be true to her ally and fight by her side."

Dr. von Bethmann-Hollweg did not mention either Russia or Servia, but this was unnecessary, as every one understood, and, with the exception of the Socialist deputies, every one applauded when the Chancellor added that he was sure that in this event the Government would have the nation at their backs.

A few remarks followed about Germany's attitude in the Turkish-Italian war, in which the Chancellor maintained that German policy had resulted in retaining the goodwill of the leading statesmen of both these Powers.

He concluded by expressing his belief that the active exchange of views between the Great Powers which was proceeding would have a satisfactory result.

In the discussion which followed Herr von Kiderlen-Waechter referred to the growing intimacy between Germany and England.

Austria was firmly resolved that the Servian troops should evacuate Durazzo, and all other Albanian territory at the conclusion of hostilities : to support her diplomacy she massed large forces in Southern Hungary destined to act against Belgrade and Semendria, and to invade the Morava Valley, whilst her forces in Bosnia and Herzegovina were to advance against Western Servia and the Sanjak of Novi-Bazar. Two armies were collected to hold Russia in check.

The first or northern army was to defend Galicia, and was concentrated in the fortified triangle formed by the towns of Cracow, Przemysl, and Tomaszow, the two former being fortresses of the first class. The rest of the province is a flat plain offering little resistance to cavalry. Here entrenchments were dug round the capital Lemberg and on the frontier, and vast stretches of wire entanglements were erected over the plain, in order to check the Cossacks, of whom there were many amongst the half million of men whom Russia, in answer to the

Austrian demonstrations, had massed in her Polish provinces. A second Austrian army was collected in Bukowina and Transylvania to threaten Podolia and Volhynia, whilst a visit of the Crown Prince of Rumania to Berlin was followed by rumours of a partial Rumanian mobilisation. Rumania has not, indeed, forgotten how Russia deprived her of Bessarabia at the Congress of Berlin, and is, consequently, the faithful servant of the Triple Alliance. Moreover, she had already raised claims to receive compensation from Bulgaria for having remained neutral during the war. It was thought that she would support them by force of arms.

Russia, however, was most anxious to preserve peace, and used her utmost efforts to induce Servia to give way.

In vain Russia warned Servia that it was a dangerous delusion for her to suppose that Russia would champion her cause whether right or wrong, and endeavoured to induce the Belgrade Cabinet to reduce their demands within reasonable limits. Russia suffered the penalty of her diplomatic methods of former days. Servia had not forgotten what King Milan once said, that when he was rebuked by official Russia for doing what he was recommended to do by her unofficial representatives at Belgrade, he always received a Russian star shortly afterwards. Servia believed that she had nothing to lose and much to gain by a European war, and consequently persisted in her defiance of Austria, despite the warnings addressed to her by Dr. von Bethmann-Hollweg in a speech which gave satisfaction at Paris, and in which he said that the Triple Alliance was firmly united in carrying out its policy, although he was accused by the Socialists of having given a blank cheque to Austria. As regards the general policy of Germany the Chancellor said : " We hope that our friendly and active relationships with the Balkan States will be improved through their indubitable accession of strength, especially in economic respects. At the same time it will continue to be our object to maintain Turkey, after the conclusion of peace, as an important economic and political factor." French observers remarked that these words might well have been spoken by a French statesman. Yet Austria continued despondent under the influence of the suffering occasioned by her military expenditure, and the feeling " that the Servian abscess in the side of Austria must be finally eradicated " was spreading everywhere. However, both Austria and Italy were firmly determined to prevent the advent of a third Power in the Adriatic. Three hundred thousand men were assembled in Hungary within striking distance of the Servian frontier ; Austrian gunboats patrolled the Danube and the Save, and a flotilla of river craft was collected for the transport of troops.

Servia still refused to comply with the Austrian demands, and since Austria appeared determined not to enter into a European Conference before she had come to a settlement with Servia, the outlook was gloomy. However, Servia professed herself ready to accept the decision of the Great Powers with regard to all the points at issue.

By December 4, German newspapers were announcing that the Ambassadorial Conference proposed by Sir Edward Grey would be held in London " as the most neutral town," concurrently with the peace negotiations between Turkey and the Balkan Confederation.

The *Tribuna*, a journal in close touch with the Servian Foreign Office, said on December 3 :

" According to our information, not one member of the Servian Government has declared that Servia waives her right to Albanian territory. Servia maintains her old standpoint, namely, that what she needs is an outlet to the Adriatic Sea through her own territories. But Servia respects the Powers, and is ready to meet their wishes and to accept their decision.

" Generally speaking, the attitude in Belgrade circles is calm and correct to-day, but, according to information from various sources, the war preparations of her northern neighbour and the latter's concentration of troops on the frontier are being carried out to such an extent and with such haste, that Servia will find it necessary, in order to safeguard her interests, to make similar preparations, and unforeseen provocation from irresponsible factors on either side at any moment may render the situation far more serious."

Fortunately not only was Count Berchtold resolved to display the utmost forbearance, but M. Sazonoff and M. Kokofftseff did their utmost to persuade Servia to keep the peace.

Outside diplomatic circles, however, this optimism was not shared, and the situation was again considered dangerous, " in consequence of a petition presented to the King and the Government by the Servian merchants, who occupy a very powerful and influential position, urging that Servia's claims for an Adriatic port be strongly upheld."

Fortunately, however, the Prochaska affair proved to be far less serious than had been supposed in Vienna.

" According to trustworthy reports from Prizrend, the Prochaska affair seems to have been exaggerated. The facts seem to be that General Jankovics, one of the most intelligent officers in the Servian army, who has passed many years at Court, became very angry with M. Prochaska, owing to his failure to pay the usual visit after the surrender of Prizrend. The Consul was allowed to attend to his usual duties, with the exception of those which he is entitled to perform under the Capitulations, but he could not use the telegraph, which was entirely occupied for military purposes.

" On the other hand, investigation has so far failed to furnish any proofs of the Consul's personal agitation against the Servian Government, but sufficient proof is obtainable regarding the agitation made by the employés at the Consulate." *

In due course the Austrian Government received the

* *Daily Telegraph*, Monday, December 9, 1912.

report of its envoy Herr Edl, and, in consequence of it, the tension grew considerably less.

In the Duma at St. Petersburg fiery speakers belonging to the Right, the Nationalists, the Centre, the Constitutional Democrats, and the Progressive parties joined in declaring that no war would be more popular than one in defence of Servia against Austria, that historical enemy which, as one speaker, M. Purischkowitsch, said, was " the monarchy of shreds and patches "; and the Belgrade papers declared that if " Austria went to war with Servia, she would have to exterminate the entire Servian nation before conquering it." But diplomats took a calmer view of the situation than did the journalists, and by December 8 it was known not only that M. Jovanovitch, the newly-appointed Servian Minister to Vienna, was bringing with him proposals which might possibly lead to a solution of the conflict, but that the Emperor William had remarked, " I do not understand the continual excitement and fear of war, since the danger of fresh warlike complications is finally put aside."

In the meantime the Ambassadorial Conference assembled in London under the presidency of Sir Edward Grey, and on December 21 an official notification was issued that as a result of their conversations the Ambassadors had recommended to their Governments and the latter had accepted the principle of Albanian autonomy together with a provision guaranteeing to Servia access to the Adriatic. Subsequently it became known that the Conference had recommended the neutralisation of the whole of the Albanian coast-line. But for the fact that the Russian representative had not received the necessary instructions from his Government, they would, at the same time, have recommended the neutralisation of the whole of Albania. The news was published simultaneously in the various European capitals, and was everywhere regarded as a clear indication of the accord with which the Triple Entente and the Triple Alliance were working in their efforts to bring about a definite and permanent settlement of the Balkan question.

For a time the Servian question was at rest ; it continued so until it became merged in the larger questions concerning the delimitation of the Northern and North-eastern frontiers of Albania, which for so long threatened the peace of Europe. Servian troops, in the meanwhile, continued to occupy Durazzo, where quiet was only disturbed by disputes with Italy, because the seamen of the Italian steamer *Caprera*, which had been placed at the disposal of the Consulate, were forbidden to communicate with the shore. Some surprise was excited by the appointment of Colonel Popopovitch, a regicide, as commandant of Durazzo, but it was explained that the appointment was necessary on account of the lack of officers, owing to the losses during the war.

Meantime the Servians despatched the bulk of their forces to assist Bulgaria in the lines before Adrianople and Montenegro in the siege of Skutari, where their presence occasioned many protests from the Austrian Government. Even though the Austrians began to disband their forces in Galicia, they yet continued to keep their reservists under arms in their provinces on the Servian frontier, and ill-will continued to prevail between Vienna and Belgrade. Servian diplomacy confined itself to an endeavour to obtain as many Albanian towns for Servia as possible. Ipek, Prizrend, and Dibra were readily conceded by the Conference, but great difficulties were raised about Djakova and the monasteries near it. Ultimately after much wrangling the district was left to Servia. In return for the concession Servia, as we shall see, eventually withdrew her troops from the lines before Skutari and from Durazzo, which was thereupon occupied by the Albanians, aided by Turkish troops who had left Skutari on its surrender.

A SUBALTERN'S LETTERS
TO HIS WIFE

Dean Hole in *Then and Now* (Hutchinson & Co., 1902), pp. 168 169.—" We have been told that drunkenness is the cause of all the evil in our midst. I have just read in one of the cleverest, wisest, and most entertaining books on that same South African War, *A Subaltern's Letters to his Wife*, the passage following: 'Coffee is the Boer's beer. The co-existence of a distinctive immorality and a distinctive teetotalism goes far to disprove the cant teetotal argument that alcohol is responsible for all the vices.'"

The Times, 27 August, 1901.—" Some of the writer's impressions show much discernment."

The Daily Mail, 16 April, 1901.—" In the fast-growing literature of the S. African War *A Subaltern's Letters to his Wife* deserves to take a very high place."

The Academy, 13 April, 1901, reviews " A Book that Counts ": *A Subaltern's Letters to his Wife*.

Saturday Review, 4 May, 1901.—" This is one of the few good books on the War."

Military Mail.—" There is not a dull page to be found in the book."

The Spectator, April 6, 1901.—"*A Subaltern's Letters to his Wife* is one of the most striking and readable books we have yet read in regard to the war. The author of these letters knows what he means and means that you shall know it too, and hence a delightful sense of vigour and vitality. There is not a dull or languid page from first to last, and he will be an exceptional reader who will be able to put it down till he has got to the last page. The present writer thought that he was far too old a literary hand to be kept from his sleep by any subaltern, either in the smoking-room or on paper, but the subaltern in question taught him his mistake."

JOHN LANE THE BODLEY HEAD LTD., VIGO ST., W. 1

*

IN MOROCCO WITH GENERAL D'AMADE

This book was favourably reviewed in one hundred and seventy-five papers, some of which gave separate notices both of the English original and of the French and Spanish translations.

Of these papers

49 were English	98 French, Algerian, Tunisian
1 Canadian	and Moroccan
1 South African	1 Russian (in French)
2 Australian (one of which	1 Belgian
was in French)	1 Mexican (in French)
9 United States of America	1 Argentine (in French)
1 Austrian	3 Italian
2 German	2 Spanish
	4 Swiss

❧ ❧ ❧

This book was translated into French and Spanish. Lord Haldane writes from the War Office, 22nd October, 1908: "Dear Sir, I have to thank you for your book on the French Campaign in Morocco. I have already read it through with keen interest and have directed notes to be taken of some of the points to which you draw attention. . . . If you will allow me to say so I think you have succeeded in writing a very interesting account of the Campaign. Yours sincerely, R. B. Haldane.

"The War Office, *mirabile dictu*, gave me £20 for my notes!"

JOHN LANE THE BODLEY HEAD LTD., VIGO ST., W. 1